WHEN MEN BECOME GODS

STEPHEN SINGULAR

WHEN MEN BECOME GODS

Mormon Polygamist Warren Jeffs,

His Cult of Fear, and the Women

Who Fought Back

ST. MARTIN'S PRESS ❧ NEW YORK

www.stmartins.com

Book design by Jonathan Bennett

Library of Congress Cataloging-in-Publication Data

Singular, Stephen.
    When men become gods : Mormon polygamist Warren Jeffs, his cult of fear, and the women who fought back / Stephen Singular. — 1st ed.
        p. cm.
    ISBN-13: 978-0-312-37248-4
    ISBN-10: 0-312-37248-5
    1. Polygamy—United States.   2. Jeffs, Warren, 1955–   3. Mormons—United States—Biography.   4. Forced marriage—United States.   5. Mormon fundamentalism—United States.   6. Fundamentalist Church of Jesus Christ of Latter Day Saints.   I. Title.
    HQ994.S56 2008
    306.84'23092—dc22
    [B]
                                                                    2008006670

First Edition: May 2008

10   9   8   7   6   5   4   3   2   1

To Laura, Gary, Elaine, Sam, Sara, Elissa, and All the Rest Who Resisted

CONTENTS

You can have power over people as long as you don't take everything away from them. But when you've robbed a man of everything, he's no longer in your power.

—ALEKSANDR SOLZHENITSYN

PROLOGUE

D RIVING NORTH OUT OF LAS VEGAS AT TWILIGHT, you see the Strip spread out in a valley below you, glowing in the rearview mirror. Its neon signs and casinos represent several of the deadliest sins, from gluttony to lust to greed. Along Interstate 15, you pass the ragged-edged mountains that ring the city, dull red against the evening sky. The wind blows across the highway, sending discarded garbage and tumbleweeds spinning through the air and ramming into grilles. A few cars stream up and down the pavement, but the desert night is left mostly to predators—the coyotes and snakes creeping through the darkness, looking for an easy kill. Just before nightfall, the desolate countryside surrounding Las Vegas takes on an edge-of-the-world emptiness, as if one could disappear from I-15 without a trace. It's a great place to go underground.

Since the start of America's War on Terror in late 2001, police officers across the nation had been trained by the Homeland Security Department to look for signs of trouble. In big cities, they studied behavior on street corners and subways, but in the open expanses of the West, state troopers watched out for suspicious vehicles transporting questionable passengers. Along the Utah–Arizona border, a different kind of terrorism had been unfolding since the start of the new millennium, in a different sort of war. Law enforcement needed to be aware of it, too. At 9:00 P.M. on a warm late August evening in 2006, Nevada Highway Patrol Officer Eddie Dutchover was observing the cars and trucks heading north on I-15, their headlights cutting through the indigo night.

As a Cadillac Escalade passed by in near darkness, Trooper Dutchover

1

noticed its temporary license plate. Something was wrong. The writing was partially obscured, which was a minor violation, but these days you couldn't be too careful. The officer hesitated: Should he stop the car and correct the problem or let it go—the sort of split-second call a patrolman has to make every day. Instinctively, he pulled out behind the Escalade, moving in closer and then lighting it up on the highway. At four minutes past 9:00 P.M., the Cadillac came to a stop on the I-15 shoulder. Dutchover stepped outside, approaching the driver's seat in routine fashion, but trained to be ready for anything.

A man sat behind the wheel of the Cadillac, with a male and female passenger in the back seat. Dutchover looked closely at all three, settling his eyes on the man in the rear, who was eating a fast-food salad. He looked out of place beside the Vegas Strip's excess—he was gaunt and spindly and very pale. At six feet five inches and 150 pounds, he was a skeleton wrapped in skin. His posture was ramrod-erect, even inside the crowded quarters of the Escalade, and he had an oddly delicate face. One moment his eyes seemed gentle and open, the next icy and blank. His cheeks were pockmarked and sunken, his chin weak.

Seated beside him was an attractive woman—one of his countless wives.

By the evening of August 28, 2006, fugitive Warren Jeffs had been riding around like this for more than two years, zigzagging throughout the western United States and up to the Canadian border, down by Mexico and dipping into Texas, once taking a side trip to Florida to visit Disney World. He'd covered thousands of miles by car, constantly circling back to his home base on the Utah–Arizona border, just below Zion National Park. Late at night, members of his Fundamentalist Mormon church, which included the local police, sneaked Jeffs into the twin communities of Colorado City, Arizona, and Hildale, Utah, to perform secret ceremonies and rituals. As the leader of his Fundamentalist Latter-day Saint congregation (as opposed to the official Latter-day Saint Church in Salt Lake City), he'd married teenage girls to older men. On other visits, Jeffs took new wives for himself and was married to thirty or forty or fifty younger women; some people said the correct number was three or four times that high. He could demand sex from them whenever he wanted to, and they'd been taught to obey his every command.

Since 2004, cops in two states had been hunting for him, along with the Washington County (Utah) Sheriff's Department, a Mohave County

(Arizona) criminal investigator, and the FBI. A private investigator had been tailing the man for more than 100,000 miles, always one step behind. Back in the spring, the feds had placed him on their Ten Most Wanted List and boosted the reward for his capture to $100,000. Night after night throughout the past summer, his picture had appeared on national and international television, alerting viewers to be on the lookout for his lean body and long face. Four months had passed since he'd made the FBI list without a single sighting of the fugitive or a decent lead.

The Utah and Arizona authorities had lately been applying financial pressure to the border towns, and their strategy was effective. They'd won a number of recent victories, but frustration was growing because they hadn't been able to catch this one man. He was too elusive, with too many resources and too many people willing to hide him, just as others had hidden Western outlaws in previous centuries. Estimates of his congregation throughout North America ran as high as twenty to thirty thousand worshippers. To the faithful, Jeffs wasn't merely their pastor but their Prophet, the only person on earth who took orders directly from God. For the past two years, he'd assumed legendary status among his flock, the phantom ruler who'd never be brought to justice, the spiritual guru who mocked the law and government as he left them in his dust.

That August night as Dutchover surveyed the three passengers, the interior of the Escalade remained silent, a hint of panic filling the small space. The threesome had never been stopped before, despite the all-points bulletins issued in connection with Jeffs. Their good luck had made the three a little cocky and a little sloppy—the flawed temporary tag had escaped their attention. For months while on the run, the fugitive had worn disguises but then relaxed the practice. Jeffs had taken off his wig, shaved his beard, and stopped wearing caps all the time, and he now looked just like his wanted poster, plastered across the Southwest. His tall, lean figure was cramped inside the SUV, his bony knees barely fitting within the Escalade, and he badly needed to stretch his legs. His neck was pulsating. For the first time in his life, the fifty-year-old religious leader was encountering authority outside of the border towns, without the protection of his father or his church.

In the past few years, religious extremists of different stripes had been showing up all over the globe, convincing others to strap explosives to their chests and kill themselves in a busy marketplace or fly airplanes into buildings—all for the glory of God. From Jakarta to London, New York to Madrid, they'd been acting out stories and myths hundreds or even thousands of years old while spilling blood for their faith. Like the radical Muslim leaders who promised their suicide bombers scores of virgins in heaven for fulfilling their deadly missions, Warren Jeffs had long ago learned how to exploit the critical connection between erotic impulses and violence. He'd issued orders that had ripped apart families, reassigning one man's wives and children to another; banished hundreds of boys from the community and left them to fend for themselves; and called for the mass extermination of pets. Since coming to power, he'd also left a trail of suicides behind him—a homegrown version of the kind of terrorism that had been emerging worldwide.

Until tonight, it was something he and his faithful had been getting away with in a distant corner of the country for decades.

I

SEX AND TERRORISM

I

THE BORDER CONNECTING UTAH AND ARIZONA, just below the canyons and mesas of Zion National Park and just above the northern rim of the Grand Canyon, is perfectly isolated and perfectly beautiful. Covered with red cliffs, wide-open vistas, endless fields of sage, and shafts of light shining down with an illuminating glow, this piece of the Southwest conjures up the desert landscape of the Old Testament or the Valley of the Kings in Luxor, Egypt. It lends itself to the notion of mystical breakthroughs and heartfelt revelations, to nakedly worshipping the grandeur of God or embracing nightmarish visions of the Apocalypse. Black and blue clouds ride atop the cliffs, shifting and splitting during late-afternoon thunderstorms, rain and wind raging across the hillsides and leaving everything washed and altered. It is exactly the sort of place Joseph Smith, the founder of the Mormon religion, might have imagined when first delving into the spiritual realm. From the start of his amazing journey toward faith, he lived in that space between what can be experienced and what can be proven to others. Ask three serious Mormon scholars about who Smith was or the nature of his mystical adventures, and you'll get three different answers. Nobody knows for sure where his ideas came from.

A conservative religion never had more unconventional origins. Official Mormon history tells us this: as a fourteen-year-old boy living in upstate New York in 1820, Smith saw two angels appear before him, one representing the Lord, the other Jesus Christ. The teenager was confused about what branch of faith to accept as his own, so he asked "the Personages who stood above me in the light which of all the sects was right. I was answered that I must join none of them, for they were all wrong; and the Personage [representing Jesus] who addressed me said that all creeds were an abomination in his sight."

It was an extreme statement, and when Smith came out of his vision and told people what had happened, he angered other Christian believers. While suffering a "most bitter persecution" from those around him, he refused to stop talking about his discoveries. Three years later another angel, named Moroni, came to him.

"His whole person was glorious beyond description," Smith recollected, "and his countenance truly like lightning."

Moroni told him about some hidden golden plates, covered with hieroglyphic-like writing, and about two stones wrapped in silver bows, which would help the young man decipher the foreign text. Moroni eventually led him to the buried plates, Smith translated them into English, and these evolved into the Book of Mormon. They revealed an astounding tale that refuted the Judeo-Christian tradition and the Bible itself: 2,600 years ago, the lost tribes of Israel were not the Jews of the Old Testament, but a different group that had left the Middle East, sailed across the Atlantic Ocean on wooden boats, and resettled in what would become America. Centuries passed, and following the crucifixion and resurrection of Christ, Jesus appeared before the transplants and spoke to them of their special destiny. They'd reached the Promised Land of Scripture, where they'd create a new religion and restore Christianity to its earlier, purer form. This brand of faith would be driven by men like the spiritual giants of old, and they'd be called not mere believers or worshippers, but "Latter-day Saints." After Smith had finished translating the golden plates, he returned them to Moroni and they were never seen again, deepening the mystery of the teachings' origins.

Many have suggested that when founding Mormonism, Smith was exposed to several other world religions and even borrowed key elements from the Muslims. Both faiths embrace a belief in divine revelation, delivered straight from the mouth of God to one chosen man, known as the Prophet. For Mormons, these messages represented the only true view of Christianity, and anyone failing to embrace them was an "apostate" or "gentile." When it came to dealing with apostates, "blood atonement" might be necessary. Converting others to your beliefs was also important; every good Mormon should serve time as a missionary and grow the new religion. Both Islam and the Latter-day Saints banned drinking alcohol and practiced polygamy. To be exalted in heaven, Mormon men needed at least three wives.

Smith initially had one intelligent, strong-willed spouse named Emma, and she and Joseph were partners in getting their religion off the ground. One day he told her that he'd received a divine revelation to the effect that a man needed to wed a handful of women, if not more, to achieve salvation. When he started practicing this "spiritual principal," Emma became enraged—and she was hardly alone. As word of Smith's polygamy spread, he met resistance from other religious leaders and began moving his Mormon tribe west, all the way to Missouri, which he labeled "the new Zion." He chose Independence, Missouri, for the Promised Land and five thousand people followed him there. They were so unwelcome that the natives burned down their homes. Missouri issued an extermination order for the Mormons—the first in American history—and Smith himself was tarred, feathered, and driven out of the Show Me State. This established a pattern, as both persecution and the Biblical theme of exodus became central to the new faith. So did going to jail for one's beliefs.

Smith then led his congregation into Illinois and resettled in the town of Nauvoo, where the locals were terrified of his efforts to baptize the dead and to marry more than one woman. Everything about polygamy ran counter to the nation's puritanical roots. The "perfect theocracy" Smith hoped to create in Nauvoo was seen by others as a perfect threat to the government and its belief in the separation of church and state. Smith ignored public opinion, and in the early 1840s the Mormon Prophet deepened the hostility toward him by deciding to run for President of the United States. When the town's newspaper, *The Nauvoo Expositor*, wrote about his practice of polygamy, he was charged with treason and faced with arrest. He had a chance to escape Nauvoo and keep running from his tormentors, but this time he decided to stay put. He was incarcerated, and prison would be his undoing.

An enraged mob—two hundred men with faces painted black—stormed the jail and murdered the Mormon founder in 1844, only fourteen years after he'd started the new church. But it had already gained traction, and a sense of victimization may have united the believers. They were bound together against a common enemy and for a common cause: their own survival and blood atonement for those who opposed them.

Another strong leader, Brigham Young, emerged as the next Prophet. He,

9

too, lived out the "sacred principle" of polygamy, marrying as many as fifty women. Young felt that the Mormons should get farther away from the established order, so he pushed on, he and his followers marching across the Midwest in wintertime, on foot and in covered wagons, losing many along the way, until they reached the Great Salt Lake in the Utah Territory. It was a massive trek toward freedom, but no sooner had they resettled than the U.S. government began trying to end the Mormons' sexual and marital practices. In the 1850s, President James Buchanan ordered one-fifth of the American military to invade the region and wipe out plural marriage. Force did not accomplish this goal but only left the faithful more determined to resist authority, driving polygamy underground.

At times, the struggle to survive and take control of their new land in the West overwhelmed the better instincts of the Mormons. In the summer of 1857, they learned of a group of emigrants—nearly 140 men, women, and children from Presbyterian and Methodist families—making its way from Arkansas to California. The Fancher-Baker wagon train was following the Old Spanish Trail, wending through the southern Utah territory and coming into a valley known as Mountain Meadows, thirty-five miles north of modern St. George. On the morning of September 11, 1857—what would much later be called "America's first September 11th" by Mormons—John D. Lee led an assembled Mormon militia. He'd recruited a few men from the Paiute Nation, a Native American tribe based in the Southwest, while the Mormon warriors had dressed themselves up to look like Indians, so they could be blamed for what happened next. The militia attacked the traveling party with knives, rocks, hatchets, and "black powder weapons," killing 120 of the emigrants. Only seventeen children escaped with their lives. John D. Lee was eventually tried and executed for his role in the September 11 slaughter.

"It was," says western historian Will Bagley, the author of *Blood of the Prophets: Brigham Young and the Massacre at Mountain Meadows*, "the saddest, darkest, ugliest day in Utah history."

The strategy to blame the savagery on the Indians worked well for about a century, until a writer named Juanita Brooks began digging into the facts behind the Mormon propaganda, publishing *The Mountain Meadows Massacre* in 1950. The Paiutes' role in the tragedy wasn't entirely clear, but they were not the culprits in planning or carrying out the attack. Nor was John D. Lee the only Mormon villain, and in future decades some argued that Brigham Young himself bore a share of the guilt. The Church of Jesus Christ of Latter-day Saints was painfully slow to acknowledge all this, and 150 years would pass before it began to come to terms publicly with the butchery at Mountain Meadows.

By 1890, the Utah territory was eager to become an American state, but the federal government said no—not until the Mormons gave up plural marriage. The majority went along with this demand, but others saw it as a direct attack on their faith and their survival. In the 1800s, six out of ten babies born in the region did not see their first birthday, so there was a Biblical need for the pioneers to "be fruitful and multiply." Hadn't Joseph Smith himself married approximately thirty or forty women? Hadn't Brigham Young? These men would never have accepted this kind of compromise. The entry in Young's *Journal of Discourses* dated August 15, 1876, reads, "There are only two churches on the earth, only two parties. God leads the one, the devil the other . . . Apostates are literally tools of the devil." For the true believers, the Mormon Church in Salt Lake City was about to join forces with the devil.

When the church officially denounced plural marriage in 1890 and Utah achieved statehood six years later, the hard-core polygamists felt betrayed. How could their leaders have changed their views, denying the core tenet that most distinguished Mormonism from all other Christian denominations? Why had the one true faith caved in to a secular authority?

In a sense, the LDS Church wanted to have it both ways. While publicly decrying plural marriage, it never removed its founder's divine revelation on polygamy or "Celestial Marriage" from the Book of Mormon. In 1831, according to the church's *Doctrine and Covenants*, God had addressed Joseph Smith on the issue of "having many wives and concubines":

Celestial Marriage and a continuation of the family unit enable men to become gods . . . For behold, I reveal unto you a new and everlasting covenant; and if ye abide not that covenant, then ye are damned; for no one can reject this covenant and be permitted to enter into my glory . . . And if he have ten virgins given unto him by this law, he cannot commit adultery, for they belong to him, and they are given unto him; therefore is he justified.

If Joseph's wife did not want to go along with this revelation, God had some words for her as well:

And I command mine handmaid, Emma Smith, to abide and cleave unto my servant Joseph, and to no one else. But if she will not abide this commandment, she shall be destroyed, saith the Lord; for I am the Lord thy God, and will destroy her if she abide not in my law.

If the Lord had told Joseph Smith that Celestial Marriage was the pathway to becoming a god, and if Brigham Young had lived out this principle, why should the faithful now behave any differently? Shouldn't Mormons be prepared to sacrifice for their religion, as their founder had done, even if that meant going to jail?

A small but committed minority of believers, who would eventually be known as the Fundamentalist Latter-day Saints, refused to knuckle under to Utah, the American government, or the LDS power structure in Salt Lake City. They'd been sold out by the "corporate church," which had fallen under the control of "apostates" and "gentiles." They would side with Joseph Smith and Brigham Young no matter the cost. The time had come to break off from the LDS and begin looking for a new home—far away from both the official church and the long arm of the police. In the 1920s, they struck out for the southern part of the state and put down roots in the tiny village of Short Creek, called "Short Crick" by the natives or just "The Crick," which straddled the border between Arizona and Utah.

Because Short Creek was located in two states, its legal jurisdiction was more complicated than in most towns and enforcing the law there was more difficult—exactly what the locals wanted. They soon established their own city government and police department, both run by polygamists.

2

THE CRICK WAS HUNDREDS OF MILES from the region's major urban centers, Salt Lake City and Phoenix, and set in a distant corner of massive Mohave County, Arizona. The high-desert plateau that spreads out above the Grand Canyon, known as the Arizona Strip, was virtually empty and in coming decades would attract tax resisters, survivalists, drug dealers, sexual cowboys of every stripe, and other outlaws. The wide-open, rolling landscape, covered with red dirt, jackrabbits, and stray dingo dogs, had a woolly feeling, as if modern civilization was unwelcome here. You moved to the Strip to get away from the cops and the conventional judgments of more tame Americans. The West would eventually be dotted with pockets of revolt—nudist hot springs, old-time bootleggers, wild-eyed men running meth labs, secret energy experimenters looking for the breakthrough that would replace fossil fuels, UFO enthusiasts, countless spiritual retreats—and the Strip was just one more. The Mormon Fundamentalists had found a home in the part of Utah called "Dixie," because Brigham Young had insisted the people of this region grow cotton for their clothing and as a cash crop.

The folks of Short Creek got busy multiplying. The men took as many wives as they could and at least one of their brides was supposed to have a baby every year; it wasn't uncommon for families to have fifty children. Money wasn't a big issue because the settlers were largely self-sufficient. They lived off their orchards and gardens, their canned fruits and vegetables. They milked cows or butchered them for beef, raised chickens for meat and eggs. A general store provided them with flour, sugar, and a few other staples. They ran a dairy and a bakery—turning out cheese products, breads, cakes, and pies—while sewing their own clothes and trimming their own hair. Utah was called the "Beehive State" because Mormons were highly industrious and natural-born carpenters, building farms and houses everywhere.

The original population of around four hundred began to spread, pushing outward and upward and sideways, moving onto hillsides and across the flat patch of desert that lay in the great shadow of the Vermilion Cliffs. The locals dubbed this mesa overlooking the village "Canaan Mountain." Out on the Strip, under a vast sky and surrounded by the natural beauty of the Southwest, people could easily imagine that they were re-creating life from Biblical times and starting the human story over from scratch. Joseph Smith's original vision, watered down in Salt Lake City, began to flourish in The Crick. Inbreeding was common, and nearly half the locals were blood relatives of the town's two founding families, the Barlows and the Jessops (97 Jessops are listed in the current Colorado City phone book). The genetic consequences of marrying first and second cousins wouldn't be seen for decades.

In 1942, the FLDS established the United Effort Plan to manage church members' real estate and other financial assets, which by the end of the century amounted to well over $100 million. The original UEP Trustees were John Y. Barlow, Leroy Johnson, Joseph Musser, Marion Hammon, and Rulon Jeffs. All land and homes were placed under the control of the UEP, run by the Prophet and Trustees, making The Crick different from every other community in the United States. Despite its distance from Salt Lake City, the FLDS's financial and marital habits made the official church nervous. The LDS was after respectability, wanted to assimilate into American society as quickly as possible, and didn't need any trouble down in Dixie that might smear its own name.

In 1935, the LDS Church excommunicated twenty-one men from Short Creek after they refused to renounce polygamy. Three of them—Price Johnson, I. C. Spencer, and John Y. Barlow—were charged with unlawful cohabitation; Johnson and Spencer spent nearly a year in a Florence, Arizona, prison. A decade later, forty-six Utah adults, some from Short Creek, were charged with unlawful cohabitation; twenty-four went to state or federal prison, but ten were freed after signing an oath to give up polygamy. Yet plural marriage continued to spread in The Crick, as did its scandalous reputation. One man was certain that he knew what to do about this.

As the Republican candidate for Arizona governor in 1950, Howard Pyle won an upset victory over his Democratic opponent, and he was eager to make his imprint on one part of the state. He'd heard the stories coming out of Short Creek about rampant polygamy, child brides, communal living, and tax fraud—maybe even socialism. The son of a Baptist minister and a deeply religious man himself, Pyle was offended by the plural marriage lifestyle, but also saw the situation on the border as an opportunity to advance his political career. For many years before becoming governor, he'd been a popular radio broadcaster, the vice president of the Arizona Broadcasting Company, and the best-known voice in the state. He believed he had a keen understanding of the power of the media and how to use it for political ends.

Like many others who viewed polygamy from a distance, the governor judged it in black-and-white terms: it was bad for all involved and should be stamped out. Pyle was untroubled by human complexities and by the freedoms promised religious minorities in the First Amendment to the United States Constitution: "Congress shall make no law respecting an establishment of religion, or prohibiting the free exercise thereof; or abridging the freedom of speech . . ." Things needed to be cleaned up along the border, and a few simple actions would take care of the problem. Not only would this increase the governor's stature throughout Arizona, but future generations living in The Crick would thank him for it.

On Sunday, July 26, 1953, Pyle ordered a massive raid, police descending on the community during the darkness of a lunar eclipse. Locals had gotten wind of this and arose early to meet the police face-to-face at dawn in the streets of Short Creek. As Truman Barlow ran the American flag up a pole, townspeople gathered round him and sang "My Country, 'Tis of Thee, Sweet Land of Liberty" and "God Bless America." They kept singing as the startled officers confronted them with pistols and machine guns, placing them under arrest. More true believers were headed to jail.

The police barged into homes, entered bedrooms, and shone lights into the eyes of families who were still asleep, dragging the men out at gunpoint. They didn't go quietly into custody.

"We have rights under the Constitution," Leroy Johnson told the invaders, "and this soil will drink our blood before we will run another step."

World War II and Korean veterans who now lived in The Crick protested the raid by showing their wounds to the officers, saying they'd gone abroad to fight for their country and religious freedom. Neither the soldiers nor the locals backed down.

"If there is a scrap of red-blooded manhood among you," Short Crick native Clyde Mackert told those who arrested him, "you will turn around and go back where you came from. We are living higher principles of Americanism than you know anything about."

As Arizona jailed the men and rounded up hundreds of women and children, headlines across Utah and Arizona announced that the "Nest of Polygamists" had been routed at last.

Governor Pyle proudly delivered this proclamation:

Arizona has mobilized and used its total police power to protect the lives and future of 263 children. They are the product and the victims of the foulest conspiracy you could possibly imagine. More than 120 peace officers moved into Short Creek, in Mohave County, at 4 o'clock this morning. They have arrested almost the entire population of a community dedicated to the production of white slaves who are without hope of escaping this degrading slavery from the moment of their birth . . . In the evidence the State has accumulated there are multiple instances of statutory rape, adultery, bigamy, open and notorious cohabitation, contributing to the delinquency of minors, marrying the spouse of another . . . along with various instances of income tax evasion, failure to comply with Arizona's corporation laws, misappropriation of school funds, improper use of school facilities and falsification of public records . . .

THE STATE OF ARIZONA IS UNALTERABLY PLEDGED AND DETERMINED TO STOP THIS MONSTROUS AND EVIL GROWTH BEFORE IT BECOMES A CANCER OF A SORT THAT IS BEYOND HOPE OF HUMAN REPAIR . . . THESE CHILDREN HAVE THE RIGHTS OF ALL NATIVE-BORN AMERICANS—THE RIGHTS THAT WERE WRITTEN INTO THE DECLARATION OF INDEPENDENCE . . . THE RIGHT TO LIFE, LIBERTY, AND THE PURSUIT OF HAPPINESS . . . WE COULD DO NO LESS THAN THIS.

The governor had made several miscalculations—but one was huge. The press had known of the coming raid but held off reporting on it until it took place. Now the media repeatedly showed heartrending images of families torn apart by law enforcement, with FLDS men being hauled off to jail as their wives cried and reached out for the children they'd just been separated from. Photos from that time show the adults males of Short Creek being treated no differently from thieves or murderers. Confronted with these pictures, the public confounded the governor and began to feel sympathy for the people of Short Creek. What right did Arizona have to tell these folks how to live? They weren't harming anyone, so why not just leave them alone? Neither polygamy itself nor the problems surrounding it were as black and white as the governor had imagined (both then and now, some women much prefer plural marriage to conventional matrimony). There was more to life in The Crick than sexual license.

1953 became a pivotal year in the history of the FLDS, both in the way authorities would now look upon the border towns and in how fundamentalist Mormons would regard the outside world. Unexpectedly, Pyle lost his bid for reelection in 1954, and for the next half-century the government backed away from Short Creek. The message was clear: using force was counterproductive in rooting out religious sects, and such moves could destroy one's political ambitions. Further, though it was illegal to practice polygamy in Utah, nearly every politician in the state had ancestors or relatives who'd done precisely that. If anyone made too much fuss about reforming the FLDS, somebody was sure to point out that the critic's father or grandfather or great-grandfather had married a score of Mormon women and sired two or three dozen children. Why bother taking the political risk?

In Short Creek itself, the raid lived on and expanded in the memories of the community. The fundamentalist church had long viewed its members as a special group in the eyes of God, subject to a special kind of persecution— just as Joseph Smith had been hounded and then murdered for refusing to buckle under to fear and convention. Governor Pyle's actions only deepened and solidified these feelings. Locals had earned the right to be afraid, even paranoid. From generation to generation, church members handed down horror stories about the raid and what they'd suffered, the event shaping and haunting FLDS parents and kids for decades. The message was clear: strangers could never be trusted, outside law enforcement was evil, apostates were lurking everywhere and deserved blood atonement for their sins. The invasion only drove polygamy, and some of its darker sexual offshoots, further underground.

Throughout the 1960s and 1970s, as America underwent a cultural and political revolution, the women's movement declared emphatically that females were not the property of men and had the right to choose what to do—or not to do—with their own lives and bodies. All females, including teenage girls and young children, needed to be protected from violence, male aggression, and sexual abuse. Change was stirring across the nation and filtering out toward the hinterlands, reaching as far as Short Creek. FLDS views were in direct conflict with the ideas developing elsewhere, and the two forces couldn't be kept apart forever.

3

IN 1954, LEROY JOHNSON BECAME THE PROPHET and reigned for the next 32 years. Many church members saw "Uncle Roy" as a reasonable and decent ruler during his first couple of decades in power—at least, before he became closely allied with Rulon Jeffs, one of seven men on the Priesthood Council running the FLDS. The Prophet was the Council's senior leader, but all seven shared power, made decisions, performed marriages, and delivered sermons. They voted on important issues and served as a system of checks and balances to keep anyone from having too much control. One-man rule was always a danger to religious communities. In the 1970s, another Southwestern polygamist leader named Ervil LeBaron, head of the Church of the Lamb of God, put together a "Bible" for his flock and declared that anyone violating his commandments would experience blood atonement. In 1981, LeBaron died in prison after being convicted of ordering the murder of rival leader, Rulon Allred.

LeBaron had left behind a "hit list" of enemies and during the next few years, several people on it turned up dead. Four murders were carried out on one day, June 27, 1988, at approximately 4:00 P.M. in Houston and Irving, Texas, all the victims slain by shotgun blasts to the head. In 1992, federal prosecutors in Houston charged six people with conspiracy, racketeering, and murder in connection with LeBaron's final wishes.

A few years after Leroy Johnson was chosen Prophet, the part of Short Creek located on the Arizona side was officially renamed Colorado City, while the remainder that lay in Utah was called Hildale. The twin communities had long avoided giving anyone too much clout, but in the 1970s the

FLDS foundation began to shift. The aging Johnson and the up-and-coming Rulon Jeffs had started pushing for one-man rule over the protests of others on the Priesthood Council. A civil war was building inside the church and would burst open the following decade.

Jeffs had been a successful accountant in San Francisco before relocating his family to Little Cottonwood Canyon, outside Salt Lake City, in the 1960s. He lived on a large spread with a colossal home featuring a restaurant-style kitchen and a living room with a baptismal font and enough space to hold a couple hundred people for Sunday sermons. A public road ran in front of the house, but a massive concrete fence kept passersby from seeing into the compound. As it would be later on in the border towns, privacy was paramount for Jeffs. Behind the concrete fence were perfectly manicured trees and a groomed, spotless lawn. Green and white pillars stood in front of the mansion, creating the impression of a grand colonial estate, and those living here were expected to contribute to this flawless facade. Trash was immediately picked up, and if cracks appeared in the wall or one of the estate's roads, they were quickly repaired. When children went outside to play basketball, they weren't supposed to be loud, to quarrel among themselves, or to become disobedient toward adults. When it was time to go inside, they lined up in rows and walked in quietly, single file. The atmosphere was orchestrated to reflect harmony, order, and not just the possibility but the realization of human perfection.

On Sundays, families traveled from Colorado City and around the region to attend services at the Jeffs's home. Worshippers entered through sliding glass doors off the living room and were seated on chairs on the immaculate green carpet according to their importance in the church, the most elite near the front, the less so behind them, and the unruly teenagers at the back. Highly placed elders were always referred to by the children as "Aunt" or "Uncle." The Council of Seven occupied chairs at the head of the sanctuary, and two or three of the men gave sermons each Sunday. Next to them was a person translating the words into sign language, along with Norma Jeffs, one of Rulon's many wives, who played the piano. Songs came from LDS hymnbooks and were often about the Mormons' difficult pioneer roots. When speakers took to the pulpit, fire and brimstone were unleashed, with references to the 1953 raid and the actions of the evil gentiles in the outside world of "Babylon." The Second Coming of Christ was imminent, and in a blaze of flames and glory, the Lord would reach down and destroy the LDS church in nearby Salt Lake City, kill the apostates who prayed there, wipe out governments from coast to coast, and put FLDS members back on their natural footing as the Chosen People of God.

One young worshipper attending services at the Jeffs's house in the 1970s and 1980s was Laura Chapman Mackert. Born in 1963 to a family with four mothers and thirty-one children, she grew up in Sandy, Utah, not far from Little Cottonwood Canyon, the shadow of the FLDS hovering over her and her ancestors. Her great-uncle, Rulon Allred, had been murdered by the LeBaron gang and her own father, Clyde Mackert, had been taken into custody in the 1953 raid. In the Jeffs's home on Sundays, she obediently listened to the sermons of the Priesthood Council, trying to follow and believe in what she heard, but the room was claustrophobic and the speeches often confusing. Everybody was told to be kind and loving and sweet, but when she tried to do that, trouble erupted. One day after attending kindergarten in a public school, she brought home an African American child. Instead of welcoming the girl to their home, Laura's mothers took their daughter aside and explained that if she ever did this again, her father could go to prison. When she asked why, they said that if any females in the church became involved with a black man, they'd be killed.

FLDS racial attitudes had been clearly laid out by Brigham Young, who'd said this about the "cursed" black race: "Any man having one drop of the seed of [Cain] in him cannot hold the [Mormon] priesthood and if no other Prophet ever spoke it before, I will say it now in the name of Jesus Christ. I know it is true and others know it."

What went on inside Laura's home was beyond confusing. When she was four, one of her stepbrothers tied her to a bedpost and tried to rape her. Three years later, her father began coming into the bedroom where she and her older sister, Rena, slept; quietly, he put his hand over her mouth, lifted her up, and carried her to another room. When she tried to fight him off, he backhanded her across the mouth. She learned not to resist, but to try to ignore what he was doing and stare up at the ceiling, telling herself that he could do this to her body, but he'd never have her soul. Her father came from a rigid German military background and she'd always been terrified of him, even before his nighttime visits to her bed. She couldn't say anything about what he did—not to him or to her sisters, who were also being visited in the dark. She didn't dare speak to her mothers, because they'd beat her—or worse. One of them, her own mother's sister, already liked to hit her with hangers and a yardstick.

As a teenager, Laura lay awake at night, unable to sleep, listening to the wind blow across her bedroom sill and stir the curtains back and forth, the soft sound she always remembered when thinking of her childhood. As she got older, she'd recall her father's smell, a combination of cheap cigarettes and Brut cologne, which evoked both terror and the coldness of his personality. In her thirties and forties, whenever she encountered this particular scent, it made her nauseous.

Church elders at the Jeffs's home constantly preached that women and girls were supposed to "keep sweet," no matter what happened, just "keep sweet for the Lord." Stay obedient and quiet and always be pleasant, regardless of what you are feeling or thinking. To reinforce this idea, Laura taped the words "Keep Sweet" to her bathroom mirror. The only way she could do this now, when seeing her father in the house or at the dinner table or passing by him in the hallway, was to convince herself that none of this had really happened, that she'd just dreamed it all up after falling asleep.

A photo of Laura at age thirteen shows a dark-haired girl with long, tightly wound ponytails, dressed up to her neck in nineteenth-century pioneer clothing. Her face isn't open or childlike, but fearful and mistrustful, her mouth curved downward and her eyes glancing away from the camera with timidity and pain. The numbness she'd felt when hearing her father step into her bedroom at night had been embedded in her features, covering up and deadening the anger just below the picture's surface. "Soul murder" was how she later described this feeling. Her greatest pleasure back then, sometimes her only pleasure, was to get out of the house and ride her horse, her hair blowing behind her as she rode faster and faster through the spacious countryside, free and in control of her life for a few moments, until she went home and waited with dread for the bedroom door to open again.

Laura was ashamed when she went to her non-FLDS public school, carrying cheap sandwiches, old brown bananas, or other pieces of fruit into the cafeteria in a soiled paper bag. She wished she could eat a hot meal for lunch like other kids who weren't in the FLDS, but her parents made her bring her own food, and it was so unappealing she couldn't trade it for something better. She wished she could dress like the other girls who didn't go to her church and were now imitating the big hair and flashy clothes of the latest TV star, Farrah Fawcett-Majors. Instead, each morning she had to put on the "sacred long underwear" of her faith.

"The undergarment's fabric," Laura says, "was a lightweight white nylon that didn't allow much airflow, so it was hot but not too heavy. We sewed it ourselves and it covered the body from our collarbones down to our ankles. We wore thick support pantyhose over it or tights, and sometimes jeans on top of all this. In the summer, the temperatures reached 110 degrees where I grew up, but we still kept it on. I like to call the sacred underwear 'polygamy's burka.' "

One day in the school cafeteria, when a woman server asked Laura if she'd like a bowl of hot chili, the surprised girl gratefully accepted. The woman was a gentile, and Laura had always been told of their wickedness, but this one was kind and generous—a fact that confused Laura.

She also didn't understand the conflict building inside her church and slipping out in the sermons. Leroy Johnson and Rulon Jeffs were supporting one-man rule now, but others on the Priesthood Council were strongly opposed. Johnson and Jeffs thought the Prophet should have all the power and be the only one to decide who could get married and who couldn't. Their attitude didn't sit well with some FLDS clans. The Jessops and the Hammons, for example, had ancestors who could be traced back to the pioneers who'd settled Utah, and they regarded their bloodlines as royal. Rumors were surfacing that several men on the Priesthood Council were thinking of breaking away and starting their own church and community.

There were other signs of conflict. If church leaders weren't supposed to touch alcohol, why did Uncle Rulon have a wine cellar in his home? Worshippers had seen him staggering around, losing his balance and talking too loudly, spit flying from the corners of his mouth. It was disturbing to observe a member of the Priesthood Council drunk. Yet one had to be careful about criticizing Jeffs. People whispered that he had spies everywhere, reporting back to him about who supported his desire to be the next Prophet and who did not. Everybody knew who his chief spy was. During church services, one young man usually stayed in the back of the main room and watched everyone else or walked up to the front and spoke softly in Rulon's ear. He was a head taller than most, with a lanky build, a long thin face, and a sanctimonious air that the congregation instantly picked up on. His name was Warren Jeffs, and he was his father's favorite son and favorite watchdog. The two of them were locked in a relationship that nobody else could penetrate, as it had always been.

Following the 1953 raid, Short Creek residents had begun to scatter all over the western United States, many hiding out in California. In Sacramento on December 3, 1955, the first son of Rulon's fourth (and most favored) wife, Merilyn Steed, entered the world a couple of months prematurely. Rulon was called upon to help deliver tiny Warren Steed Jeffs, small enough to fit into a shoebox with room to spare. His father's childbirthing efforts and the infant's survival were seen as miracles. The experience created a special bond between Rulon and his son, leaving the youngster with his own sense of destiny. God had saved him for a purpose and, just like Joseph Smith, Warren had grand things to accomplish. He grew up hearing stories about the tribulations and murder of Smith, and about the ugliness of the 1953 raid, developing an absolute disdain for any authority but his father's and his own. He heard about Smith's revelation concerning the "one mighty and strong" who would be sent by the Lord to purify the community and "to set in order the House of God." Warren and his father were the only truly principled followers of the first Prophet. Everybody else was subject to corruption.

If Warren saw himself as ordained for greatness, few others did. As a child he was sickly, gawky, and frail-looking, his young life filled with physical and emotional challenges. It was difficult enough to get noticed inside a large family, but even more so if you were constantly criticized for your bad health. Boys rarely chose him for their games, and the girls likewise avoided him. He found himself drawn to artistic endeavors, singing or playing music or putting on plays, while most of his brothers were rougher around the edges. Warren's muscles didn't develop, but his mind did, and he became good at plotting strategy and ratting out his siblings if he felt they'd done something wrong—or just to get even. He was fanatically jealous of his father's attention and always trying to get more of it. One time his snitching became so offensive that he was thrown out of Rulon's house, made to go away and think about his sins and repent, before confessing to his dad and being let back in. The banishment from home and separation from his mother made a permanent impression on the young man, who never forgot the shame of being singled out for punishment and humiliation.

From boyhood on, Warren was fascinated with power and eager to get some for himself, which his mother didn't discourage. As a plural wife, Merilyn Steed Jeffs's own dreams were buried behind helping raise scores of children and countless domestic chores. Because Warren was her favorite child, she nurtured his ambitions instead of her own. As he got older, he loved reading about historical figures, like Napoleon and Hitler, and became obsessed with the lives of famous men. He was also developing an obsession with improving the human race—just as Joseph Smith had been hoping to do with his perfect community of Nauvoo, Illinois, inside his perfect theocracy. Jeffs himself didn't need to be perfect, but to surround himself with those who were. If he ever had his father's power, or the power of the Prophet, he'd find a way to improve everything and everyone around him.

As Warren grew taller and taller, he remained thin as ever, his neck so flimsy it hardly looked able to support his head. He was pale, wore glasses, and had a very prominent Adam's apple, which seemed to jump out of his throat when he talked. His eyes drew you in, then repelled—and his face held a false sensitivity. Because his father had for decades been one of the Mormon elite, the young man felt that he, too, should be viewed and treated in this manner. Others didn't regard him as a prince about to inherit the throne but as a sickly, awkward-looking, mostly ineffectual young man. They didn't hesitate to poke fun at his appearance or his weakness. Only his mother saw him for what he actually was—born royalty—and he was determined to prove her right. Maybe someday he could be the one mighty and strong.

4

A FTER GRADUATING IN THE TOP 3 percent of his class and with honors from Jordan High in Sandy, Warren briefly worked at his father's accounting business. When Rulon opened Alta Academy in 1973, a private school on his compound in Little Cottonwood Canyon, the seventeen-year-old Jeffs became a teacher of math, science, computer programming, and FLDS priesthood history. Warren had studied the life of Joseph Smith in depth: his visions and revelations, his direct pipeline to God, his sense of persecution for having plural wives, his resistance against the outside world, his need to keep moving the faithful, and his arrest and death in jail. The young man was absolutely certain that Smith had discovered and launched the one true faith, and he closely identified with the struggles of the Mormon founder. Starting in the first grade, kids at Alta Academy learned about Smith from Jeffs, along with the trials and glories of the other Prophets from Brigham Young to Leroy Johnson.

Each morning following a conference with his father, Warren walked over to Alta, held a meeting with the children, sang songs, offered up prayers, and asked them to give testimonials about being a real Mormon, as opposed to the apostates in Salt Lake City. He'd been given the chance to exercise power and would make the most of it, keeping the boys and girls segregated from one another at school and safe from the modern influences of the outside world. He insisted that they cover their bodies with long dresses or pants and long-sleeved shirts buttoned up to the collar. Their skin was never to be exposed to the sun, so it remained as white as possible.

Race was part of the educational process at Alta, where teachers tried to use textbooks without pictures of African Americans, Mexicans, or anyone with dark skin. If they couldn't find such books, they went through others and meticulously cut out the images of people of color so the children wouldn't have to look at these faces (the official LDS Church had refused to accept blacks as priests until 1978). Warren taught American history, but only up through the writing of the U.S. Constitution, dismissing the rest of the nation's past and denying many recent events, including man's landing on the moon just a few years earlier. The Constitution was a critical document for the FLDS, which practiced its beliefs under the protection of the First Amendment. As U.S. citizens, fundamentalist Mormons felt they had the unconditional right to live out the practices of their faith, regardless of the laws of Utah, Arizona, or the American government.

Warren wrote hymns about his faith and an ode to his father called "He Will Be Renewed." The younger man liked to sing his own material to audiences, but other kinds of music, especially those rooted in the African-American experience, disturbed and angered him. Rulon had once declared that the penalty for being homosexual or for an FLDS worshipper marrying an African American was "death on the spot." At the school, Warren shared his ideas on this subject with the students:

You see some classes of the human family that are black, uncouth, or rude and filthy, uncomely, disagreeable and low in their habits; wild and seemingly deprived of nearly all the blessings of the intelligence that is usually bestowed upon mankind.

So I give you this lesson on the black race that you can understand its full effects, as far as we are able to comprehend. And that we must beware—if we are for the prophet, the priesthood—we will come out of the world and leave off their dress, their music, their styles, their fashions; the way they think, what they do, because you can trace back and see a connection with immoral, filthy people.

It was necessary that the Devil should have a representation upon the earth as well as God. So Ham's wife that was preserved on the Ark was a Negro of the seed of Cain and there was a priestly purpose in it, that the Devil would have a representation as well as God.

So the Negro race has continued, and today is the day of the Negro as far as the world is concerned. They have influenced the generations of time; they have mixed their blood with many peoples, until there are many peoples not able to hold the priesthood . . . And the lesson is, if anyone mingles their seed, their bloodline, with the seed of Cain, the Negro, they also would lose all rights and priesthood blessings.

When Rulon later picked his son to become school principal, Warren was given a bigger platform for leadership. He began each day with a one-hour devotional filled with sermons, hymns, and the reading of scripture—but not the Pledge of Allegiance. At Alta, the authority of the federal government was nothing compared to God's authority—or Jeffs's own—and he constantly enforced his own brand of discipline. Sloppy handwriting or a casual remark led to verbal humiliation from the principal. If a boy's shirttail wasn't fully tucked in, he was lectured or whacked with a yardstick or belt-whipped. If a girl's skirt was too short or she smiled at a boy, she could be suspended. For his own amusement, Jeffs made kids stand in the classroom and flex the muscles of their buttocks in front of others. He liked to sneak up behind girls, grab their necks, and squeeze while asking, "Are you keeping sweet or do you need to be punished?" He shocked the children by grabbing a first- or second-grade boy by the ankles, flipping him upside-down, and saying, "I'm shaking the evil out of him!"

Students weren't allowed to wear red clothes (the color of the devil) or anything with stripes. Some days Jeffs let them eat lunch during the noon hour, but other days he switched the time, and occasionally they didn't get to eat at all. From moment to moment, he acted like their best friend or flew into a rage, keeping everyone and everything off-balance. He hated snowball-throwing or water fights, which could lead to expulsion. He took youngsters into a small room and interrogated them about their parents—getting information to be used later on.

Mothers and fathers of Alta children assumed that someone, most likely Rulon, would eventually step in and tone Warren down, but that never happened. Rulon was a vengeful man himself, long ago embracing blood atonement toward his enemies, and the need for violence.

"I could refer you," he once said,

> to plenty of instances where men have been righteously slain for their sins. I have seen scores and hundreds of people for whom there would have been a chance (in the last resurrection there will be) if their lives had been taken and their blood spilled on the ground as a smoking incense to the Almighty . . . The wickedness and ignorance of the nations forbid this principle being in full force, but the time will come when the law of God will be in full force.
>
> This is loving our neighbor as ourselves; if he needs help, help him; and if he wants salvation and it is necessary to spill his blood on the earth in order that he may be saved, spill it.

At the academy, Warren implemented his favorite motto: "Perfect obedience produces perfect faith, which produces perfect people." If children weren't perfect in his eyes, he simply got rid of them, expelling dozens of kids without regard for what would happen to them or their education. Yet he wasn't always fearsome and could be quite childlike, letting the students see a gentle and humorous side. Some of the children greatly respected and admired him; he was a strong leader and they were eager to follow his commands. He enjoyed sledding with them, playing softball, or telling jokes. He did slapstick imitations of Groucho Marx and Jerry Lewis, which left the kids roaring. He put on plays at the school and delivered long speeches to his captive audience, giving his voice a lulling, hypnotic quality, repeatedly driving home his central point: perfect obedience leads to perfect faith, perfect lives, and perfect people.

Jeffs treated the academy as his personal laboratory for experimenting with various human emotions, but particularly fear. For years he'd read about the rise of Adolph Hitler and absorbed the story of Nazi Germany, paying close attention to the relationship between sex and power (the Nazis had designed one program in which SS officers were bred with carefully chosen blonde, blue-eyed women in order to produce the next generation of elite Germans). One of Warren's half-brothers was Ward Jeffs, and some family members believed the two siblings had grown up as rivals. Ward didn't blindly support his father in all things; he wasn't devoted to one-man rule for the FLDS and felt the church was better served by keeping its Priesthood Council and its system of checks and balances intact.

In 2004, decades after Jeffs had become Alta's principal, one of Ward's sons filed a civil lawsuit against Warren for his actions at the school. For years Brent Jeffs had kept quiet about his experience at the academy and his recurring nightmares as he'd gotten older, but the denial and silence gradually became intolerable.

"Don't hurt me!" he'd wake up screaming in the darkness as a young man. "Don't hurt me!"

In his suit, Brent alleged that when he was five years old, Warren and two of his brothers, Blaine and Leslie Jeffs, would slip away during church services, lead him out of a basement room where the children studied Sunday school lessons, and take him into a bathroom, where they sodomized him. According to Brent, the three adults told him that this ritual was God's will and the way for him to become a man. Two of Brent's brothers had also stepped forward to back up this claim. Before Brent could work up the courage to file the suit, one of the brothers supporting his confession, Clayne Jeffs, shot himself in the head. The suicide was a major motivation for Brent finally taking legal action.

5

UNLIKE WARREN, who was eight years older, Laura Chapman Mackert was forbidden from attending Jordan High School. Because she was female, her public education stopped at the fifth grade, and she also wasn't permitted to get a driver's license. On her sixteenth birthday, her father took her into Salt Lake City in his new Cadillac. As they headed to a fancy restaurant to celebrate the occasion, he commented on her developing figure and announced that it was time for her formal "Sexuality Lesson"—the same one he'd given his other daughters when they'd reached this milestone. The Sexuality Lesson was his way of legitimizing the intimacy he'd already had with them; and his way of commanding them, with force and clarity, not to talk about any of this with their mothers. At sixteen, they were supposed to start thinking of themselves not as his children but as his wives, and what went on between them could never be discussed with the other women. Listening to him talk in the car, Laura wrapped her fingers around the door handle and squeezed, wanting to fling it open and leap out, but the Cadillac was traveling sixty-five miles an hour and she was frozen with fear. She often wanted to die—to make her breathing stop or her heart quit beating—but the impulses passed and afterward all she felt was numb.

Two years later, in 1981, she and her father traveled down from their home near Salt Lake to Colorado City for the wedding of one of her sisters at Uncle Roy's house. Laura was eighteen and had fallen in love with a young man for the first time, but when his family advised him to marry someone else, he'd followed their orders. She was still trying to heal her crushed expectations.

After her sister's wedding ceremony, her father took Laura's hand and led her up to Uncle Roy.

"She's eighteen now," he said to the aging Prophet, implying that his daughter was quite old to be single. "She's ready to get married."

Laura's cheeks colored, shocked by his words, but the shock was about to turn to anger.

As she stood by, the men conferred. Then Uncle Roy told her that another young man attending the wedding, the pale-skinned Philip Barlow, who was a member of the Barlow clan, had just been chosen as her new husband. Since they were already doing one ceremony today, they might as well perform a second. Was she ready to go to the altar or did she need a few minutes to get prepared?

Laura stared at her father, a pleading look in her eyes, but she was afraid to speak up.

He told her to do what the Prophet had instructed.

All she could think about was the young man she loved, and that she had to come up with a plan—immediately—to keep from marrying Philip.

"I need to pray about this decision," she stammered to Uncle Roy. "I need to be alone and have time to pray."

He granted her request and she was led to a back bedroom, where she sat down by herself, trying to shove aside her growing sense of panic. Glancing at a window, she considered climbing out and running until she was away from all of them, but they'd catch her and bring her back and force her to wed the boy, whom she wasn't attracted to at all.

Her older sister, Carol, knocked on the door and stepped inside. She said Uncle Roy had just had a direct revelation from God that Laura's salvation depended on her marrying Philip this afternoon. If she didn't go through with the ceremony, she would be damned for eternity.

"I have to think about this," she told her sister. "I don't have to do it right now."

Carol rolled her eyes.

"A roomful of people are waiting for your answer," she said as she left.

Laura knew that she had to do something nobody in her family had ever done before or maybe even thought about doing: defy the Prophet and his revelation from the Lord, or at least stall Uncle Roy for a little while. The hell with salvation—she couldn't marry Philip Barlow.

As she sat on the bed, it didn't occur to her that she had legal rights in the state of Utah about deciding whom she married, and when, and under what circumstances. She didn't know that if a woman was forced into wedlock against her will, the man performing the ceremony could be subject to punishment under the law, including charges of being an accomplice to rape. She didn't even know that for years she'd already been a victim of various sex crimes—after all, so many of the young females around her had been treated the same way. She knew twenty girls in her position, just off the top of her head, maybe more. It was normal, so normal that no one ever thought of it as illegal.

When Laura got off the bed and rejoined the other guests at the wedding party, they crowded near her and once again encouraged her to get married this afternoon. Summoning all her courage, she asked Uncle Roy if she could have just a few more days to fast and pray about her decision.

The old man with bushy eyebrows and hands that were bent and gnarled by rheumatoid arthritis looked puzzled by her request. Young women didn't act like this, not the ones he was used to dealing with; there must have been something wrong with Laura. After considering her request, he said yes, she could have some time to think things over. With this reprieve, she and Philip left Uncle Roy's and went to his family's house, where he was eager to introduce Laura to her soon-to-be relatives. His father gave him $25 to entertain the woman he would marry, and they rode around town in a pickup. Philip kept putting his arm around Laura and trying to pull her closer, as she tried not to squirm or jump out of the truck.

She returned home to Sandy but still had to give Uncle Roy a final answer. When she met with him again a week later in Salt Lake City, she'd had time to devise a subtle strategy. Laura told the old man, who was in failing health and addicted to morphine, that God had revealed to her through her prayers that she should not become Philip's wife. With the same befuddled expression as before, the Prophet nodded and asked if she wanted to marry somebody else. She'd anticipated his question and had her answer ready. She mentioned George Barlow, another member of the local clan, whom she wasn't in love with but who was more appealing than Philip. Uncle Roy accepted this choice and a date was set. During the ceremony, Laura and George enacted the secret FLDS handshake, clasping palms and folding the middle finger down into the wrist of the marriage partner, sealing the wife to her husband forever. After both were dead, the husband, if he believed his wife worthy of the honor, would call to her from the grave by a special name—usually "Sarah"—and she'd be resurrected and greet her spouse in the afterlife with the secret handshake.

At Laura and George's reception, Warren Jeffs played a starring role, crooning "The Wedding Song" by Peter, Paul, and Mary in the same soft, droning tenor voice he used when speaking to the children at Alta Academy. His first wife, Annette, accompanied him on the piano. After Warren finished performing, he sat quietly at the reception by himself while Annette got up and circulated among the guests. She was the sister of Laura's new husband, and the bride couldn't help noticing the changes in Annette since she'd become Warren's wife.

Before her marriage, Annette had been considered a prime catch inside the FLDS, the young woman whom all the young men wanted to take to the altar. Five feet two, with blond hair, blue eyes, an explosive smile, and a radiant personality, she was popular enough to buck some of the harsher fashion restrictions imposed on other female church members. She didn't wear long cotton dresses or elaborately woven braids that trailed down her back. Her clothes were more modern and her style much freer—until she got married. Then she began looking more and more like the other women around her, acting much more subdued in public. Under other circumstances, people might have been surprised by her marriage to this homely young man, so stiff and reserved and self-righteous, but he was the favored son of a leader on the Priesthood Council, so he could have anyone he wanted for a wife. After marrying Annette, he married her sister, Barbara.

Mormons weren't supposed to drink, but many did in private and some even did publicly on certain occasions: at weddings or when men gathered for professional football games on autumn Sunday afternoons. Annette was usually more restrained, but at Laura and George's reception she drank too much wine and got tipsy, her pretty face flushed, her laughter returning. Her husband kept a constant eye on her. In church, at school, or around Rulon's compound, Warren made mental notes on who was having too much fun or becoming too rowdy, and this included his own wife.

II

ONE-MAN RULE

6

OR A DECADE, turmoil had been growing inside the FLDS, finally emerging in the 1980s. After thirty years as the Prophet, Leroy Johnson's health was failing, Rulon Jeffs had positioned himself as his successor, and other Priesthood members had started dying off without being replaced. By mid-decade, only four men were left in power—Johnson, Jeffs, Alma Timpson, and Marion Hammon—instead of the usual seven. Since the 1920s, the Priesthood Council had played an important role in keeping FLDS leadership at least somewhat democratic. They'd advised the Prophet, had input on major decisions, cast votes, and applied the brakes if any one man was assuming too much control. They worked together to keep the system, and one another, in balance. Toward the end of Johnson's life, some within the church had encouraged him to move away from the past and institute one-man rule, but he never accepted this idea. As he neared death, another faction inside the FLDS pushed Rulon Jeffs to establish himself as the new Prophet—under one-man rule. Things would be run more efficiently this way, they argued, and much more would get done with a single person in charge.

But there were serious doubters about how the church was evolving.

"Back in late 1970s, Uncle Roy got up in a Priesthood meeting and said that the people of Short Crick had been weighed in the balance by God, and we'd been found wanting," recalls Benjamin Bistline, a former resident of the border towns and a local historian. He's written two books about the history of the FLDS. "Uncle Roy said that if we didn't truly repent and change the way things were going, the Lord would slough us off. No one ever spoke a truer prophecy."

In 1986, Johnson died and the conflict erupted. Alma Timpson and Marion Hammon, who represented the slightly more progressive wing of the FLDS, fervently opposed one-man rule. They didn't see this as a positive movement toward "theocracy," as some had labeled it, but dictatorship. They decided to break away from the church, removing the last remaining barriers to the Jeffs takeover. Timpson and Hammon packed up their families and left Colorado City to launch the new town of Centennial Park, a couple of miles south on Highway 59. Their new settlement would come to be known as "the second ward." Rulon was left alone to rule in the first ward, and the system that had been in place for decades was suddenly gone, but the full effects of this wouldn't be felt until Rulon himself had died many years later.

As the new Prophet, Rulon continued to live up north in Little Cottonwood Canyon, but his word was law down in the border towns. It wasn't long before his absentee leadership and high-handed attitude had people in Colorado City grumbling. Because Jeffs came from the more urban environment around Salt Lake City, locals felt that he looked down on the rural folks of southern Utah and northern Arizona. He was more sophisticated than they were, in his own mind, more outspoken and critical. Small towns often have a live-and-let-live attitude, but the new Prophet was quick to point what was wrong with how this person dressed or that one spoke or behaved in public. Worse still, he didn't confront an individual face-to-face, as Uncle Roy had, but went behind his back and spread gossip, which then snaked around town and got back to the offender. People in Colorado City weren't used to this; despite occasional infighting, the border community had always maintained a fierce sense of loyalty and unity against the outside world. If the leader had an issue with someone, he was supposed to go to that man or woman and say it straight out. Backbiting was ugly, even more so when it came from the Prophet.

And there were other complaints. Jeffs rarely traveled to Colorado City, except for one purpose.

"He didn't think the faithful were tithing enough to the church," says Ben Bistline, "so he started coming down to collect the money himself."

While Rulon took over the FLDS, Warren continued holding court at Alta Academy, enforcing his own one-man rule inside the school. He used the morning devotional to hone his leadership strategies and inculcate the children with his beliefs, angers, and fears. He gave lessons from the Book of Mormon and from his own teachings, lashing out at the authorities who'd made the "sacred principle" of polygamy a crime and promising they'd receive retribution from God. He told and retold the story of Short Creek being raided at four in the morning by 120 Arizona police officers, giving thanks that nothing like this had happened since 1953.

"The Lord has turned the key," Warren said to the children on March 25, 1997, "and made it so even the government has not persecuted us for forty years. We're teaching you openly the grown-up things you must do, the laws you must live and prepare for."

Be ready to defend our way of life, he told the boys. Keep sweet in all things, he emphasized to the girls, keep sweet in thoughts and deeds, stay true to their faith, and one day they'd be blessed by living the polygamous lifestyle.

But all marital unions had to be arranged by their leader.

"The Prophet," he said, "doesn't make mistakes as far as marriages are concerned. What he appoints—it can be eternal if the people who got married will live faithful. If ever a marriage fails, it's not the Prophet's fault. It's the people who lived it wrong . . . You are the children of Zion today, and you are offered to live it [plural marriage] no matter what the world thinks. This law is the greatest and most holy law that will exalt men and women."

Despite all the talk of marriage, contact between boys and girls was off-limits at Alta. Warren told the opposite sexes to treat one another as if they were "snakes." Part of his teaching concerned the importance of "male leadership," and how girls should never date and women should always obey their husbands. Every Friday, while the boys attended construction class, he spelled out for those in home economics their coming duties as wives, quoting from a book called *Enlightened Truth*. Girls shouldn't talk to their mothers, sisters, or female friends about sex because when it came time for them to learn about this "sacred matter," their husbands would show them all they needed to know.

"Warren instructed girls on how to be a good mother—the highest honor of the religion," says Rebecca Musser, who both attended and later taught at the school. "He went through keeping house, learning to cook, comforting husbands, and raising kids to be loyal and obedient. Everything was devoted to the father. When girls got married, they were supposed to transfer all ties and loyalties to their husbands and have perfect obedience to them, because their husbands were their direct ties to God. Warren talked about girls 'belonging to' young men.

"He taught us to be submissive to our husbands in every way. Never, ever stand up against him. Never say no to your husband, especially in front of your children. If anything went wrong, it was your fault because you didn't have enough faith. He said that our joy should come from loving our fathers as he loved Rulon, not from Rulon loving him. Our joy was to come from loving our husbands, not from our husbands loving us."

On January 30, 1998, Warren spoke to a class of seventh- and eighth-grade females: "A girl's emotions and feelings can be led by the wrong things if she's not careful. After all, who knows the spirit of revelation better—you or the Prophet . . . ?"

Sometimes he demonstrated his teachings about female obedience and male leadership with cruelty. His first wife, Annette, had become Alta's home economics instructor, and one morning in front of boys and girls gathered in the meeting hall, Warren and his spouse were addressing the audience. He grabbed Annette's long braided hair, twisting it slowly around his hand, tightening his grip until she dropped to the floor, her face turning crimson and contorting in pain. She didn't make a sound or movement of protest. He let go and quietly left the room with no explanation to the students and no apology to his wife, who stood up, straightened her hair, and went back to teaching. She'd grasped well the concept of "keeping sweet."

One young student named "Zeke" (not his real name) was quite close to Jeffs at the academy. Many mornings before the school day started, Warren singled the small boy out on the playground and made a point of shaking his hand and asking him questions. Zeke was obviously bright, had tested very high at Alta, and the principal seemed to identify with him more than with the other kids. The slightly built Zeke had intense and sensitive eyes; words poured from him on every subject, and he was the most articulate child at the school. Early on, Jeffs began grooming him for a high position inside the church, and the boy greatly admired him. As Zeke moved through the grades at Alta and excelled in his classes, Jeffs continued to pay him a lot of attention. Zeke was flattered and eager to spend more time with the man.

Years later, he was asked if he'd ever been molested at the academy.

"Not by Warren," he said. "He always had his eye on me, but *he* didn't assault me."

What struck Zeke was that Jeffs not only dwelled on powerful historical figures, but acted as if he wanted to become one himself, craving recognition beyond the boundaries of a tiny school in an obscure setting.

"Warren really wanted to become somebody," Zeke says. "Somebody whose name people knew."

It was obvious to the young man that the principal had much bigger plans than running Alta, and he was preparing his favorite student to be part of them. Zeke had his own ambitions, and for years he wanted to be a part of Jeffs's future—until he matured and got to know Warren better.

At the academy, Jeffs was honing his leadership skills and learning several key lessons that he'd one day apply in Colorado City: small children, adolescents, and even their parents would obey his demands, regardless of how outlandish they became. They trusted his authority simply because he was the principal and his father was on the Priesthood Council, assuming he knew what was best. They didn't question things or wonder what was being born inside the walls at Alta.

7

IN THE LATE 1990S, Rulon decided to relocate his family from Little Cottonwood Canyon to the border towns in preparation for the new millennium, which would bring disaster to mainstream America and the official Mormon Church. Only those church members who'd been sufficiently obedient and had already achieved salvation in the eyes of the Prophet would be blessed enough to depart the earth in a blast of divine deliverance, while the wicked ones left behind would feel the wrath of a terrible scourge. Long-standing prophecies were about to be fulfilled. In 1984, Uncle Roy had proclaimed: "The redemption of Zion . . . according to the revelations of God, is to commence in the seventh period of time. According to our reckoning, that seventh period of time is only about sixteen years off."

With the approach of widespread death and destruction, Rulon was certain that his own kin would be much better off in an isolated rural setting, beyond the reach of big government, big media, law enforcement, and other gentiles and their destructive ways. The Jeffs of Little Cottonwood Canyon cleaned out their mansion, closed down Alta Academy, and headed south to Dixie.

Rulon had shut the school so that Warren could come with him and be his closest adviser. By the time the family resettled, the Prophet was almost ninety, and a severe stroke in August 1997 had left him much weaker and less capable mentally. His hearing was fading and his attention wandered. He had trouble formulating whole sentences or tracking a conversation. He needed other eyes and ears, and Warren had made himself into his father's indispensable adviser and enforcer. Traditionally, the Prophet's "first counselor" was considered the second most important post in the church. After first coun-selor Parley Harker passed away in 1998, Warren assumed this role without fanfare, managing church details and various leadership functions. All he had to do now was wait for his father to die.

Once the family had moved into a massive new home in Hildale, Warren took over his father's office and kept almost everyone away from the older man, not wanting them to see how incapacitated he'd become. He told his brother Issac to guard the compound's front door and let in only a select few. Warren took Rulon's calls, handled his appointments, and offered counsel to those with problems, gradually making more and more of the FLDS's day-to-day decisions, choosing who could get married and who couldn't. If any man in the church wanted to take another wife, he first had to get Warren's ap-proval. He made these marital choices partly on the physical and genetic makeup of each man and woman, in order to keep the FLDS "racially pure."

"The devil," he told church members, "is trying to get people to go out and marry and mix with the world, even different-colored people. That is why we marry *only* who the Prophet says."

Rulon predicted the world would come to an end on June 12, 1999, the 111th anniversary of Leroy Johnson's birthday. That morning, the faithful arose early and gathered in a local parking lot to sing hymns and form a prayer circle. Many had brought an extra supply of groceries and lots of wa-ter, so they would have plenty to eat and drink in the next life. As the long day wore on and darkness gradually fell, they marched to a grassy field near the town's cemetery—known as the "launching pad"—where past Prophets had brought them when the Lord was supposed to reach down from heaven and "lift them up." Nothing had happened on those occasions and nothing hap-pened at midnight on June 12, the prophesized moment for the transition into the celestial realm. They lingered at the launching pad for a while longer before going home tired and disappointed, Rulon having explained to them that God had decided to give everybody a reprieve. They had six months to become more obedient and pray more fervently before the grand event.

When the new millennium came and went without incident, Rulon of-fered a similar explanation, indicating that his flock wasn't yet worthy of leav-ing the earth. His next prediction concerned the 2002 Winter Olympics, held that February in Salt Lake City: the Games would bring monumental tragedy to Utah and the LDS Church. But that promise also turned out to be wrong.

While the Colorado City and Hildale residents had their gaze focused on impending disaster from the heavens, they failed to notice the monster approaching from a different direction.

For a while, the emergence of Warren as the power behind the throne was hidden from the community, but Rulon himself began observing the changes taking place around him. One day over lunch at the thirty-thousand-square-foot compound, father and son were sharing a meal together and the old man had become particularly quiet. He suddenly leaned forward and pounded on the table.

"I want my job back!" he said.

Warren smiled and nodded gently. In his smoothest and most reassuring voice, he said, "Now, Father, I'm just helping you out."

For years Rulon had told people that he'd live to be at least 350, or until Christ returned to rule the earth and all the gentiles had been destroyed. And with the latter about to happen, church members were encouraged to take out as many loans from their lending institution—the pink adobe Bank of Ephraim up on Highway 59—as they could. Since the world was about to end, borrowers would never have to pay back the money. When the faithful did as instructed, the bank collapsed. It was obvious to some that Rulon was becoming more erratic.

"I didn't know exactly where things were heading in the late 1990s, but I could see they were moving toward chaos," says local historian Benjamin Bistline. "The Barlow boys in town, and there were eight important ones, turned to the elderly bishop, Fred Jessop, for leadership, instead of to Rulon or Warren. They wanted Fred to back *them* as the next heads of the community and church, but Fred told them to go along with what was happening and the Lord would take care of everything. They listened to him. They rolled over and played dead."

Many church members still assumed that if Rulon did in fact die, the next Prophet would not come from inside the Jeffs clan but from an older, more established local family. That was how things had usually worked in the past—but not now. As Warren bided his time, it was critical that his decisions and actions appeared to be based on orders from the Prophet, so his statements to the congregation often began with, "This is what Father wants me to tell you . . ."

Once the Jeffs family had relocated to southern Utah, Warren summoned Zeke, his protégé at Alta, to join him on the border. Zeke was now a teenager and became a religious instructor at one of the private schools run by the FLDS.

"I moved down there and began teaching the Book of Mormon to youngsters," Zeke recalls. "I was a rising star in the church and could get away with more than most people. When my brother drank and caroused at night, Warren kicked him out of the community. I did some of the same things just to see if he would boot me out, but he didn't. I could see that he made up the rules to suit his plans for the future. I was still useful to him and in favor."

Jeffs and Zeke met at least once a week, and the closer the young man got to him, the more concern he felt. Despite his indoctrination at Alta about the infallibility of FLDS leadership, Zeke began to have doubts. Warren gave him the impression that he consulted with God on a daily basis—and that God was telling him to deliver severe punishment to those He disapproved of. This contrasted sharply with Rulon, who'd often prayed with and then forgiven his followers for their sins. If Warren saw conflict in a local family, his first instinct wasn't to confront or try to heal the problem, but to break it up and reassign the family members. Both his manner and his blind will increasingly frightened Zeke.

"Warren had a way of intimidating you just by looking at you," the young man says. "He wouldn't threaten you himself, but threatened God's wrath on you in the form of eternal damnation. He used only a few words to do this and did it very quietly. He was extremely precise and calculating and manipulative in everything he did."

With Rulon less and less able to lead, Warren began making more outrageous demands on worshippers.

He ordered families to cut off all ties with the modern media—to get rid of television sets, satellite dishes, newspapers, magazines, and Internet connections. Radios were allowed, but he told them to stop watching movies. He banned anything with the color red, children's videos, and musical recordings, unless they contained the songs he'd written and performed. Just as he'd done at Alta, he scheduled closed-door meetings with parents, criticizing their clothing, dress, and attitudes, castigating them for an unsnapped button or an out-of-place lock of hair. Men were told to be obedient and women were instructed to keep their children in check and their homes spotless. He brought together gangs of young men, called "Uncle Warren's Sons of Hela-man," and sent them into the houses of possible apostates, which they in-spected for neatness, dust, or questionable behavior.

He encouraged children to inform on their parents for minor rule viola-tions, banished traditional FLDS holidays and dancing, forbade swimming and other water sports. He told business owners to turn over their assets to him and insisted that they give the church the money they'd placed in 401(k) accounts. Some did as asked, but this demand was so potentially ruinous that several families resisted and then left Colorado City, restarting their lives in an Idaho settlement headed by Winston Blackmore, leader of the Canadian FLDS. Following the 1953 raid, a branch of the congregation had migrated north and eventually put down roots in Canada. In 1986, Blackmore became a trustee of the church and presided over the second-largest FLDS commu-nity, in Bountiful, British Columbia, just across the border from Idaho. He was considered the most serious rival to Rulon's leadership, and in the late 1990s the aging Prophet kicked him out of the church, a move that many felt his son had orchestrated.

Warren made youngsters stop playing basketball and told people not to leave town to eat in restaurants—a waste of time and money. Parents were or-dered to throw away their Bibles and Book of Mormon storybooks, but some stashed their favorite reading material in garages or closets so that when visi-tors or the Sons of Helaman came by, they wouldn't see the offending mate-rial. Warren was particularly disturbed by Dr. Seuss books depicting animals with human characteristics; they also had to go. When a family's dog attacked a two-year-old boy inside the city limits, Jeffs told his minions to round up all the canines in town, take them to a ditch outside Colorado City, and exe-cute them. The town no longer held the sound of barking dogs. When War-ren needed more cash, he gathered up the animals in the town's small, quaint zoo and sold them off, the bears, goats, and zebra. He closed the library.

Warren had survived a miraculous birth, endured a painful childhood, and become a grown man for just this moment and this opportunity. God had clearly chosen him as the natural leader of the Chosen People, and he now stood at the threshold of his dream. His mission was to cleanse and perfect the followers of the FLDS, and nothing could be allowed to stop this pro-gression. Like Joseph Smith in the 1830s, Warren had only one goal—to re-turn Christianity to its pure form as the one true faith.

He wasn't the first American religious leader to embrace this kind of vision. Two decades earlier, the Aryan Nations Church in northern Idaho, led by Reverend Richard Butler, had churned out sermon after sermon about the need for a radical restoration of Christianity and a purging of the nation's ethnic melting pot. The script for that purging had been laid out in a 1978 blood-soaked, anti-Semitic novel, *The Turner Diaries*, written by William Pierce. The book featured a small group of white supremacists, known as the Order, who kick-started a revolution that led to the "Day of the Rope," a day on which white women who'd slept with black men were hanged, along with lawyers, judges, teachers, journalists, editors, preachers, bureaucrats, and other enemies.

The Aryan Nations church would go on to draw racists from all over the nation, and in the early 1980s it became the founding place of a small neo-Nazi gang that called itself the Order, after the group in Pierce's novel. Like the fundamentalist Mormons, the Anglo-Saxon men in the Order believed that they, and not the Israelites of the Middle East, were God's Chosen People. Those who now called themselves Jews were impostors and the spawn of Satan. African Americans were regarded as subhuman "mud people."

In 1984, the real-life Order stole more than $4 million, assassinated a Jewish talk show host in Denver named Alan Berg, and murdered four other men, unleashing the largest investigation into domestic terrorism in U.S. history. The federal government soon broke up the group and killed its founder, Bob Mathews, in a shootout near Seattle, but the Order's legacy resonated darkly. Timothy McVeigh studied the same violent literature as Aryan Nations members had, before bombing a federal building in Oklahoma City in April 1995 and killing 168 people.

The rise and fall of homegrown neo-Nazis had shown law enforcement that white separatists and offshoot religious sects could be extremely dangerous. The 1993 FBI standoff with followers of David Koresh at the Branch Davidian compound at Waco, Texas, had left scores dead and created within the government more concern about such groups.

Since the fall of the Order in the mid-1980s, religious fanaticism had begun intensifying elsewhere. As Jeffs gradually took over the FLDS, the American military began locking itself in combat with Islamic fundamentalism in Afghanistan and Iraq. In Indonesia, Pakistan, India, Lebanon, Israel, Palestine, England, the United States, and Spain, spiritual warriors were coming together to kill "the enemy" for their God. The twenty-first century hadn't brought an end to life on earth, as the FLDS and others had prophesized, or ushered in a New Age of peace and love. It had triggered a hardening of beliefs and a deepening intolerance.

Groups became convinced that their definition of religious truth was right. Ancient myths were resurfacing with a vengeance, and across the planet young men who hadn't separated spiritually or politically from their fathers were filled with an anger, fear, and violence far more pronounced than their ancestors'. They'd prove just how righteous they were through blood atonement.

As stories of the rise of Warren Jeffs began filtering out of the twin communities, the authorities' concern about where this might lead only increased. By 2002, the Arizona attorney general's office had generated a memo referring to a "Waco-level problem" among the polygamous communities in Colorado City. Rumors were seeping across the high desert plateau and reaching officials in Kingman and Salt Lake City about the emergence on the border of something like an American Taliban.

But something else was emerging right alongside it—a new generation of women waging their own war against the FLDS.

8

SOON AFTER MARRYING IN 1981, Laura and George Barlow began having children, four girls and a boy in the next seven years. Their son developed autism and was eventually institutionalized. Overwhelmed by the endless demands of small kids and housekeeping, Laura asked her husband for help with the household chores, but he didn't know how to respond. One day she asked him for more "emotional intimacy," which he thought meant having more sex. After discouraging his advances, she spelled out that these two words could include his offering to help dry the dishes or pick up one of the crying children or simply ask her about her day after he came home from work. He tried to do some of these things, but none of this behavior came easily to him. In his culture, twelve-year-old boys were initiated into the "Aaronic Priesthood," which instantly gave them more authority than their mothers and caused many to start acting superior, or indifferent, to the females around them. To make things worse, Laura didn't enjoy the way he made love. It was repetitive and distant, just like the rest of their relationship.

Laura had been raised amidst rumors that FLDS men occasionally traveled to the Middle East to learn more about how these ancient societies kept women under control (in some Muslim countries, mothers still had to ask their young sons for permission to travel). The more Laura uncovered about the practices of Islam, the more parallels she discovered between that faith and the FLDS. Muslims, for example, were promised scores of virgins in heaven if they were willing to become martyrs for their "jihad," or war against the non-Muslim world. One of Joseph Smith's most controversial revelations regarding plural marriage had read: "*And if he have ten virgins given unto him by this law, he cannot commit adultery, for they belong to him, and they are given unto him; therefore is he justified."*

Boys raised inside the FLDS were subtly discouraged from becoming too attached to any one female. Polygamy depended on a man desiring multiple wives and being available, emotionally and physically, to all of them. The odds against real intimacy developing between a husband and one wife were steep. Laura knew all of these things going into her marriage, but hoped that her husband would love her enough to be different from the other men in her community.

Their life together was shaky long before George decided, on their tenth anniversary, to take a second wife (when Laura told him she was finished having children after giving birth to five, her husband said they were finished making love and he needed to find a new partner). The one he found was sixteen. Like Emma Smith before her, when Joseph Smith announced he was marrying another spouse, Laura rebelled, declaring that she was leaving and taking the children and half of George's income. In 1991, the twenty-eight-year-old mother fled the FLDS for northern Utah and filed for divorce, but George never came to court and refused to sign any legal papers, even after the judge demanded it. Once the divorce was granted, she raised her kids as a single mother and put herself through college, then started a career in social work. In time she reported to the Mohave County police that they should investigate her husband for marrying a sixteen-year-old, but law enforcement was reluctant to look into something that was hundreds of miles away and commonplace in Colorado City.

Now that Laura had small children of her own—and could see and feel their complete vulnerability in the emotional and sexual arena—she finally began to pry open the closed doors of her past. Her father's smells and the sound of him coming into her bedroom in the darkness were still alive within her, causing recurrent nightmares. They needed to be confronted and perhaps healed before she could do what she most wanted to: become a political activist and challenge the foundation of the FLDS. Her most painful memories unfolded in flashbacks triggered by a touch or an odor or the sight of curtains blowing across a windowsill, pulling her back into being used by her father, who had "priesthood power" inside her home. No one ever thought about resisting or challenging what he did. As an adult woman, Laura knew what she hadn't known a decade earlier: she'd been the victim of a crime that nobody had ever been held accountable for. It was time for this chain of molestation to stop.

Years after their divorce, her husband came back to Laura and asked to spend time with their daughters in his home in Centennial Park, but she said absolutely not. Away from her and alone with their father, the girls could be funneled into the system of arranged marriages, just as she'd been. It was the thought of what could happen to *them* that finally pushed Laura to act. She went to court to fight her ex-husband's request, spending $5,000 in legal fees and becoming the first woman ever to keep her polygamous spouse from having unsupervised time with their children.

In the 1990s, Laura read the history of African American women during slavery, and she'd also begun to identify with the struggle of women in Muslim countries and elsewhere. She wasn't as isolated as she'd imagined; women around the world had begun to come together to change their political status and living conditions, and this thought emboldened her. In 1998, she wrote a letter to Utah Governor Mike Leavitt, who'd recently portrayed the people of southern Utah as good, hardworking folks. He added that polygamy was protected under the First Amendment and that his state had a long history of handling this particular situation in its own way, within its own borders. The distant shadow of the 1953 raid on Short Creek obviously still lay over the politicians in Laura's home state.

She wrote the governor that Utah had a long history of *ignoring* polygamy and its children, who were denied a public education, information about the outside world, and choice when it came to selecting whom and when to marry. Women in polygamist communities weren't provided equal protection under the law—weren't given the freedoms granted all full-fledged citizens of the United States. Another activist and friend of hers, Vicky Prunty, told Laura that letter-writing wasn't enough and that they needed to protest the governor's remarks on the steps of the state capitol in Salt Lake City. On July 28, 1998, Laura, Vicky, and two other women did just that, attracting widespread media coverage and bringing their cause to the public for the first time. A new generation of women who'd escaped polygamy was loudly raising questions that Utah had for so long managed to dodge. The main one was: Why did the authorities refuse to enforce existing laws or pass new ones to help women and children still trapped inside the FLDS? Laura joined a group in Salt Lake City called TAP—Tapestry Against Polygamy—headed by Vicky

Prunty. A large part of its strategy was to shame state leaders into action. The July 1998 protest had generated national attention and Laura did numerous interviews, speaking out against the abuses she'd endured.

Word of her efforts quickly got back to the Fundamentalist Mormon Church and Warren Jeffs. In FLDS meetings, he'd begun talking about the activist women, calling them the "daughters of perdition," saying they'd taken on "the spirit of Lucifer" in order to harm God's work. They weren't behaving like any women in the community before them and they weren't keeping sweet. They had to be stopped—now—before their ideas spread.

Laura's sister, Rena, also joined the activist fight. Ten years older, Rena had been molested by their father starting at age three. The beatings came later. She attended Jordan High School with Warren and was one grade ahead of him. The young man already had a strong air of self-importance and self-righteousness.

"He just creeped me out," Rena recalls. "It wasn't anything he said or did, but just the way he was. He had this attitude that he was on a higher level with God than anybody else and he let you know that."

Rena was more outwardly rebellious than Laura and by her junior year she'd developed a reputation as a "bad girl," sneaking her brother's guitar into the school and playing rock music. Her father's sexual abuse and violence had made her question her faith and would eventually push her toward hard drinking and drug addiction. At seventeen, she was forced into marriage with her stepbrother and soon had three children. Five years passed and, struggling with severe emotional problems, she approached Uncle Roy and tried to tell him that her father had molested her, but the Prophet said she was lying. When Rena decided to leave the church and the region, her father kept her children against her will. She fled to Southern California, where she met an attorney who explained to her that she had the legal right to prosecute her dad for taking her kids. Nine months later, she returned to Utah, confronted her father in the middle of the night, and told him that if he didn't give her back her children, he was going to prison. The threat worked.

"I put my kids in the car," she says, "and drove like the devil was chasing me all the way to Nevada. I was the first woman in the history of Colorado City to get my children back after they'd been taken from me."

Rena had won this legal battle, but it would be years before she'd defeat alcohol and cocaine. Her emotional and psychological scars pushed her further into the drug world, and she was surprised to find that these connections led her back to her religious roots.

"In the early 1990s," she says, "I inadvertently got involved in moving ten pounds of marijuana that had been cultivated and grown by people in the FLDS. Their thing was that the outside world was going to hell and they were going to help it along. They weren't using the pot themselves, but selling it to other people so that *they* could go to hell. I eventually went to the FBI and told them about the marijuana in Colorado City, but they said the information was too old to be pursued."

Ben Bistline was also convinced that in the 1990s the border towns became a distribution point for drugs, including cocaine and heroin moving from Texas to California. Occasionally, the Colorado City police blocked off access to the local airport when small planes were coming in at night, which deepened Bistline's suspicions. He believed that church leaders received a share of the substantial amounts of cash this underground business generated.

"A few of us," Ben says, "went to narcotics officials at the Drug Enforcement Administration and asked them to investigate this, but they put the burden back on us. They told us to bring them evidence of this activity before they'd look into it. They wouldn't do any surveillance themselves and that really ticked me off. The heads of the church back then had their hands out for a piece of this money—there were people around here who never worked a day in their lives and lived like kings. Drove big new cars and had fine houses and no source of income that you could see. They figured that people someplace else were going to take the drugs anyway, so they might as well get in on the good end of it."

A step at a time, a man or woman at a time, the revolt against the FLDS was slowly building momentum.

9

ACH SPRING THE FLDS HELD A GENERAL CONFERENCE in Colorado City, designed to mimic the much larger LDS conference held annually in Salt Lake City. Prominent elders spoke to the faithful, marriages were arranged and performed, and everyone was encouraged to make a renewed commitment to the church and the Lord. The conference was usually held around April 6, the date that fundamentalists believed was Christ's actual birthday. In March 1999, just before the conference was set to begin in the border towns, Laura was contacted by two sixteen-year-old girls from Sandy, Utah, Sarah Cooke and Kathy Beagley. Both had been told by their parents that they'd be getting married soon, and Sarah felt certain her wedding would take place during the conference. The girls were panicking, and Sarah felt suicidal. Their plight evoked Laura's past, as well as fears for her own daughters and other young women. It was her chance to do for someone else what had never been done for her.

At 10:30 one night in late March, the girls sneaked out of their houses to meet Laura on a Sandy street corner, where they discussed this legally complex challenge. If Laura referred them to Child Protective Services, the state would likely return them to their parents, pending an investigation. If their parents turned them away, which had happened before in FLDS families after youngsters had rebelled, the girls would have to fend for themselves in the adult world. Neither alternative was good, so Laura began looking for someone who might offer them a home and stability. She found a local couple and ran a background check on them. The husband was a police officer, the wife a nurse, and they had a daughter just one year younger than the girls; the family's reputation was sterling.

Late one night, Laura introduced Sarah and Kathy to their new foster parents, and they soon arranged to leave home and move in. The first things the teenagers indulged in were the stylish hairdos and makeup they'd never been allowed. Kathy couldn't adjust to the radical change or being away from home and soon returned to her family, but Sarah stayed with the couple and became a high school honor student before earning a degree from Nebraska's Creighton University. When graduating from college, she told Laura that she'd saved her life and given her the most important gift she'd ever received: her freedom. Laura then helped a young mother with two small boys leave the FLDS, and years later Kathy herself was successfully able to break away from the church.

Laura's growing activism brought her more media attention and more threats. At the end of the 1990s, she appeared on CBS's *48 Hours* and ABC's *20/20* (but only after the official LDS power structure had made certain that FLDS activities would not be associated with the branch of Mormon faith represented by the church in Salt Lake City). She was featured in the *New York Times Magazine* and the *Denver Post*. During thirty interviews, she used her exposure to bring more awareness to the legal problems surrounding polygamy—and more embarrassment to Utah authorities for neglecting these matters for decades. If she couldn't change or enforce existing laws regarding sexual abuse and underage marriage, she and other civilian women could keep raising their public voices to vent their frustration and goad politicians.

Laura's activism did not come cheap. Her mother, Myra Tolman, bitterly chastised her for going public with the secrets of the FLDS, feeling that her daughter had betrayed her and her religious background in front of the whole world. While helping Sarah Cooke and Kathy Beagley escape their homes and find a new family, Laura began receiving nasty calls at 3:00 in the morning, telling her to stop what she was doing because she had no business "messing with children born under the Covenant." An unknown person put sand in her gas tank, while someone left more ominous messages on her phone, insisting that she'd committed a sin she could never repent for and should have her blood spilled as atonement to God.

In the late 1990s, her sister Rena was working in a convenience store in

Midvale, near Sandy, when someone taped a note on the front door: "We know where you are." She, too, had been identified as one of the "daughters of perdition" and was now contacted by people close to the fundamentalist church, who said her life was in danger. In private meetings, Warren Jeffs was preaching "blood atonement" for Rena as well.

"This meant that the only way for me to achieve salvation," she says, "was by having my blood spilled by a worthy priesthood holder whose mission was to save my soul."

The more Laura and Rena pushed to expose the faith they'd been raised in, the more it pushed back. Groups of FLDS men began showing up in the convenience store parking lot and staring at Rena. They came inside and one man pointed his finger at her as if it were a pistol. When a car parked near her house at night, she called the police, but the threats continued. Rena and her husband decided they should leave Utah for good. They packed up and never returned.

Laura also moved to a secret location, vowing never to live in Sandy again. She'd done everything she could in her home state short of bringing legal action against the FLDS, but a younger generation of women would later take that momentous step.

10

BY 2000, WARREN JEFFS WAS IN THE AWKWARD position of impatiently waiting for his father to die, while trying to appear reverent toward Rulon. The old man had faded so badly that he couldn't monitor everything his son did, and Warren had begun speaking for the Prophet about ridding the FLDS of enemies and apostates, laying the foundation for his coming reign. On July 17 of that year, at the LJS Meetinghouse in Hildale, he seemed to represent his father, who waited in the wings as Warren addressed the congregation:

> I ask Heavenly Father to strengthen me at this time to deliver the message our Prophet has directed we receive this day ... Let there be a separation of this Priesthood people from associations, business, and doings with apostates ... An apostate ... is the most dark person on earth. They are a liar from the beginning. They have made covenants to abide the laws of God and have turned traitor to the Priesthood and their own existence, and they are led about by their master, Lucifer ...
>
> And if you are choosing to socialize with apostates, to join with them in any way, you are choosing to get on the devil's ground ... Stop patronizing businesses of the apostates ... If you are in partnership with apostates, come away from them is the call of our Prophet, for your labors of earning money is strengthening their hand against this Priesthood ...

Echoing Brigham Young's entries from 1876, Jeffs said, "The great challenge among this people is the apostates who are our relatives. If a mother has apostate children, her emotions won't let her give them up and she invites them into the home, thus desecrating that dedicated home ...

"Your only real family are the members of this Priesthood who are faithful to our Prophet . . . If any among this people work in a job for an apostate, he wants you to find a different job."

After Warren finished, his father commended him on the excellence of his sermon and repeated the same sentiments.

"Apostates," Rulon said from the pulpit, "have ingratiated themselves with their friendly relatives and it is poison. So let us separate ourselves and stand with the true cause of God and the Priesthood. It is all the way or nothing at all . . . So take this counsel that I have asked Brother Warren to deliver to this people today. God bless you. I pray in the name of Jesus Christ, amen."

In August 2000, Warren ordered all FLDS parents to pull their boys and girls out of the public schools serving Colorado City and Hildale, ending the children's interaction with gentile teachers and classmates who came from nearby Centennial Park. Enrollment at Phelps Elementary School dropped from 350 to 16. Washington County (Utah) eventually closed Phelps. The FLDS community tried homeschooling, but when it became too burdensome, the families organized more formal private schools. One was the Jeffs Academy, which moved into Phelps after the district sold it to the Twin Cities Improvement Association for pennies on the dollar. The result of all these changes was that local children were more isolated from the outside world and fell further and further behind in their education.

Another institution was coming under Warren's control as well, and he was exercising it far from The Crick.

The 160-mile drive from Colorado City to Caliente, Nevada, winds along the two-lane Route 56, leading through Utah's Antelope Mountains and across the Escalante Valley. By 2001, Nevada had become the best choice for FLDS wedding ceremonies, as Utah and Arizona authorities were finally stirring from their decades-long indifference to underage marriage. That year Utah Attorney General Mark Shurtleff had prosecuted one of the state's most notorious polygamists, Tom Green, who'd openly flaunted his lifestyle by claiming that he had five wives and twenty-nine children. Green was convicted of child rape for having sex with his first wife when she was thirteen. His legal troubles had widespread implications. They motivated pro-polygamy female activists—led by Marianne Watson, Mary Batchelor, and Anne Wilde—to form the advocacy group Principle Voices and to start networking with other Mormon fundamentalist women. Their mission included telling the media that they did not condone underage or arranged marriages, but that for consenting adults plural marriage could be a healthy choice. They also recommended that everybody should be at least eighteen before entering into wedlock.

Warren had followed the Tom Green case and decided that the border towns were no longer a safe haven for performing "celestial marriages." The isolated Caliente Hot Springs Motel in eastern Nevada was not only owned by church members, but was tucked far enough away to be safe from Utah and Arizona law enforcement.

Room 15 had no pews, arbors, pipe organ, or candlelabra, only a plain wooden dresser, bed, table, and sofa. The motel featured therapeutic waters for people in search of healing or relaxation, but those traveling in caravans from Colorado City to Caliente for as many as ten weddings back-to-back were too busy to think about soaking in the hot springs. On weekends, they arrived as a pack and waited until most of the other guests had checked out of the motel or left for the day so strangers wouldn't see what they were doing. The brides usually came with their mothers or fathers, while the grooms brought along a few of their plural wives. During the ceremony, one of the wives usually held the bride's hand and placed it in the groom's, as a way of accepting her into the new family as a "sister wife."

In the spring of 2001, a fourteen-year-old girl named Elissa Wall was living in the Hildale home of ninety-year-old Fred Jessop, a bishop and the third-in-command inside the FLDS behind Rulon and Warren Jeffs. Elissa had grown up near Salt Lake City and attended Alta Academy before her family was broken up because of her father's behavioral problems. The church leadership decided he needed an "adjustment," and he was sent away. Elissa, her mother, Sharon, and her sisters were "reassigned" and moved in with the Jessops in Hildale. As a child, Elissa had spent time on a farm in southern Utah and gotten to know one of her first cousins, Allen Steed. Elissa had several pretty sisters and was attractive herself, with pink cheeks, long flowing blond hair, and an innocent smile, but she'd always been a little overweight and self-conscious about it. Allen criticized her appearance, calling her "Tubby Tubba" and other hurtful things. One time he shot Elissa with a hose filled with cold water, and she never forgot how it felt. To her, Allen was a mean-spirited bully.

The home Elissa's family moved into was vast, with forty bedrooms and half as many baths. Fred Jessop needed a lot of space to accomodate his fifteen or so wives and the three or four dozen others who lived there—after Elissa's mother came to stay with the old man, he married *her*. One April evening, Fred appoached Elissa and mentioned that the Prophet "had a place" for his girls now, code language meaning that some of the local teenagers were about to be wed. FLDS girls had been taught at Alta, at home, and at church services that being selected as a marriage partner was the highest honor they could hope for. And then to have lots of children.

"There is no greater goal," they were told, "than to be a mother in Zion."

Fred looked surprised when Elissa didn't seem happy about this news. In fact, she didn't respond at all—assuming that he was talking about other girls in the community and not her. He repeated himself and this time made his message more clear: the Prophet had chosen a place for her.

Even as the words sunk in, she wasn't certain that Fred was serious.

"I don't feel," the ninth-grader told the ninety-year-old, "this is what I should be doing."

He calmly nodded and suggested she go into her room and pray about her situation.

"Who am I supposed to marry?" she asked, but the old man refused to give her an answer.

After thinking about what Fred had told her and praying for a couple of days, she went back to him and said that she definitely wasn't ready for all the responsibilities of being a wife. The bishop listened patiently and then told her to go speak to the Prophet.

She phoned Rulon's compound and reached Warren, explaining that she was too young to get married and wanted to ask his father for advice. Warren also told her to pray about her situation, and said that he'd soon let Fred know what the plan was. Later that week, Warren contacted Jessop and said that God had called Elissa to be married now. When Fred conveyed this to the girl, she was stunned, but didn't express her feelings or argue with him. Since the first grade at Alta, she'd been taught that the Prophet was not just the church leader but God on earth and whatever he said wasn't just his opinion, but a direct command from the Lord. Still, she doubted she'd be forced into marriage at fourteen.

One spring night at a family gathering in the Jessop home, she was sitting next to her mother, and on her other side was an empty chair. Other women kept walking by and asking if she was excited about her upcoming wedding, but she didn't know what to say. No spouse had been chosen for her and, in her mind at least, the matter seemed to be fading. Looking around the room, she spotted her first cousin, Allen, who walked over and sat down beside her. Her mind suddenly clicked—this was the young man they'd selected as her husband! He wasn't just a close relative whom she disliked, but a bully.

Her cheeks flushed a deep shade of pink as she jumped up and hurried away.

Elissa ran into her mother's bedroom, lay down on the pillows, and began to sob.

Her mother came in and sat next to her.

"I can't marry him!" the girl said. "He's my first cousin! I won't do this!"

Talk to Fred, Sharon told her in a reassuring voice. He'll know what's right. Just go talk to Fred.

When she confronted the old man and said that she could never be with Allen, he spelled out to her that this was how things worked in the FLDS and that she needed to understand and accept that. Uncle Rulon had ordered this wedding because it was the fulfillment of God's will. Elissa just needed to settle down and offer the Lord more prayers for her good fortune.

"You wouldn't defy what the Prophet wants, would you?" he asked.

"No," she replied. "No, I wouldn't. I just don't want to marry *him.*"

Uncle Fred was taken aback. Why would a young woman being given the chance to enter into a good marriage be so distaught? This wasn't the way things had been done in the past, when teenage girls in the church had said yes to their weddings and made far more of an effort to keep sweet. Fred was so bewildered that he told Elissa to go back to the Prophet and seek his counsel again.

She called Warren and made an appointment to see his father, but when she arrived at the Jeffs's compound, the younger man spoke to her alone in Rulon's office. She tried to explain that she needed time to grow up before becoming someone's wife, but Warren gazed at her with a confused expression, just as Fred had done.

Why, he asked her, would she or any other girl in the congregation not be thrilled to be getting married? This would give her a lifetime of security and respect within the church and the community. It was a great privilege to be joined with somebody from one of the more prominent FLDS families, and to receive the protection and support of her husband.

"Have you prayed about this?" Warren said.

"Yes, I have," the girl answered. "Many times. Everything inside of me is telling me not to do this."

Didn't she understand that the Prophet had received a revelation from God about her marriage to Allen?

She didn't know how to respond to his question, so they stared at one another across Rulon's desk.

"I need to hear it from the Prophet," she said.

Warren took her into the dining room, where his father was eating lunch with several of his wives. As the younger women hovered around the elderly man, Elissa knelt down at the Prophet's knee and said what a wonderful honor it was for her to be allowed near him. Surely, he would listen to her.

With his broad face and white hair sweeping back from his wide forehead, Rulon smiled at her gently.

"What can I do for you, sweetie?" he asked.

"I'm not trying to defy God's word," she said, "but I want to wait two years before I get married. Just two years."

The old man gave her the same perplexed expression Fred and Warren had. Why was she acting this way?

He didn't seem to know what to say.

"If I can't wait two years," she told him, "I can never marry Allen. Maybe someone else."

Rulon leaned in closer and cupped his ear.

"Sweetheart," he said, "I can't hear you. Can you repeat that?"

Elissa glanced up at Warren, who slowly explained to his father that the girl didn't want to marry her first cousin.

Rulon reached down and patted Elissa's hand.

"Follow your heart, sweetie," he said. "Just follow your heart."

11

A WAVE OF RELIEF SHOT THROUGH THE GIRL, then a happiness so strong she thought she might cry. His words had been so kind and so wise. Someone had finally paid attention to her feelings and understood. She knew the Prophet would not deny her wishes. Elissa rose from the floor and gave the old man a glowing smile of gratitude, thanking him for his help. She and Warren walked out of the dining room and returned to the Prophet's office. Elissa was anxious to leave the compound and share the good news with her mother and siblings. Lowering himself into his father's chair, Warren told her to sit down, and she obeyed.

Remembering Rulon's words of a few minutes earlier, she said, "My heart has told me that this marriage is all wrong."

"Your heart," Warren said softly, "is in the wrong place."

She stared at him in disbelief. Hadn't he heard what Rulon had just told her?

"But the Prophet—"

Raising his long thin hand, he cut her off and bluntly said that she needed to proceed with her wedding plans.

She was too stunned to argue. Maybe if she didn't put up a fight, Rulon would talk some sense into his son. Warren led her out of the office and to the front door, thanking her for coming to the compound.

After returning to Fred's house, she approached him and described what had happened and how she felt about it. Even though Warren had ignored his father's words and talked about her upcoming wedding, she couldn't go forward with the marriage.

Fred wasn't as patient as before.

"If you don't do this," he said, "your future here will be in jeopardy."

She was shocked by the force of his words. This was a direct threat coming from one of the most highly placed elders—and its meaning was clear. If she didn't follow his orders and become Allen's wife, she'd lose her home and her welcome in Hildale/Colorado City, her place at school and in the church. She'd lose her mother and sisters, her friends, everything. The fourteen-year-old could no longer hold back her emotions, breaking down in front of Fred, begging him to help her, saying that if she had to get married now, at least let her pick someone else for a husband.

"I'm very disappointed in you," he said, "for being so defiant."

Elissa went back to her room and cried some more.

When her mother heard about the girl's discussion with Fred, she took Elissa aside and insisted that she go through with the wedding. This was how things were done inside the FLDS and how they'd always been done; no woman had the power to change that, and more was at stake than just marrying her first cousin. Elissa's eternal salvation was at risk if she continued to oppose the men in charge of her church, community, and home. If she pushed too hard, she wouldn't just lose her support system, but her chance at heaven.

Elissa's older sister by ten years, Rebecca Musser, had attended and then taught at Alta Academy after graduation. When she was nineteen, the eighty-six-year-old Rulon asked her to marry him (he had as many as 65 wives and 75 children). Inside her family it was considered a great honor to wed the Prophet, but Rebecca had some questions and doubts, deciding to go to Canada for a while to think it over. Like all the girls Warren had instructed at Alta, she'd been taught to "keep the bars up" sexually around males, but if she married Rulon she'd have to "let the bars down." She didn't know if she was ready to do that, especially with an octogenarian. Rulon had begun pressuring both Rebecca and her father, Lloyd Wall, to make her return from Canada and become his wife. People within the FLDS were constantly saying that Rulon's age was irrelevant; God was going to make him young again and he'd be able to father many more children.

In 1995, Rebecca married the old man, in part to avoid embarrassing her family. Later that decade, she moved down to Hildale with the rest of the Jeffs clan and lived in the Prophet's compound with his other wives. In 2001, she was present as Elissa's upcoming marriage to Allen was discussed by Rulon and Warren. When the younger man told his father that Fred Jessop had placed the fourteen-year-old with her nineteen-year-old first cousin, Rulon was startled by the girl's age.

"What the hell is Fred thinking?" he asked his son.

Warren calmed his father down by saying they should honor Fred's request because of his position as bishop within the church. Plans for the wedding were going forward.

Elissa kept trying to think of a way out of her troubles, but felt doomed and trapped. She had no experience living outside the FLDS, no money, no other resources, no father to help her, nowhere to go, and even if she had, she was terrified of leaving behind her mother and sisters. They were the only people anywhere who really cared about her. What else could she do but agree to marry Allen?

The night before the wedding she stayed up late, her sisters scurrying around her as they worked on her hair and clothes. They couldn't get her to stand still so they could sew the lace on her dress, worried about poking her with a needle. Nor would she stop crying. God was punishing her, she kept saying through the tears, but she didn't know what she'd done to deserve it. They were barely able to get the lace on in time to leave for Nevada.

Early the next morning, she put on the gown for the long trip to Caliente, but was told to change into something else until she got to the motel; it looked too suspicious for a fourteen-year-old to cross a state line dressed for her wedding. She rode to the ceremony with Allen and his folks, while Warren, Rulon, Elissa's mother, and some others went in separate cars, the caravan making its way over the wending 160 miles to the secret location. There would be two other FLDS weddings in Caliente today. At the motel, Elissa slipped into the gown, tears covering her face as she stood in front of a mirror and tried to collect herself. She couldn't go through with this, she kept telling one of the women helping her. Nobody could defy the Prophet, her companion said.

When Elissa had dried the tears and was calm enough to walk, she made her way to Room 15, where Allen eagerly awaited her. Hardly able to stand up beside him, she stared blankly around the wedding suite, at her mother and sisters, at Warren and Rulon, and at the guards watching the door in case any outsiders got too close. Warren came up to the young couple and smiled, welcoming everyone to the sacred event and reading some verses to commence the proceeding.

When he told Elissa to take Allen's hand, she refused. He told her again, more insistently this time. She put her fingers next to the young man's but refused to intertwine them. Warren read more prayers and then asked if she took Allen for her husband for eternity. Everyone in the room strained to hear her response, but she stood silent, hanging her head, her cheeks burning, embarrassment and shame filling her throat. She couldn't speak. As the seconds ticked away, Room 15 became perfectly still and the ceremony came to a dead stop.

Warren told Elissa's mother to take her daughter's other hand and again he asked her to receive Allen in marriage, but she wouldn't raise her head or make a sound. People were becoming restless and Warren shifted his weight from foot to foot, growing annoyed, staring right at the teenager with the same look of quiet disapproval and intimidation he'd long ago mastered at Alta Academy. A third time, he posed the question.

"Yes," she mumbled, the word barely audible.

The room came alive with a feeling of relief and the sounds of nervous laughter.

Warren grinned at the couple and pronounced to the groom, "You may kiss the bride."

As Allen bent down and pursed his lips, Elissa closed her mouth and turned away.

"You may kiss the bride," Jeffs said again.

She looked up and gave Allen a peck.

"Go forth and multiply and replenish the earth with good Christian children," Warren declared, beaming at the newlyweds and bringing the event to a fast conclusion. No marriage certificate or other documentation of this event existed, so there was no paper trail establishing that a nineteen-year-old man had just taken a fourteen-year-old girl, his first cousin, for a wife.

The moment the wedding was over, Elissa ran into the bathroom and locked the key, collasping into sobs and telling her mother and a stream of other visitors who knocked on the door to leave her alone. She wanted to jump through a window and run away from her husband, but she was a very long way from home and had no resources, no choices left. She was stuck forever with someone she couldn't stand to look at or be around. But at least she'd avoided a worse fate: she hadn't lost her salvation and wasn't going to hell.

When she emerged from the bathroom, drying her eyes and straightening her dress and hair, everyone came up and congratulated her, saying how happy they were for the girl. She and Allen would make a fine life together and have many wonderful children. Elissa tried to smile and say something back, but she felt empty and numb, speechless as she watched the guests chatter and enjoy themselves. When she searched Room 15 for Warren, hoping to be able to talk to him, he was gone.

That evening the wedding party returned to Hildale, where Fred welcomed her with a big hug and told her how proud he was of her. Elissa's sisters had rearranged the sleeping quarters inside the crowded house, creating a "honeymoon hideaway" for her and Allen with a heart-shaped symbol on the mattress encircling a pile of homemade cookies. Elissa didn't know what to expect after she entered the suite, having never been taught anything about sex at Alta Academy and trained never to raise the subject, not even with her mother or sisters. It was up to her husband to inform and instruct her about marital relations after she became his wife.

All the time she was growing up and attending school, showing bare arms or legs had been considered offensive to society and God. She was unprepared for seeing a man naked, or being naked in front of one. That night, when the festivities were completed and Allen and she lay down in the bedroom her sisters had beautifully decorated with roses, chocolates, and confetti, they slept in their sacred underwear, their bodies further covered by pajamas and a silk nightgown. Elissa was horrified that he might try to touch her.

He didn't, but still she tossed and turned until morning.

1 2

I T WASN'T LONG BEFORE Warren heard about Elissa's unhappiness inside her new marriage. He eventually went to her sister Rebecca and told her that it was important for Elissa to get along with her husband and not cause trouble over this issue. Utah's laws were changing regarding underage marriage, and the FLDS didn't need any more notoriety focused on this practice. If the girl drew too much attention to her situation, it could hurt everyone.

Although Jeffs and his father knew that conducting underage marriages in Caliente was a criminal risk, they ignored the danger and continued doing so. Rulon's concerns were captured in his last recorded sermon to his devoted congregation, made in 2002. Warren prompted the dying Prophet, to keep him focused on his message.

"I am going forward," Rulon said weakly, "and continuing building the storehouse and living the holy united order, and God is going to handle anyone who fights against it."

After a long pause, he asked, "Do we have the lawyers?"

"Yes," Warren replied, "we do."

"We have the lawyers!" Rulon said. "We have the lawyers!"

Then he added, "And God will fight our battles."

Looking out at the assembled worshippers from behind his spectacles, the old man said, "Are you worried about what the state of Utah and the state of Arizona are going to do?"

"No!" the faithful shouted back at him.

"Okay. We'll go on . . . Smile! God will fight our battles."

As the church elders rose and joined the Prophet at the altar, a voice next to him declared, "They have already started their attack."

"They have already started their attack!" Rulon echoed, "but we are going to go on . . . God is on our side."

The crowd rumbled its approval.

"God bless you in the name of Jesus Christ," Rulon said to end his sermon.

The Prophet did not live to be 350, as he'd repeatedly promised his followers. He died on September 8, 2002, with Warren and Fred Jessop huddled over his bed. They exchanged a few words about who would become the next Prophet, but Fred was in his mid-nineties and Warren was already operating as the new FLDS leader.

He did not seem fazed by his father's passing. Two days after Rulon's death, he gave the morning devotional at the Jeffs Academy in Hildale, where he was making the transition from church leader to a direct conduit to God. In his repetitive, hypnotic, and overly sincere manner, he spoke as the new Prophet and hinted of things to come:

> This is a wonderful occasion. We are privileged to meet in priesthood schools, even with the whole wicked world wanting to destroy us . . . Let there be no disputations or fightings among us. The rules of every priesthood school is the will of the Prophet, the will of God to us through him . . .
>
> We were sent to this earth to learn who God is and how to become like him. Prophets have been sent who, through obedience, became like God . . . Let it be written in every mind and heart the call of our Prophet. Keep sweeter and sweeter. Live in the increase of the holy spirit of God and smile. That is how our Prophet knows you love him and you are with him . . . You cannot be like the world and be with our Prophet. You must come out of the world and clean up your minds and your lives . . . There is a pruning going on. We want to be perfected and step up, not cast off. And the Lord is about to clean house . . .
>
> I say this rejoicing in God and the Godhead and our Prophet and all the Prophets, for you will learn this year about them, that you may know how to become like God. That is why we look up to the Prophets. Each in their day, they were the example of godliness to the people . . .

Jeffs had recently orchestrated the excommunication of Winston Blackmore, who was the head of the Canadian branch of the FLDS, and gradually isolated the Barlow men, who occupied key political offices in Colorado City. Instead of the power passing to the most worthy or most senior man, as had been church custom for decades, it was now handed down informally from father to son. Warren never directly declared that he was the new Prophet and neither did FLDS officials.

The first Sunday after the funeral, he sat in his father's chair at the temple, completing the transition. Fred Jessop soon disappeared, later surfacing in a Colorado hospital before passing away (some locals believed that he'd been kidnapped by Warren's minions and hidden until his death). If Jeffs's brazen defiance of tradition unsettled and frightened many, it captured the imagination of others and gave them a sense of his strong leadership; he'd protect them and keep them safe. He seemed more defiant of outside authority than Rulon had been, willing to go to prison or perhaps even die for his convictions. Belief wasn't something that could be compromised to fit changing circumstances: a man embraced and practiced the divine revelations of Joseph Smith or he did not. One had to be either willing to denounce human laws for the laws of God or he was an apostate. Giving in to the gentile world was not an option. As Warren took hold of the church and this attitude hardened inside the top ranks of the FLDS, it was clear that a war was coming. The new leader was both ready and eager for it.

Right after his father died, Warren told the congregation, "Our Prophet and the Celestial Law . . . are under attack. There is a combined effort in the state of Utah and the state of Arizona to come against our Prophet and this people, trying to stop the work of God."

He then called on "Brother Sam Barlow" to give a full report of the impending struggle between their faith and the society that wanted to shut down the "spiritual marriages" of young girls to adult men.

Barlow, a former town marshal and church leader, answered the call by saying that law enforcement had "taken this on under a pretense that they are going to protect young women from being coerced or levered or pressured into a marriage union with men that are older than them . . . And they suppose that we are evil as they are evil. So therefore they accuse us of being lewd and lascivious and that we enter into these marriages for the purpose of exploiting the young women and satisfying the physical urges of our body under the guise of religion . . ."

Barlow was not a hothead or rabble-rouser. He spoke in quiet, solemn tones and with a touch of religious poetry, sounding very much like a church elder who saw serious trouble coming straight at the congregation. With gravity and precision, he laid out the profoundly American conflict between religious freedom and the laws of Utah and Arizona, adding that the FLDS was entering territory it had spent decades attempting to avoid.

"I'm trying to be careful," he said,

> because we're not talking about a civil lawsuit like we were a decade ago, when they made an attack on the United Effort Plan to try to interfere with Uncle Rulon's work. We are now talking about criminal conduct, things that by statute they have now legislated purposefully to bring us into collision with the judiciary . . .
>
> This family order that we have engaged in, that we organize our families under, is rooted in antiquity. It goes back into Biblical days and finds resting place with Abraham and Isaac and Jacob, and it comes forward to the days of the Prophet Joseph. And a new revelation was given and the Prophet Joseph and his brethren entered into it at great risk. It came on down, was attacked and been through a war . . . of more than 150 years of attack. Our forefathers, the forefathers of this congregation of men, maintained it through some very, very difficult times . . .

This was "the most dangerous, far-reaching time . . . since the raid of '53," and could lead to an economic hemorrhage for his church. Yet there was no compromise for Barlow or the faithful.

In the past, he said, FLDS women had needed to be strong when facing the prospect of being dragged into court and testifying against the men or their religion. They might be called upon to do this again. Near the end of his speech, he rallied the troops with a reminder of who they were and what they were committed to as members of their church.

"We are born to this conflict," he said.

> We cannot shirk it, leave it or turn aside for even a moment without an element of cowardice growing in our souls . . . It is our job to come here and . . . preserve the celestial law so that a royal priesthood can be raised up and we can enter the millennial reign with . . . people that will serve the God of life at all hazards . . .
>
> The apostates have bragged that they will take down certain men and then they will take the whole Short Creek down, meaning Uncle Rulon's work, or the forward motion of the cause of Zion that has been developed here in this land, in this valley, in these sacred lands.

That could never be allowed to happen—the moment had arrived to take a stand. The FLDS wasn't fighting this battle with guns or ammunition, but lawyers and legal strategies. The church not only had to have strength but money, lots of it. The attorneys they'd hired had asked for a $30,000 retainer, plus fees of $500 an hour.

"That will give you," Sam Barlow soberly told the congregation, "an idea what kind of lurking problem we're facing."

He was worried about the women who'd remained in the FLDS and might one day be called into court to defend their faith or their Prophet, but he should have been more concerned with another group. The women who'd left the church behind represented the far greater threat.

13

IN THE EARLY 1980s, Laura Chapman Mackert had been forced into
marriage with a man she didn't like or respect in order to avoid a worse
match. By the late 1990s, having broken away from the FLDS community, she'd begun to protect youngsters from sexual molestation and encouraged several girls to escape the fundamentalist church. Rebuffed by the Utah
authorities, she and a handful of other women had then carried their fight to
the national media. After a Denver University professor read about Laura, she
contacted a human rights activist in New York City, Donna Sullivan. Laura
and one of the young girls whom she'd helped flee, Sarah Cooke, went to
Manhattan to meet with Donna. They worked with New York University
Law School to identify human rights violations in Utah's polygamist communities.

In March 2002, Laura and Sarah were invited to Women's Conference
Week at the United Nations, where they listened to stories of Japanese sex
slaves in World War II; of the oppression of Muslim women in Third World
countries (each year hundreds of Afghani females tried to escape forced marriages and domestic violence by setting themselves on fire); and of ten-year-old
African girls who'd been raped on the way to school and then turned away by
their families because they were no longer virgins. From education to work opportunities to birth control, abortion, and the freedom to choose a husband,
societies were now being judged on a worldwide stage by their treatment of
women. The United States had its own version of these problems but, along
with Somalia, was one of only two countries that continued to refuse to sign
international treaties protecting the rights of women and children.

At the United Nations, Laura shared her experience with a global audience, drawing attention to the contrast between America's current war against radical Islam and its ongoing refusal to deal with similar troubles at home. A publication accompanying this event, put out by New York University's School of Law and the International Human Rights Clinic, echoed this point:

> *In recent months, the United States has championed the cause of women's human rights in Afghanistan and condemned religious fundamentalism in other countries. Yet in the U.S. itself religious fundamentalists are allowed to violate women's human rights with impunity.*
>
> *Media and activist sources have documented a pattern of human rights abuses in polygamous families in Utah and neighboring states. Women and girls are subjected to violence, sexual abuse, incest, child marriage, trafficking, and coerced or forced marriage. Many live in closed religious communities where they are denied education and access to information from the outside world. Although both international human rights law and U.S. law prohibit these abuses, local and national officials have failed to ensure that these legal guarantees are observed in practice.*

Despite Laura's recognition and a growing awareness of these issues, Utah's state government still failed to confront the problems in Dixie. But more and more women who'd been raised inside the FLDS and then broken away were starting to tell their stories. Led by Laura; Vicky Prunty of Tapestry Against Polygamy; two ex–church members, Flora and Carolyn Jessop; and others, they formed support networks, shared their intimate experiences, wrote about them, made documentary films, appeared on television and radio, created Web sites, and contributed to blogs. Generations of keeping quiet and sweet were giving way to an eruption of confession and catharsis.

Sara Hammon's father, Marion, was the FLDS leader who'd rebelled against Rulon Jeffs in the mid-1980s before going on to found Centennial Park. Sara (her given name was Roberta) was born in Hildale in 1974 and had seventy-four brothers and sisters. Her nineteen mothers dressed their forty daughters in traditional long cotton dresses and white socks, making them tie their hair in pigtails. As a young girl, Sara once saw in a magazine a picture of a businesswoman in a handsome dark suit working in a corporate office. The photo inspired in Sara a dream—nothing more than a wild flight of fancy—but she nurtured it anyway. When she became an adult, she'd find a way to get out of the clothes FLDS women were forced to wear, cut her hair the way she wanted it, and look like the woman in the suit.

Sara remembered that, when she was still in diapers, a brother molested her with his hands. Other siblings in her family later did the same thing, and so did her father, regularly slipping his fingers up her dress. If she or her sisters tried to talk about this with their mothers, they were given a straightforward, consistent response: boys had strong sexual urges, it had always been this way, and the best solution was to avoid contact with them. By thirteen, Sara had been repeatedly sexually abused by the males in her family and was plotting ways to escape. Her deepest fear, besides being raped or beaten, was that she'd turn into the women around her. She couldn't understand why they acted as they did and why their personalities changed whenever her father came into the room. They never raised their voices around the man or spoke up against him. The only emotion her mothers were good at displaying was anger, after one of the children had violated a minor rule. They'd briefly explode, before becoming docile again and reminding themselves that their goal was to "keep sweet for the Lord."

Sara was growing less sweet and more rebellious by the day, ditching school, pushing the limits of the despised dress code, and mouthing off to her elders. She decided to call a meeting of all her sisters so they could talk about being sexually abused and how to stop it. Nothing like this had ever happened before: no female in her family had ever taken a stand against this behavior. One day Sara charged into the house wearing a knee-length skirt and a see-through shirt with a tank top beneath it. One of Sara's nonbiological mothers stopped her and took her aside for a proper scolding.

"You have no business trying to embarrass the boys by talking about these secret things," she said. "They have a sex drive and that's that."

The teenager tried to put up an argument but was overmatched.

"You can't blame boys for acting that way," the woman said. "And you deserve what you get for dressing like that."

"I didn't dress this way," Sara replied, "when I was five."

The woman moved in closer, bringing her chin right up to the girl's until they were almost touching. Reaching down with both hands, she grabbed Sara's knees, jerked them apart, and slammed them back together—a lesson in how females were supposed to act. The conversation was over, but Sara was just beginning to fight back.

From television and radio broadcasts, she'd found her two biggest heroes and role models: singers Tina Turner and Dolly Parton. As the daughter of FLDS parents, Sara couldn't have picked a more inflammatory choice than Turner. Since taking over Alta Academy decades earlier, Warren Jeffs had preached that nothing was more offensive than a black man, like Little Richard, ferociously performing music onstage—wild hair, wild shaking hips—except perhaps for one thing: a black woman doing the same.

Sara didn't want to be forced into an arranged marriage, so at fourteen she asked to be engaged to a young man. This would get her out of the house and away from her abusive brothers and father, while keeping her family and church leaders from choosing a husband for her. The wedding was scheduled for her fifteenth birthday, but before the date arrived, she ran off and moved in with a foster family. Her relief at getting out of her former home was short-lived. She recalled her new father making suggestive remarks to her around the house and molesting her when his wife was away. When Sara told her foster mother about this, the woman said, "This is just how he is. You're taking it the wrong way."

One day when she was home alone, Sara began cutting on her wrist with a knife, slicing it open. Much later, she'd joke that because she hadn't paid attention in her high school anatomy class, she didn't know where to find her main arteries. The first cut didn't work, so she tried again. As she was lying on the floor bleeding profusely, her biological mother called to ask how she was doing and Sara said everything was just fine. The older woman sensed otherwise and sent one of Sara's brothers-in-law over to the house. He rushed her to the hospital and Sara escaped with her life.

She left Utah for Westport, Connecticut, to work as a nanny. Since she was living near New York City and had read that Dolly Parton kept an apartment in Manhattan, she bought a "Star Map" and discovered where one of her role models could be found. Sara camped out at the singer's apartment building, got to know the concierge, and talked him into letting her meet Dolly in the lobby. It was her biggest thrill ever, and it convinced her to keep pursuing her dreams, but her upbringing still haunted her. She moved to Tennessee, where she lost herself in alcohol for several years before resettling in Michigan and then Mesquite, Nevada. In 2002, she became sober, started attending therapy sessions, and began to confront her family history. She landed a job at a high-end real estate office and went to work wearing the stylish suits she'd first seen in the magazines of her childhood.

Sara began speaking in public and through the media about her experience and the need to reform the FLDS, reaching a national and international audience on CNN. Overcoming her resistance to revealing her past and her own sense of shame, she told the world about being molested by her father, even as he lay on his deathbed, when he'd tried to reach out and touch her genitals.

In her home in Mesquite, Sara took in a struggling teenage girl from the Canadian branch of the FLDS, about the same age Sara herself had been when she'd left home and others had provided shelter for her. If she ventured back to the border towns now, it was to offer assistance to women trying to escape the church and the chokehold of Warren Jeffs.

14

THROUGH THE PUBLICITY GENERATED by these female activists, word of the new Prophet's activities and racial attitudes began spreading beyond Colorado City, reaching outside law enforcement. Jeffs had nothing to fear from the homegrown police force—the town marshals were FLDS members and many were involved in polygamous marriages themselves—but the rest of the world wasn't so forgiving. A highly visible and respected civil rights organization in Alabama, the Southern Poverty Law Center, was about to place the FLDS on its list of American hate groups. And there was trouble closer to home.

As Utah Attorney General Mark Shurtleff, whose own ancestors had been involved in polygamy, described it, state authorities were considering three options. One they called "the scorched earth policy," which meant arresting all the polygamists they could find. The problem with that, Shurtleff said, was that they'd have to build a lot more jails to hold the offenders. Also, they'd tried this strategy in 1953 and it had only left the polygamists—and the predators who thrived inside the structure of plural marriage—more isolated, able to get away with more and more serious crimes. The second option was labeled "Mary Had a Little Lamb," which meant leaving the community alone and letting it resolve its own problems. But that hadn't worked in the past, and the new leadership of the FLDS was sending signals that it intended to be even more resistant to Utah's government than in previous decades.

The third option was enforcing the state's existing laws, which had been essentially unenforced in the border towns for half a century.

"This," Shurtleff said, "was the constitutional choice, the legal and right choice."

His office released a public warning that child bigamy (marrying a second wife under the age of 18) and having unlawful sex with a minor would no longer be ignored. The church was facing a clear-cut decision: tell your fundamentalist congregation to withdraw from these marriages or they'll be prosecuted.

When Jeffs learned of this ultimatum, he didn't just refuse to end child bigamy, but made it a test of faith for worshippers. If they were truly committed to their beliefs and to their new Prophet, they would risk enduring prosecution for him. Jeffs may have also harbored the view that if church members didn't cave in to these demands, the authorities would eventually back down.

It was the stance of someone who'd spent his life in a world safely sheltered from intrusion. Before becoming Prophet, Rulon Jeffs had been a practical man with years of experience as a CPA away from Utah. But his chosen son had never ventured beyond the confines of his family or the FLDS. Since childhood, Warren had lived a privileged existence, never having to leave home, earn a living, or interact with outsiders. He hadn't ever been on a date—when he wanted a new woman, he simply married her.

"Unlike Warren," says Ben Bistline, "Rulon had some compassion and forgiveness for people who weren't his relatives. He'd ask you to confess your sins, then forgive you, rebaptize you, let you come back into the church, and you'd feel good about all this. It was genuine. Warren had none of these qualities—no feelings at all about what he was doing or asking others to do. Just a massive ego."

Jeffs had a premonition of what was coming, spelled out in a speech made to a group of men and recorded in 2005:

The Lord revealed to me that in 2003, a secret combination was in place between the apostates everywhere, many of them, and the government officials, and also traitors and half-hearted men, false brethren among the Priesthood people. And that conspiracy involved the passing of these laws, to call us criminal by performing marriages, so-called "under-age" marriages . . .

The Lord showed me they were going to take away our lands and houses. He showed me that it was the intention of our enemies to pull me and many people into court and turn

traitor by bearing witness in court of my father's doings and my doings, concerning the
Celestial Law of Marriage, the judging of the people, bringing God into question and what
He does among His Priesthood people and on His Priesthood lands in His Celestial Law.
And I say to you brethren, no person, no court, no government, no people on the face of the
whole earth has the right or authority to bring God into question what He has His Prophets
do in the Celestial Law among his Priesthood people on His consecrated lands.

This time Utah didn't back down. On March 5, 2003, fifty years after the raid on Short Creek, the state legislature kept its promise to enact tougher penalties for men who took young girls as their plural wives. Child bigamy was now punishable by one to fifteen years in prison. In Arizona, meanwhile, polygamy was constitutionally prohibited, but not a punishable crime. However, it *was* a Class 6 Felony to engage in sexual activity with anyone under eighteen, unless that person was a legal spouse, and this carried a sentence of up to two years.

Back in 1998, one Hildale resident, policeman Rodney Holm, had entered into a "spiritual marriage" conducted by Warren Jeffs. The officer had wed a sixteen-year-old girl, Ruth Stubbs, who was his wife's sister. Five years later, after endless prodding by female activists about the problems inside the FLDS, Utah and Arizona used his case to launch one of their first successful assaults.

In August 2003, Rodney Holm was tried and convicted on one count of bigamy and two counts of unlawful sex with a minor, receiving a one-year sentence. Holm loudly protested his conviction, which he appealed all the way to the U.S. Supreme Court. His defense was that with the widespread popularity of cohabitation in modern America, the traditional view of marriage should no longer apply to everyone. In response to this strategy, a national organization based in Washington, D.C., the Family Research Council, filed a "friend of the court" brief urging the nation's nine highest justices to reject Holm's petition because of its "contemporary efforts to redefine and undermine marriage." The Supreme Court refused to hear Holm's case.

Following the 2003 conviction, Utah attorney general Shurtleff announced plans to investigate the entire Hildale police force and recommend that all officers with multiple wives be decertified, losing their jobs and income. Having made good on their threats so far, state officials now sought peace with the church and its new Prophet, holding a summit in nearby St.

George, Utah, to discuss polygamy issues and the law. Jeffs failed to show. But a month later a group of plural wives in Centennial Park took the attorneys general of both Utah and Arizona on a tour of their community, explaining why they'd freely entered into this way of life and how no one was being harmed by it.

These women and others spoke out in favor of polygamy to CNN and ABC, citing various reasons. They liked knowing where their husbands were at night; sharing their sexual duties with other women; having several mothers around to help take care of all the children; and a stable environment that provided them with the financial, emotional, family, and spiritual resources to assist them in every phase of living. They enjoyed belonging to a culture and a faith that offered them religious absolutes, moral clarity, and protection from the external world. They didn't approve of what America had become—particularly its political leadership and emphasis on consumerism—seeking instead to separate from mainstream values and beliefs. Sex was far less important in their lifestyle than outsiders believed: they simply didn't place that much emphasis on it. Like Warren Jeffs himself, they felt they were answering to a calling higher than secular law, and any sacrifices or hardships endured were for the glory of God and their own salvation.

Some of the women mentioned the specific psychological benefits of polygamy. Plural marriage had helped them come to terms with difficult feelings like jealousy, insecurity, competition, and thinking that they "owned" their spouse. Instead of denying these complex emotions, they'd been forced to confront them in order to make their marriages work. They saw all this as a growth experience—a lifestyle that was not only tolerable, but preferable.

The most visible supporter of plural marriage was LeAnne Timpson, the administrator of the Masada Charter School in Centennial Park. Timpson, who described herself as a polygamist and a feminist, had attended Harvard's Kennedy School of Government and was outspoken about her legal right to be a plural wife and the virtues of her choice. She considered her activism civil disobedience and eventually hoped to go all the way to the U.S. Supreme Court to have plural marriage decriminalized. Within her community, she often appeared before civic groups and the media to show that a woman with her educational background could embrace plural marriage. One of her patented replies to the charge that polygamists were abusing polygamists was that "monogamists are abusing monogamists."

LeAnne brought out the irreconcilable conflict between those females who felt that plural marriage could be beneficial and those who despised it. In her youth, Brenda Jensen had lived in Colorado City before her father moved the family away from the border towns because of his disillusionment with the FLDS. After raising three daughters herself, Brenda had come back to the region and would eventually help others escape Mormon fundamentalism.

"Polygamous women like LeAnne Timpson," she says, "have their own work outside the house and their own money. Do you think that's the way most plural wives live? LeAnne gets to travel and have her own living space. She got to make choices about going to school, about what clothes to wear, and about who to marry. If she was speaking for all the women in her community, that would be different, but she isn't. She's got a very privileged existence, compared to most of them.

"All my life I've seen the weeping, unhappy, gossipy, hateful women raised inside that religion who felt deeply about so many things that they couldn't or weren't allowed to express. I felt their sorrow and their heartache. I watched them turn wonderful women into empty hulls. They were treated with absolutely no respect by the men around them and this colored everything they felt and did. When you're hurt by those you instinctively care about, it kills your ability to love."

After Utah and Arizona officials ended their tour of Centennial Park, they restated their point of view: they weren't against polygamy among consenting adults and weren't going to investigate or prosecute that. They were only interested in pursuing cases involving sexual abuse, forced marriages, and crimes against minors. If the FLDS wanted to be reasonable, this was their opportunity. If not, the two states would have to turn up the heat.

When Jeffs ignored this latest warning, a subpoena was issued for him in a second child bigamy case, but he refused to answer it. By mid-2003, he had begun traveling in and out of Colorado City with growing frequency, often moving in secret to avoid detection. When he was gone, trouble emerged at home. That summer, he became enraged at a group of FLDS members, led by Mayor Dan Barlow, who hadn't sought his permission before dedicating a local museum and monument to the community for surviving the 1953 raid. After learning of it, Jeffs ordered the monument torn down and broken into pieces, its remains scattered over the hillsides. He justified this action to the congregation on July 27, 2003, invoking the words God had allegedly spoken to him:

Verily I say unto you, my servant Warren, my people have sinned a very grievous sin before me, in that they have raised up monuments to man and have not glorified it to me. For it is by my almighty arm that my people have been preserved, if they are worthy . . . And you must seek my protection through the repentance of your sins, and the building up of my kingdom, my storehouse, my priesthood on the earth. And if you do not, I shall bring a scourge upon my people to purge the ungodly from among you. And those righteous will suffer with the wicked, if I will preserve the pure in heart who are repentant. I, the Lord, have spoken it and my word shall be obeyed if you would receive my blessings . . .

Angered and stung by the defiance toward his leadership, Jeffs declared FLDS members no longer worthy of future blessings—such as new marriages, baptisms, and confirmations—or even of attending their own church.

"Jesus is weeping," he proclaimed, "because of the wickedness of the people of Short Creek."

The large white FLDS meetinghouse, evoking a rambling ranch-style home and seating nearly three thousand people, now stood empty in the heart of Hildale, no cars in the parking lot and no children playing around it, slowly going to seed for lack of repairs. The border towns had been defiled by apostates, so Jeffs decided it was time to start looking elsewhere for new, unsullied outposts for the FLDS.

In a fit of spite, he ordered the faithful to stop laughing, saying that it drained them of the spirit of God. To be prepared for the Apocalypse—which was coming next week or next month or next year—believers needed to purify themselves. God was about to impose a test like no one had yet seen or imagined seeing, and once the tribulations had passed Jesus Christ would make his victorious return to earth. Only the strongest, the most perfect and obedient, would survive to see that wondrous day. The Prophet alone would decide who was worthy of staying in the church and receiving the blessings of deliverance from the cleansing ahead—and who should be excommunicated before the Second Coming.

By 2003, Jeffs was so busy making messianic plans for the Apocalypse, that he barely noticed Elissa Wall and Allen Steed's deepening marital problems.

15

WITHIN DAYS OF THEIR WEDDING IN APRIL 2001, Fred Jessop had sent the bride and groom, along with two other young couples, on a honeymoon to Carlsbad Caverns, to help the marriages get off to a good start. On the trip, Allen began fondling his fourteen-year-old wife in ways that shocked and disgusted her. Her resistance was so obvious that the group made jokes about it, offering Elissa money if she'd allow Allen to kiss her. She occasionally gave in and took the cash, but they didn't consummate their marriage during the vacation. One evening a month later, she and Allen were walking in a park near Fred's home when the young man asked her to sit down beside him on the grass. As she stretched out on her back and took in the glorious spring night, stars spread out above her in the Southwestern sky, he exposed himself. She screamed, leaped to her feet, and ran all the way back to Fred's house, escaping into her mother's room and staying there until she assumed Allen had returned and fallen asleep. As she would later recall in a courtroom under oath (and Allen would dispute), when she finally came to her own bedroom that night, her husband was awake and waiting for her.

Allen made an advance.

"Please don't touch me," she said, pulling away.

He reached out for her again.

"I don't want anything to do with you or anything to do with sex."

Allen tried to explain that this was what men and women did after they were married, but Elissa became so upset that she spent the night in her mother's bed.

Another week passed before Allen led her into their bedroom and announced that his patience had run out: it was time for Elissa to fulfill her wifely duty. Undressing his trembling bride, he said they were going to have children and that "male–female relations" were necessary for this to happen, adding that he'd always wanted to see a naked woman and tonight he finally would. Ashamed, Elissa tried to cover herself and hold him off, but she couldn't, shaking the whole time. When it was over, she lay in silent pain, unable to stop the tears, feeling as if God were punishing her again. What had she done to deserve His wrath?

At least once a week, according to her testimony years later, Allen insisted on having sex. She learned to give in without a fight.

Later that year, she and Allen traveled to British Columbia to visit Elissa's older sister Teresa, who was associated with members of the Canadian FLDS. When Elissa privately told her how much she feared and despised intercourse with her husband, Teresa said she didn't have to keep enduring it. She suggested that Elissa speak to Warren Jeffs about it. He was the Prophet now and would know how to advise her.

Back in Hildale in late 2001, she made another appointment to see Jeffs at his father's compound. Warren greeted her warmly and seemed much more open to her questions and feelings than before she'd gotten married. She relaxed in his presence, telling him how much she disliked being with her husband.

But Jeffs suddenly changed his demeanor and his message: Allen was a good Christian man and in time she'd come to love him.

No, she wouldn't, Elissa argued. Allen insisted on doing physical things to her that were simply wrong—based on everything she'd been taught by Jeffs as a child at Alta Academy.

"He's your husband," Warren explained softly, in the same drone he'd used for decades as the school principal. "You're supposed to be obedient and submissive to him. He knows what's right for you and he'll lead you to the Celestial Kingdom, but only if you're an obedient wife."

Elissa tried a different tactic, saying that this really wasn't Allen's fault and confessing that she'd failed miserably at marriage. She wasn't a good wife to him, and all she wanted was to separate from her husband.

"I can't stand him," she said, breaking down and begging Jeffs to release her from the situation.

Using the same monotone, he deflected her plea, telling her to go home and give herself mind, body, and soul to her husband.

Again, she felt as if she were being punished by God for a sin she hadn't committed.

Jeffs brought out a book called *Enlightened Truth*, which he'd taught from in the girls' home economics class at Alta, telling Elissa to study the passages about how a wife should interact with her husband. Warren wanted her to read the "Marriage Covenant" every day, as this would give her more strength, clarity, and moral instruction. He said that he didn't want the young woman to visit him alone at the compound anymore, and told her to bring along Allen next time so they could all discuss these matters together.

Leaving Jeffs that day, she felt hollow and numb, surrounded by a dull anger—the same way she felt after sex with her husband. At home, everything continued as before, with Allen regularly demanding intercourse and Elissa reluctantly submitting. Some nights she slipped away from her bed and crawled back into her mother's, where the older woman offered comfort and guidance about being a good wife. Elissa tried to follow this advice, but nothing helped. Months passed and the marriage worsened. Elissa made another appointment to see Warren but took her mother, Sharon, instead of her husband. When he asked her why she'd defied his command, she burst out that she didn't love Allen and didn't want to be married or have children with him. Why couldn't she just leave?

Warren turned to Elissa's mother and then her, asking the girl about her relationship with the woman. The two of them had a very special connection, Elissa said; her mother was her best friend.

It was time to break off this connection, Jeffs declared—time to stop seeing Sharon altogether so she could give her complete loyalty to her husband. Warren turned back toward Elissa's mother. He told her to let her daughter go, because she was standing in the way of Elissa's marriage. This was what his father, the Prophet, wanted and what God was dictating. If Elissa kept rebelling and didn't start obeying her husband, she'd lose her chance at salvation.

Departing the compound that day, Elissa ran into her sister Rebecca, who was married to Rulon.

"I'm not supposed to talk to you or any of my sisters," Elissa told her in tears. "I'm supposed to go home and obey my husband."

Elissa again tried to follow these orders, moving out of the Jessop residence and into a trailer so she'd spend less time with her mother and more with her husband, but nothing changed.

Following Rulon's death in September 2002, and Warren taking over as Prophet, she again met with Jeffs at the compound, this time with Allen. By now Elissa was pregnant, and she pleaded with Warren to let her spend time with her sister in Canada. The Prophet deferred to Allen, who made it clear that he didn't want his wife traveling north. After nearly two years of confusion and rage, the teenage girl could no longer contain her misery. She threw herself on the men's mercy, beseeching them to let her go, and they finally relented.

In Canada in early 2003, Elissa suffered a painful miscarriage and then a prolonged recovery. Depressed and defeated, she returned to Hildale to try to resurrect her marriage, but after their separation she and Allen were nothing more than strangers sharing the same living space. She spent most of her days away from the trailer and slept many nights in her truck. Unable to get a divorce, cut off from her mother, with little education and terrified of leaving Hildale, she made another effort to get help from the Prophet, again taking Allen with her. After openly telling Jeffs that she could never love or trust her husband, Warren calmly advised the couple that the answer to their troubles was starting a family; having children would not only lessen Elissa's selfishness and disobedience, but heal the marriage and make them fall in love. The young woman was just too spirited for her own good, but motherhood would change that. It was the job of females in the FLDS, Jeffs reminded her as they were exiting the compound, to "keep sweet" no matter what.

Elissa began spending more nights in her truck or else sneaked off to be with her mother.

One evening, she recollected years later in court, Allen invited her to a marshmallow roast north of Hildale, and afterward they went for a ride in his pickup. He parked in a deserted location and asked her to lie down beside him in the back of the camper shell. If she just got pregnant, he said, echoing the Prophet, they'd start the marriage over and have much more to look forward to. He tried to make love to her but she resisted, and as they were struggling on the bed of the truck, he told her that her eternal salvation depended on her obedience to him.

She shoved him away.

"Don't!" she yelled. "Don't touch me!"

"You're my wife," he said, "and you will do whatever I want you to do."

"Don't!"

Clasping his hands on her shoulders, he lowered her to the hard metal surface, the old numbness filling her arms and legs and chest as she lay helplessly in the back of the truck and looked at the sky. When he was finished, Elissa reached a decision. She was going to leave Allen for good, even if that meant losing her family, friends, church, and salvation. She'd kept sweet long enough—hell couldn't look or feel any worse than this.

She still wanted to give the Prophet one final chance and made another appointment to see him, but then something unexpected occurred. She met someone new, a young man named Lamont Barlow, and began falling in love for the first time in her life. He was gentle and kind, a good friend and companion. Elissa's misery began to lift; she had more confidence than ever before when speaking to the Prophet.

This time Jeffs communicated with Elissa via speakerphone. When she admitted that she was dating somebody now, Jeffs was shocked, explaining to her that this was a grievous sin within the church. Males and females never went on dates or had intimate contact before marriage. The only way for her to repent was to "be destroyed in the flesh." He wanted her to write him a detailed letter about her adultery, adding that she could neither continue living in Hildale nor see her mother anymore. Because she'd betrayed Allen and her faith, she was being released from her marriage and her family should treat her as if she were dead.

Elissa happily accepted these terms.

Divorced, banished, and excommunicated, no longer bound by the rules of her religion, she began her break from the FLDS. With the help of her new partner, who'd one day become her husband and the father of her children, she slipped free of Jeffs's control and started spending more time with her mother and siblings. The women of the Wall family were creating their own revolt.

Elissa's older sister Rebecca had been taught that a wife should give herself "body, boots, and britches" to her husband and that he was "her lifeline to God." In her case this was particularly true because she was married to the Prophet. Throughout the first years of her life with Rulon, she'd kept sweet and been obedient, but she was changing, too. One night near the end of the old man's life, he made a sexual demand on the young woman that she found repugnant and she finally said no. When Warren learned about this, he was outraged and let her know it.

After Rulon died in September 2002, his son quickly began marrying his widows. He had his eye on Rebecca, which led to a second outburst between the two of them at the Jeffs compound.

"Warren was putting great pressure on us," she once said, "and I didn't want to be married, especially to him. He said it was God's will and Rulon's will to be married. I told him I would not choose any of this."

Pointing his finger in her face, Jeffs said in his quiet, menacing monotone, "I will break you. I will teach you to be an obedient wife. You've had too much freedom."

"Please don't do this to me," Rebecca begged him.

"You know what God wants," he replied.

In the fall of 2002, she too broke away from the FLDS, joining her younger sister in open rebellion against the church. When Elissa and her siblings got together now, they began considering the possibility that Elissa had not simply been forced into matrimony and then involved in an unhappy marriage, but might have been the victim of a crime—one committed not just by Allen Steed, but by the new Prophet himself.

While she and her sisters thought about their legal options, Jeffs was laying plans to use his power in ways he'd never tried before. The targets of his wrath never saw it coming.

16

WITH HIS THINNING BLONDISH HAIR and ruddy cheeks, his friendly country face and open, sincere manner, Richard Holm looked like a gentleman farmer. For decades he'd made it a habit not to raise his voice, to avoid swearing, at least in public, and to make his word his bond. All of this had helped him become a leading citizen in the border community and the FLDS church. Born in 1952, one year before the invasion of Short Creek, he'd grown up there in an environment filled with constant fear of governmental interference and repression.

"The raid was just a huge event," he says. "The terror of losing your family to outside influences was very great, and you could feel it for years afterward."

Holm had been an admirer of Leroy Johnson. He hadn't agreed with everything "Uncle Roy" had done as Prophet but never felt threatened by him. He saw Johnson as a beneficial leader, but in the 1980s, with the rise of Rulon Jeffs and the triumph of one-man rule, Richard became concerned.

"There was always an attitude inside the Jeffs family," he says, "and it was that they felt they were too good to live in Short Creek. They acted like they were more holy than others, more worthy. People picked up on that and tried to do some things to make a better impression on Rulon. They threw money at him and built him a big home here so he'd feel more comfortable."

Despite this, Rulon was quick to criticize local men for having their hair too long or wearing short sleeves and exposing too much skin or driving a red car. Even if the Jeffs didn't seem like the kind of small-town people you could implicitly trust, Holm extended them the benefit of the doubt, and he backed the church with large amounts of his own cash. Highly successful in real estate, Holm had donated property that contributed to the growth of the United Effort Plan, doing what he could to "Build Up the Kingdom." Over his lifetime, he estimated, he'd given as much as $10 million to the FLDS. Because of his assets and generosity, Rulon treated him with decency and respect, and Holm eventually become the vice mayor. At the same time, there were unresolved tensions.

"After Rulon took over in 1986," Holm says, "no marriages were performed here for a year or two, but a girl from Colorado City got married to a man in Salt Lake. He was rewarding the people up there, where he came from, not those of us in Colorado City and Hildale. The men around here made a real effort to get to know Rulon so we could get a first wife or another wife. He was the only one now who could make decisions about who got married in town. In Leroy's day, if young people fell in love and wanted to get married, he'd marry them. That all changed with Rulon. Then it changed even more with Warren.

"Looking back, I can see that all these feelings of nervousness and uncertainty were building up in town throughout the 1990s. Everyone was being closely observed and judged and tested for our loyalty to the Jeffs, but we didn't really understand that at the time. We weren't used to dealing with power-hungry mongrels. We might have thought that something bad could happen to someone else in the church, but it wouldn't happen to me."

After assuming power, Jeffs appointed Wendell Nielsen, owner of a large local manufacturing plant, Western Precision, as his first counselor. In August 2003, the new Prophet named twelve men, including Holm, as "high priests" in the church. During priesthood meetings, Warren turned to each man and in a very quiet voice said, "Draw in, brethren, draw in. The Lord is now choosing his people and his leaders."

He often repeated these sentences.

"What he meant," Holm says, "was that he wanted us to come in and kiss his ass, throw our money and our daughters at him in the hope that we'd be allowed to have a new wife or build a new home. Many went along with this. Almost all of the high priests had given Warren a daughter to marry to someone else. Those were the men who'd be rewarded later, but I hadn't done this for him. I didn't really understand how extreme he was. At that time, I don't think anybody did."

Yet it was becoming more obvious all the time. Jeffs set strict boundaries for intimacy in the community: there could be no premarital sex for couples, no sexual contact during pregnancy or when a mother was nursing, and no sex except for procreation. He delivered these instructions again and again in sermons, school lessons, and priesthood meetings with the men. If they obeyed his orders, they were considered pure and promised favors, but if they didn't they were threatened with being "cast out of the kingdom of heaven." When Jeffs was questioning a man's worthiness for being in the priesthood, he put him on a kind of probation during which he could not have sex with his wife or wives. The Prophet liked to counsel women about sex in his office without inviting their husbands to attend.

By November 2003, despite his misgivings, Richard had remained a true follower of Jeffs and continued offering financial aid to the church while supporting his own three wives and seventeen children. Like many in the FLDS, the LDS, and the Beehive State itself, Holm was shrewd and highly industrious. He and his younger brother, Edson, had worked together on many lucrative projects and were considered stalwart businessmen.

That month, with no warning at all, Richard received a call from his wives' father (Holm had married a pair of sisters). With a handful of words, the older man informed Holm that God had offered a revelation that deemed Richard unfit for the priesthood. By the time the call ended, Richard had been excommunicated by the Prophet and ordered to give up his $700,000 home, his spouses, and ten of his children. His father-in-law told Holm to leave Colorado City immediately and to "repent from afar." Richard was beyond stunned, certain there had been a misunderstanding.

"I began calling Warren," he says, "but it took two days to get through to him. When I finally did, I said, 'Why are you doing this to me?' He said, 'I don't know. This is what the Lord told me to do.' Then he said, 'Remove yourself from UEP property and we'll work this through.' I was stupid enough to believe him."

Holm was told to go away by himself and come up with a detailed list of his sins, which Jeffs would study while deciding whether or not to let him back into the FLDS. Holm took this demand at face value, preparing to sit down with a pen and paper and lay out what he imagined were his most intimate and darkest secrets and flaws. He'd never dealt with anyone like Warren before, and it never occurred to Richard that what he'd be putting in black and white was the very evidence the Prophet needed to keep him from ever being readmitted to the church.

After packing an overnight bag and saying goodbye to his family, Holm checked into the town's one motel, the Mark Twain Inn, just off Highway 59. He didn't take many clothes, because he imagined only being gone a day or two at the most. After thinking about it for a while, he was pretty sure that he'd figured out what was going on. This was a spiritual test dreamed up by the church's new leader, who was trying to put his own stamp on the flock. Faithful FLDS members could expect to be pushed or stretched to the limit from time to time, to determine if they were strong enough for the coming trials of the Apocalypse. Richard didn't like any of this, of course, but was willing to play along. That first night he composed a lengthy letter, describing all the terrible things he could think of that he might have done. It was hard work and he had to dredge up stuff from deep memory, because he really hadn't been that bad.

The next morning he drove over to the Prophet's compound and dropped off his list of sins. Following Rulon's death in 2002, Jeffs had quickly moved into his father's huge two-story home, enclosed by a high brick wall, with its security cameras trained on the street. The house stood not far from the town's birthing center and a cemetery that some locals believed was filled with the corpses of infants who'd died right before or after birth because of all the FLDS inbreeding (the lack of new blood in town was one explanation for the recurring facial structures and rather sleepy eyes in the population). Church members hadn't been that surprised when Warren had taken over his father's residence, but many were startled to learn that the son had quickly begun marrying Rulon's widows. He may have secretly wed as many as twenty of the women, with only a couple of them saying no. One was so appalled by Warren's advances that she left the compound on the run and never came back.

Holm awaited a response from Jeffs to his letter but received nothing, which confounded him. He'd worked so diligently, laying out his foibles, that he couldn't believe this hadn't made an impact on the Prophet or kick-started the process of redemption. After waiting a few days, he began phoning, but Warren wouldn't take his calls. Holm sat down and wrote him another letter, then another and another, each one describing more of his sins and his desires to come back to the fold. While making these confessions, he offered additional money to the church, but none of this made any difference. He never heard back from Jeffs.

Half a dozen weeks passed and Richard was still holed up at the Mark Twain Inn. It was gradually sinking in that Warren was never going to "work this through" with him. He'd been thrown out of the FLDS and his home for good. That was disturbing enough, but one day in December, when speaking with his younger brother, Edson, he learned something far more disturbing.

"Edson told me that he'd gotten married to my two wives who were sisters," Richard says. "One of the women was pregnant with Edson's child. When I heard this, I almost couldn't talk. We were brothers. Then I said, 'Edson, this is so wrong. You know this can't be right.'"

Edson offered no apologies or explanations, and by now Holm was starting to understand the depths of the deception unfolding all around him.

"When I think about what happened," he says, "I believe that Warren was extremely jealous of my relationship with his father. Rulon had treated me fairly well and that bothered his son. I just didn't realize how much it must have bothered him. Ever since the Jeffs began moving down here in the late nineties, we'd seen a river of change in Colorado City, but nothing like this. It hadn't yet turned into a stinking putrefied sewer, full of rotten bodies."

Holm wasn't a man who lost his temper easily, and he rarely took the Lord's name in vain—one of those country people raised to say good things about others or keep his mouth shut. But this had become impossible when speaking about Jeffs or his own brother and each time he mentioned them now, he groped for the ugliest words he could find.

Deeply hurt and just as deeply afraid of what he might do if he ran into Edson on the streets of his hometown, Richard checked out of the Mark Twain Inn, packed more clothes, and headed for St. George, about thirty miles away. He wasn't going back to the border anytime soon and started looking for a house to buy. As he adjusted to his new life, cut off from everything that had been familiar to him since birth, the grim story behind his excommunication gradually reached him. He'd heard that Edson had recently "gifted" three of his own daughters (ages 17 and 18) to the Prophet so Jeffs could marry them off to three of his closest followers. As a reward for handing them over, Warren had expelled Richard and "gifted" Richard's family to Edson.

To seal his power over Richard's daughters, Jeffs told them that polygamy and obedience could turn young women into goddesses. Then he wrote them a note, saying, "There is a place for each one of you in Zion. When you are ready, I will come and get you personally."

Although he'd been driven out of the church and betrayed by his brother, Holm still clung to the belief that his wives would return to him. They didn't.

"They'd been indoctrinated in character assassination against me," he says. "According to Warren and Edson, I was to be regarded as the worst of evil. For years and years leading up to all this, there were so many things going on in Colorado City, but we didn't pay attention to them. We allowed an extreme religious pervert to take over and to rape and pillage. . . ."

Another churchgoer whom Jeffs tossed out of the FLDS was forty-year-old David Draper, a loyal member of the congregation.

"Warren also ripped David's family apart," Holm says. "Like me, he went away and swore his allegiance to the Prophet and tried to crawl back to him, but Warren wouldn't let him in. David decided to kill himself by driving his car into a ravine outside of Hurricane [25 miles from Colorado City, on the Utah side of the border]. Just wrapped it around a tree.

"When I was going through all of my troubles with Warren, my brother Con died of a heart attack. Right before it happened, he'd been writing in a notebook and was very upset about the loss of my family and what had been done to me. About a week after my wives were reassigned to Edson, Con collapsed and was gone."

As he stayed in St. George and tried to make sense of his recent past, Richard realized that church leaders had had numerous opportunities to question where things were headed, but had turned away from the warning signs. Ever since Rulon had become too sick to run the FLDS, Jeffs had been carefully plotting his takeover and assembling a "royal elite," made up of men like Warren's own brothers and Edson Holm—a strike force to carry out his orders. In return, these followers were the ones enjoying the spoils under the new Prophet.

"Once Rulon was gone," Holm says, "Warren gathered the priests together and told us, 'I say to the elders of Israel regarding my father's family—hands off of them.' This meant that Rulon's widows would not be available to anyone but Warren. Long before his father died, he had everything planned out."

After the shock of his loss began to subside and he understood that he'd never be able to return to his old life without a legal fight, Richard contacted an attorney and launched a long custody battle to get visitation rights with his children and to win back ownership of his fifteen-thousand-square-foot home. Everything about this battle was costly and entangled, because the UEP Trust owned all the property in Colorado City and Hildale, but after a two-year struggle Holm obtained joint custody of seven of his kids and was able to return to the border towns and move back into his house after agreeing to pay taxes on it. Like others who'd been devastated by Jeffs, he gradually discovered that he had recourse through the very thing he'd been taught to mistrust and despise: the American court system. While gathering information about Jeffs and mounting his legal challenge, he'd kept uncovering more and more about the man who'd taken charge of the FLDS.

"I've talked to both boys and girls," Richard says, "who attended school at the Alta Academy and were molested there. It was unbelievable what Warren was doing to these children. He did this as a form of punishment and a way of controlling people. He did the same thing with sex and marriage in our community. I see so many similarities between the actions of radical Muslims around the world and what's gone on right here in Colorado City. In order to hold more power, leaders in both places create divisions between people—and those divisions make them want to kill each other."

17

ON JANUARY 7, 2004, roughly two months after Holm had been
expelled from the church, Jeffs appeared at a morning prayer service at the local meetinghouse. Standing before fifteen hundred
men and women, he unleashed a brutal tirade, chastising them for their spiritual failings and lack of respect for their new Prophet. For half an hour this
continued, growing in intensity and anger, as the congregation sat quietly, becoming more nervous and baffled. Why was he saying all this and where was
it leading? The great majority of listeners were totally devoted to the FLDS
and to Jeffs himself. They'd always placed trust in their Prophets and depended on them to know what was best for the church and community. As
the castigating went on and on, worshippers traded glances and murmurs,
shifting uncomfortably in their chairs, looking like shamed and frightened
children. Something was happening that they'd never witnessed.

Warren brought out a list of twenty-one men, reading off their names
and letting the sounds ring through the meetinghouse and above their
heads, before branding all of them "master deceivers." The list included
Colorado City mayor Dan Barlow, along with Louis, Joe, and Nephi Barlow. Dan's son, Roland, and Louis's son, Tom, were also named, in addition
to four of the Prophet's own brothers: Blaine, Hyrum, Brian, and David
Jeffs. All the outcasts were told to stand up, which they did, as everyone
else turned and stared at those who'd been singled out for public humiliation.

Jeffs instantly excommunicated the whole group with the phrase, "*You
know what you've done.*"

Then he read a decree immediately divorcing the men from their wives, separating them from their children, and commanding them to leave town.

The expelled Barlow brothers were the most stunned.

"It was the Barlow clan," Ben Bistline once said, "that for years and years had pushed hard for one-man rule and helped create a god out of Warren. They didn't count on their god turning on them."

Decades earlier, Warren's father had once severely punished his son by making him leave their house until Rulon decided to allow him to come home. The boy never forgot what that had felt like, and he now seemed to relish doing the same thing to others. This morning, Jeffs asked the banished husbands and fathers, who were still standing in front of him with bodies slumped and heads bowed, to raise their right hands if they believed that the Prophet's actions against them were the word of God. Each man lifted his hand. Warren then asked the other fifteen hundred people if they agreed that these excommunications were the work of the Lord, and all fifteen hundred lifted their right hands. He told everyone to kneel on the floor and they obeyed, as he prayed over them and ordered the banned men to repent their sins so they might be let back into the church and returned to their families. But that would never happen.

Within days of their expulsion from the border towns, Jeffs had begun reassigning their wives and kids to other men. As they were being reshuffled to different addresses around Colorado City, the women and children were told to have no further communication with the apostates.

One "master deceiver" was Isaac Wyler, a longtime FLDS member who'd been in excellent standing with the church—until now. Like Richard Holm, Wyler had no idea why Jeffs had done this to him. All he knew was that he was put under orders to keep working, making money, sending it to the Prophet, and repenting for his sins. Wyler followed Jeffs's dictates, putting together a list of his imagined transgressions, which ran to twenty-five pages, and sending it off to Warren, who never answered the letter or made any effort to contact the excommunicant. Wyler's wives and children were off limits to him and had been told that their husband and father had become "the worst of beings."

At a sermon delivered two weeks after the banishment, Jeffs revealed that he wanted to control not just the behavior of his flock, but also their feelings. They shouldn't be "disturbed" by anything he was doing or they were experiencing:

If your feelings can be disturbed and you simply need more of the spirit of God to have and earn more of that sweet spirit, you must pay the price. The price is sacrifice. Set aside any feeling or thought that disturbs the spirit of God . . . Focus your mind, your desires, your all, on keeping sweet. That is the most important work in all you do . . .

You show you love Heavenly Father, that you're thinking of Him, that you yearn to be like Him. The sign of disobedience is when you don't keep sweet . . . Go do better, ask forgiveness, stay busy in the good, govern the present moment in keeping sweeter and sweeter and He will remember your sins no more, because His sweet spirit is so sensitive to the smallest details that it does not give the least degree of allowance for evil . . .

Not everybody in town remained undisturbed: a few even dared to resist the Prophet, but not by name. On January 12, an anonymous letter was mailed out to 453 local post boxes, reading in part:

I am a young man. I am simple and do not know the proper way to address you. But I have been commanded of God to stand upon the wall as Samuel and to tell you of a dream I had . . . And darkness crept into my dream and a great fog did form. I witnessed as many of the labors of our forefathers went unrecognized and unappreciated. And I did see the world's respect begin to whither for the people's work. I beheld a harsh time in which forgiveness was abandoned. And I beheld too many families destroyed for petty reasons. I beheld children torn from their fathers and mothers torn from their husbands. I beheld the people of God crying in the darkness for God to deliver them. Fear filled my heart and I too prayed for deliverance . . .

As Jeffs's commands took hold in the community, those who remained in the FLDS went out of their way to please the Prophet by referring to people who'd been kicked out as "tools of the devil." Small boys and girls who only a few days earlier had been playing happily with their next-door neighbors began yelling over the fence:

"You are a gentile!"

"Apostate!"

"You're going to hell and so is your father!"

On January 15, 2004, the post office boxes received a second anonymous letter, this time condemning Jeffs for attempting to marry his father's wives right after Rulon had died:

A simple word, to those in Colorado City/Hildale who are currently following Warren Jeffs. Never and nowhere, in the known history of God's work upon this earth, has He condoned the marriage of a mother to her son. It is an abomination in the eyes of God and should be shouted from the rooftops. In spite of Uncle Roy's teachings to all parties, the fact that Warren Jeffs, convincing his own mothers to wed and bed him, does not make a prophet of him.

Before he died, according to the letter writer, Leroy Johnson had tried to sound an alarm to the church about the Jeffs family:

Uncle Roy felt concern for our future and so should we. . . . He said that he had run into, or was almost overwhelmed by, a power in Salt Lake City that was almost stronger than he was . . . [This] occurred at a time in our history when Warren Jeffs had been given control of the Salt Lake City Alta Academy. . . .

This new school administrator began a somewhat foreign era of physically and mentally forcing young children to be righteous through fear. Fear of being physically whipped so bad by the principal of the academy that you could hardly walk. . . . Fear of being publicly expelled from school and ostracized from your friends for small infractions of rules. . . . Warren planted small seeds in the minds of those young people that after "humbly and sweetly" informing on someone, they felt more elevated than those around them and "more worthy of building up the kingdom of God" . . .

Informants were everywhere. Children against parents, wives against husbands, and brethren against brethren. You didn't know who you could trust. Independent thinking, of any kind, was driven further underground. This force, disguised as "love," began to slowly spread beyond the confines of the school and into our Salt Lake City community. . . . It slowly, but surely, began to make its way into the Colorado City/Hildale community. . . . The clues to our future are hidden deep in Warren's past . . .

After banishing the twenty-one men, Jeffs disappeared from town but continued giving directives through his minions. He was on the lam to avoid answering the subpoena that had been issued for him in a child bigamy case. Some suspected he was down in Mexico or up in British Columbia, both of which had FLDS outposts. Before leaving, he'd told his closest circle that Colorado City had been "desecrated" by recent events, referring primarily to the monument built to the 1953 raid, so it was time to find another spiritual home. He sent church members out to purchase property in Eldorado, Texas; Mancos, Colorado; and Pringle, South Dakota. After buying 1,691 acres near Eldorado, highly placed FLDS members headed south and began erecting a village on this isolated piece of land, complete with log cabins, a meeting hall, a garden and chicken coop, a huge and gleaming white temple cut from local limestone, a dairy, an orchard, and a cheese factory. The temple was modeled after one Joseph Smith had built in the 1840s in Nauvoo, Illinois, not long before he was murdered. The FLDS has a prophecy that says, "With the laying of the last stone of the temple, the people shall be raised up to Zion"—and the new temple was clearly meant to signify their readiness to leave the earth for their celestial home.

They may have been preparing for heaven, but they were also constructing gargantuan houses on the Texas property, some measuring thirty thousand square feet. The new compound was called "Yearning For Zion Ranch" (YFZ) and had enough water and sewage infrastructure to support 2,000 people. Rumors flew around Colorado City and beyond that Jeffs was hiding in the bowels of the ranch and about to shift the core of his operations to Eldorado. He'd begun moving some of his spouses down to Texas. When his second wife, Barbara, was diagnosed with breast cancer she wasn't permitted to leave the ranch to seek proper medical care. Her condition was rumored to be left untreated until death.

Jeffs's increasingly bizarre behavior had started to attract regional and then national media attention, but people in Colorado City knew better than to talk to the reporters who showed up and hounded them for interviews. Whenever a strange vehicle arrived inside the city limits, another car (often a van) tailed it through the streets, trying to intimidate. The locals didn't seek out direct confrontation; they just wanted the visitors to go away and never come back. Since the rise of the new Prophet, the message to all foreigners was utterly clear: they were not only unwelcome in the border towns, but were being watched and stalked.

Nearing fifty, Warren had never spoken to a journalist or granted one a peek inside his church. Reporters were as irrelevant to his life as the laws of the United States and the authorities in Utah and Arizona. When TV or newspaper reporters approached Colorado City or Hildale homes to talk with families, blinds came down and doors were slammed in their faces. If they walked up to residents in parked cars, tapped on the windows, and asked for an opinion about the Prophet, the locals squealed away in a cloud of burnt rubber and red dust, shouting "Idiots!" or "Damned fools!"

While he was away, Jeffs's demands on the faithful deepened. In addition to tithing the regular 10 percent of their earnings to the church, they were now ordered to come up with another $1,000 a month for the needs of their runaway leader. He sent his brothers and closest followers out to collect the money, and sometimes he came for it himself. The scuttlebutt around Washington and Mohave County was that the border towns' police force occasionally escorted the Prophet back into Colorado City late at night to perform underage marriages in secret locations. His flock never actually saw him but heard stories of his nocturnal comings and goings, like a ghost or a god in flight. Among the faithful, these rumors only added to Jeffs's aura and status as a folk hero—a true outlaw prophet. Anybody who could move around like this must be part of an elite, with special knowledge and powers, and guidance from the hand of the Lord. In reality, Jeffs *was* well protected, with hiding houses spread across the Southwest and many worshippers willing to take him in. He could never have stayed on the run for long without the direct collaboration and financial backing of hundreds or even thousands of Fundamentalist Mormons who fervently believed in him and the principles of the FLDS.

The mounting war between the fugitive Prophet and the legal authorities stood in contrast to the silent obedience of the faithful and the quiet neighborhoods of Colorado City, where ponies grazed in side yards and roosters crowed away the daylight hours, giant clouds sweeping overhead and constantly changing the reddish face of Canaan Mountain and the surrounding mesas. Many backyards held trampolines, one of the few things Jeffs hadn't banned in the community. A visitor could still see children's heads bobbing up and down behind tall fences and hear their joyful cries and high-pitched laughter (even though the latter *had* been outlawed by the Prophet). Boys and girls still needed exercise, after all, especially once Jeffs had pulled them out of school and refused to let them play sports.

The place had an eerily quiet, strangely empty, ramshackle feel about it, as if it had been hammered together out of next to nothing, with wide-open streets and many houses that were half-finished or abandoned. The exposed siding and walls without windows looked oddly sinister. Everything about the twin communities seemed hostile and ghostly now, otherworldly and out of sync with modern time, as if something very odd or very bad was about to erupt and unleash chaos or retribution rolling out across the high desert plateau.

III

THE RESISTANCE

18

ON JANUARY 23, 2004, former Bullhead City, Arizona, police officer Gary Engels came to Colorado City for the first time, two
weeks after the Prophet had excommunicated twenty-one men. Engels had once worked with Mojave County Attorney Matt Smith, a no-
nonsense prosecutor with a crew cut, a square jaw, and an iron-fisted
handshake—a man known for not only taking on hard cases, but winning
them. In early 2004, Smith was thinking of doing something his county had
spent decades avoiding doing: investigating and possibly filing criminal
charges against members of the FLDS church. Smith had asked Engels, now
in semiretirement, to drive up to the border and poke around. Engels had
elected to come to town that day to listen to a scheduled press conference,
one that amounted to a local revolution.

In the past few days, Warren Jeffs had demanded that Ross Chatwin, another longtime loyal FLDS member, give up his wife, Lori, so the Prophet
could assign her to a "more worthy" man. While other husbands had
dropped their heads in front of the congregation and bowed down to such
outrageous orders, Chatwin chose a different response. He and Lori became
the only couple so far to publicly fight back against the head of their church.

On the front stoop of his home, with his wife and family spread out behind him, Chatwin offered a powerful rebuke to Jeffs. As bystanders and
members of the media looked on, he said:

> Recently, I joined a growing list of men who have been told to leave their homes. I can't be
> sure as to why I've been told to leave behind everything that I've worked for. I do know,

however, that the owner of the UEP land trust, Warren Jeffs, has claimed to be receiving revelations of whom to evict . . . My family and I do not plan on leaving our home anytime soon. I am pleased to report that my wife has submitted to stay by my side, regardless of Jeffs' commandment to leave me . . . It is difficult for me to find the words that can express to her how much I appreciate her . . .

As Chatwin's defiant words rang out on this cool winter morning, neither the Prophet nor his primary supporters were anywhere to be seen on the flat cottonwood-lined streets of Colorado City. Engels observed a few women darting in and out of the handful of stores in the center of town—in a hurry to get someplace without being noticed by strangers. They kept their heads lowered and eyes down, all of them wearing long-sleeved, full-length, buttoned-up cotton dresses in pastel shades of yellow, blue, pink, green, beige, and lavender. Beneath the dresses, they had on the sacred long under-wear of their faith. Their long hair was swept up in pompadour-like waves above their foreheads and tightly woven into French braids in the back, not an unruly strand in sight. None of their pale skin, except for hands and faces, was exposed.

From its outset, one of the primary goals of the Mormon faith, just as in Islam, was to downplay or obscure female vanity. Women weren't supposed to be physically provocative, and insisting on the same hairstyle and clothing for everyone took away the possibility of using one's body for creative expression. Over the decades, some of these rules had occasionally been relaxed by other Prophets in Colorado City, but Jeffs had lately brought them back full force. While Muslim women were allowed to wear jewelry and makeup beneath the fabric that covered most of their flesh, both were off limits in the border towns. High heels, mascara, and short hair were unthinkable. Jeffs had in-sisted that women return to the pioneer look that was popular when Joseph Smith founded Mormonism. The new Prophet wanted everything—clothing, hair, beliefs, and bloodlines—to be as pure as he was convinced they'd been back in 1830.

Yet, as Engels observed the town that winter day, it was clear a few things had changed. One young woman rode through the streets on horseback while speaking on a cell phone. Another broad-shouldered mother drove a minia-ture tractor to the general store and parked by the front door. Attached to the tractor was a metal scoop, normally used for picking up gravel or grain, but she'd put two small children in the metal basket and was carting them around town—a violation of the law almost everywhere else. The local police didn't arrest the faithful for breaking minor rules; they were much too busy hunting for apostates and gentiles. They'd soon bust Ross Chatwin on the trumped-up charge that he'd burglarized his own house.

"While the possibility of losing your home is frustrating," Chatwin continued before the gathered reporters,

> *the real travesty in Colorado City is the possibility of losing your family . . . I've talked with individuals who, being stunned by the magnitude of the situation, allowed Jeffs to remove their families from them. They now deeply regret having allowed this to happen. Houses can ultimately be rebuilt. Once a family is destroyed, it leaves broken hearts that can never be healed.*
>
> *Please, give it some thought before you throw it all away. There are few systems of checks and balances to govern how Jeffs operates. One of the only ways we can affect what he is doing is by letting the world know about the things that go on inside this town . . . I am sickened by the number of families Jeffs has been instrumental in destroying . . . At least fifty men have been turned into eunuchs . . .*

Most of the men and boys were absent from town that January day, as with every other weekday, working at one of the scores of lucrative construction companies owned and run by the church. It had been doing business this way for years, ignoring the child labor laws, as the United States had ignored the inner workings of the FLDS and the activities of its members. The Southwest was booming, St. George was the fastest-growing city in America, and building skills were in high demand. Some FLDS worksites were close to town, but others were in Mesquite, Nevada, seventy miles to the south and west. Each morning, boys as young as ten or eleven were hauled out to these locations and expected to put in eight or nine hours alongside their fathers. If they were too small to work a full shift, they were often left outside to endure the cold or extreme heat of the desert summers until quitting time arrived. The temperature in Mesquite in July was searing enough to bend the heads of palm trees until they were nearly parallel to the ground.

Throughout the hottest months, the men and boys were forced to work in long sleeves, their arms and legs fully covered from the sun. "Slave labor" was how some referred to this arrangement. The boys weren't paid much, if at all, but provided extra hands and extra profits for the bosses. Underpaid, under-age employees were a critical factor in underbidding other companies to get these jobs, some of which involved government contracts. The FLDS hated the American power structure but loved finding ways to take its money, a strategy they called "bleeding the beast."

Males occupied a strange position in Colorado City. They were the fa-vored children of families and church elders, but women often held more value because they could reproduce. The number of wives and children a man supported were symbols of his success, virility, and favor in God's eyes. But the inherent problem with polygamy, whether on the border or in Muslim countries abroad, is that there aren't enough females to go around. This pro-duces an excess of single young men in their physical and sexual prime, unat-tached to the opposite sex and not deeply rooted or invested in society. In every culture, men without women—drifting together in packs out of loneli-ness, boredom, a lack of identity, or a sense of adventure—raise the potential for trouble.

Jeffs's solution was simply to get rid of them, hundreds of them. Since taking over the church, he'd ordered wave after wave of teenagers and young men to leave the community. Kids were kicked out for smoking, drinking beer, or partying northwest of town at a spot called the "Edge of the World." They were banished for watching movies, talking to girls, kissing in public, or having a bad attitude—and left to fend for themselves on the streets of Las Vegas, St. George, or Salt Lake City. Known collectively as the "Lost Boys," some turned to selling drugs or prostitution. They crowded together in tiny apartments they called "butt huts," sleeping on couches and floors, if they bothered sleeping at all. One Lost Boy was Zeke, the former rising star within the FLDS. Back when he was a young student at Alta, Jeffs had handpicked him as a future church leader, and the teenager had followed Warren to Col-orado City to become a religious instructor. Despite misgivings about what Jeffs was doing to others in the community, Zeke remained faithful to him. Then, without warning, Warren announced that he was separating Zeke's grandparents and reassigning his grandmother, now in her mid-seventies, to another man. His grandfather was so devastated by losing his wife that he en-tered a mental hospital, his health collapsed, and he was soon dead.

"When Warren did this," Zeke says, "everyone in my family looked at everyone else and said, 'What the hell is happening to us?' We thought he *liked* us. In my mind, he murdered my grandfather, and that was the turning point for me. I couldn't keep ignoring or rationalizing his behavior. I'd like to see Warren spend the rest of his life in prison just for what he did to my grand-dad."

From a distance, Zeke was able to view Jeffs's tactics more clearly than when he was in the man's favor.

"Warren taught us," he says, "to have nothing to do with those who'd been banned from the church, but the worst thing he did was create a huge chasm between parents and their children. He knew exactly how to do this. When he began throwing teenagers out of the FLDS, it made kids hate their parents for listening to Warren, and it made parents hate their kids for doing things to get kicked out. This went right to the heart of the parent–child relation-ship. When you tell a mother she can't talk to her child anymore, how much more manipulative can you get?"

After his grandfather's death Zeke began rebelling openly and Jeffs ban-ished him from the border towns. At the turn of the new millennium, the teenager left Colorado City for St. George, where he used his intelligence and street smarts to adjust to the outside world. Besides smoking pot, he and other Lost Boys indulged in all the things they'd been denied: watching music videos, surfing dark corners of the Internet, dancing into the early hours of the morning, and drinking themselves into a stupor. They trashed some apartments so badly that the landlords wouldn't renew their leases. One of Zeke's friends got busted for selling cocaine, and others were regularly having run-ins with the law. "At first," he says, "we did a lot of drugs because we'd been so restricted in the past. It's like holding a rubber band on the end of your finger and pulling it back farther and farther and building up more and more tension. When you let it go, it flies as far as it can."

Local teenagers made fun of the Lost Boys for their out-of-date clothes, clumsy haircuts, speech patterns, or lack of education. Many could barely read, write, or do simple math, and most were ashamed to say where they'd come from. To stand against their tormentors, they began forming into gangs, ready to fight as a unit if necessary.

"The first few years on the outside," Zeke says, "were hell."

Like many other Lost Boys who'd escaped the FLDS—some of whom preferred to call themselves "Survivors"—Zeke had a haunted quality, espe-cially in his eyes, as if he'd been hurt in a place that would never quite heal.

But he also had his freedom. In a backhanded way, he was grateful to Jeffs for driving him out of the community when he was young, could adapt quickly, and experience another reality. He now had modern hair and clothes and the latest technology, and was earning a degree while holding a job. He and some of his friends had become success stories. When they got together, they jokingly referred to breaking away from the church as "taking the red pill."

"Once you've swallowed that pill," Zeke says, "you're never the same. Warren destroyed my hometown and I'll never go back."

Most of the Lost Boys, like the FLDS girls who'd been forced into underage marriages, didn't realize they could take legal action against Jeffs. They were too busy just trying to survive. One of them, Johnny Jessop, was ten when the Prophet expelled his father from the church and reassigned his mother to live with Bishop Fred Jessop. Three years later, Johnny was so miserable living under Jeffs's restrictions that he ran away to join some older companions in Hurricane. The thirteen-year-old began moving from relative to relative, repeatedly ending up in juvenile court. A judge ordered him returned to his mother, but Jeffs wouldn't tell the boy where she was.

Johnny wrote letters to the Prophet begging to be reunited with her, but Warren refused to respond, so the boy found a lawyer and sued him.

John Larsen of Utah's Department of Human Services had been dealing with domestic abuse and other social issues in Colorado City since the 1970s. A Utah native and practicing Mormon in the LDS Church, with decades of experience with the FLDS, he'd interviewed numerous Lost Boys and had never seen anything approaching the cruelty of the new Prophet or the scope of the current problems.

"These kids were kicked out of their homes, their church, and their community," Larsen says, "for listening to rap music or Whitney Houston. When they still lived in Colorado City, they'd go into the desert and the town marshals would follow them out there. When the police found them sitting in cars playing this music, they'd tap on the windows and haul them in front of the Prophet. He'd force them to go away until they'd repented, and their parents went along with this, which is almost unbelievable."

Larsen says the boys talked to him about their mothers, whom they deeply missed. "They all said they were now 'dead' to their parents and their parents were 'dead' to them. If their mothers and fathers even spoke to their sons, they'd also get thrown out, but some of the boys sneaked telephone calls to their mothers anyway. Or tried to sneak back into town to see them. You've got to remember that these are just little kids who are really hurting, and to be able to talk to their mothers for five minutes is their biggest joy. They've told me that they might as well have sex, get drunk, and do drugs now, since they've been excommunicated and are already doomed. One young man I spoke to kept brushing his arms, touching them over and over again. He couldn't get used to wearing short sleeves and having his skin exposed. That's how badly adjusted they are to the outside world. We don't have any good statistics on the number of these kids who were sexually molested as children, only stories from those who will talk about it, but a closed society is more prone to every kind of abuse."

19

OVERALL," ROSS CHATWIN SAID, as Gary Engels and others looked on, "Jeffs's leadership has been reckless at best. It's shocking to realize that the owner of a one-hundred-million-dollar asset could act so carelessly . . . Some people are concerned that I might be endangering my life for sticking up for my rights. I do fear that some overly zealous person from within the FLDS Church might take it upon themselves to do something rash. But . . . I feel it's my responsibility to let the world know about the situation here in Colorado City and that in doing so, I ultimately make things safer and better for everyone by limiting what Jeffs can do . . ."

Chatwin's speech and the media coverage it generated would bring more of the kind of attention to the border towns that the Prophet and his followers despised.

In Amish societies, the men traditionally came together on weekends for barn raisings for their neighbors. In Colorado City and Hildale, they now started throwing up barriers in front of their homes to keep out reporters and sightseers—walls of brick, cinder block, cement, wood, metal, and bamboo. The people inside the houses were hunkering down for a long wave of bad press and snooping around by strangers. These were homes that did not have portraits of Jesus Christ on the mantle, but a photograph of Warren Jeffs or his late father. By early 2004, paranoia, always lurking below the surface of the FLDS, was rising throughout the community.

Occasionally, tourists exited Highway 59 and came into town looking for supplies at the general store. Now they weren't just entering a place filled with nineteenth-century-looking residents, but an environment that was outwardly hostile. Visiting children wearing shorts or T-shirts were met by the stares and catcalls of local kids. Female store clerks refused to make eye contact or acknowledge their adult customers, handling their money as if it were toxic. Yet they seemed ashamed or embarrassed by their own behavior. They had the shy awkwardness of country people everywhere, whose natural instincts were to be friendly, but who weren't allowed to be. The town had taken on a poisoned edge. All strangers had come to be perceived as a threat to their religion and way of life, and the women looked deeply relieved to see them leave their place of business.

Near the general store, a broad open street ended at the metal gate of the FLDS cemetery. The first headstone belonged to Rulon Jeffs, dead on September 8, 2002, at age ninety-two. Freshly dug, fine red dirt stood atop his grave, and similar mounds covered the other plots. All faced east, the ancestral home of the lost tribes of Israel, the graves paying tribute to a spiritual past the town believed was its own. Rulon's marble headstone was chiseled with the message "Sweet and Sound," but it wasn't sweetness that one found driving around Colorado City.

"This Hitler-like dictator," Chatwin said, concluding his speech and holding up a book, "has got to be stopped before he ruins us all and this beautiful town."

The cover held a black swastika and read *The Rise and Fall of the Third Reich*.

"Warren," he said, "has studied this book for many years. It is what he uses as a guideline to govern this community and control the people."

In the early 1990s, a Colorado City boy with acute retardation had been brought into the office of a Phoenix pediatric neurologist, Dr. Theodore Tarby. A veteran of dealing with childhood illnesses, Dr. Tarby had never seen anything like the youngster and didn't know how to diagnose him. After seeking help from a pediatrics professor at the University of Colorado, he learned that the boy had an extraordinarily rare disease called fumarase deficiency, with only a few cases reported worldwide. It produced overly large heads and unusually thick features. Brains were often misshapen or had been replaced by pools of water. The boy's sister had the same illness, because both children had received a recessive gene from their parents. Fumarase deficiency, caused by the body's failure to process food properly, led to severe speech impediments, deformities, epileptic seizures, and the inability to grow normally, sit upright, or walk. The disease was soon found in two other local families, which for generations had been marrying close relatives. Tucked away in Colorado City houses and bedrooms, kept out of sight from the general population and outside authority figures, were a number of infants who could barely move their bodies.

Dr. Tarby had found that by the end of the 1990s, the inbreeding of FLDS members had produced the highest rate of fumarase deficiency in the world. The genetic defect was traced back to an FLDS founder, Joseph Smith Jessop, and the first of his plural wives, Martha Moore Yeates. In 1923, one of their daughters had wed another Short Creek patriarch who was also her second cousin and the Prophet from 1935 to 1949, John Yates Barlow. The town's power structure had essentially evolved from the intermarriage of these two prominent families, the Jessops and the Barlows, producing revered Bishop Fred Jessop, civic leader Truman Barlow, school superintendent Alvin Barlow, police officer and church leader Sam Barlow, teacher Louis Barlow, and Colorado City mayor Dan Barlow. Inside the church, marriages between first and second cousins were commonplace, and thousands of FLDS members carried this recessive gene.

Fumarase deficiency had no cure. The only way to stop the spread of the disease was through aborting the damaged fetuses or halting intermarriages, but neither alternative was acceptable to Warren Jeffs. When reports of the spreading disease reached him, he ignored them. His job was to decide who married whom, and he chose wedding partners with specific goals in mind. Not only did he want their offspring to be perfectly obedient, but also to keep racial lines within the FLDS perfectly pure, free of any influence that might darken the gene pool. Like Hitler, his goal was to use sex to build a superior race.

For decades, Jeffs's church had claimed that under the First Amendment to the U.S. Constitution, it had the absolute right to practice its religion as it chose; county, state, and federal governments had no business interfering with the FLDS and no jurisdiction over it. But what about the public benefits the community enjoyed? Colorado City had received $1.9 million from the U.S. Department of Housing and Urban Development to pave the streets and improve the fire department and water system, while Arizona had paid out more than $12 million a year to the local poor for health insurance premiums. The American government had built the town's impressive $2.8-million-dollar airport, and nearly three-fourths of those living on the Arizona side of the border received food stamps—eight times the amount of welfare handed out in most other towns or urban areas. Once a month, on Wednesday afternoons, women dressed from head to foot in pioneer garb, most of them the multiple wives of one husband, flooded the single county government building, a triple-wide trailer on the outskirts of the village, where they lined up to get their stamps. Only the first wife of a plural marriage was officially wed to her husband. All the others were only "spiritually married" to the man, so they qualified as single mothers eligible for welfare.

The FLDS loathed the U.S. government, and some church members had openly celebrated the September 2001 terrorist attacks on New York and Washington, D.C.—a clear sign from God that the long-awaited Apocalypse was near and the heathen were about to fall. Yet these same churchgoers eagerly accepted food stamps, welfare checks, and other public funds. The more money they took from the state, the more they "bled the beast." Only one American flag was seen flying in the border towns, a frayed, weather-beaten piece of cloth rising above a rooftop and mocking the most powerful nation on earth. For the past half-century, Arizona, Utah, and the federal government had left the FLDS alone, free to conduct its polygamous lifestyle and financial scams. During those fifty years, the community had avoided the reach of the law, but more and more problems and questions had started to emerge.

What about the rising costs of welfare and of treating fumarase deficiency? What if citizens across the nation with no connection to Mormon fundamentalists had to pick up the tab for other people's very expensive marital and sexual practices? What if a religious sect on the Utah-Arizona border were being run like a criminal enterprise, similar to the Mafia? Or like a terrorist outfit, answerable only to its Prophet?

20

AFTER LISTENING TO ROSS CHATWIN'S PRESS CONFERENCE, Gary Engels returned to Bullhead City, intrigued by what he'd seen and heard. He reported back to Mohave County Attorney Matt Smith, who'd decide what to do next. With stories coming out of Colorado City about a radical new FLDS regime and rumors flying about an increase in underage marriages, sexual abuse, and other crimes, law enforcement was paying more attention to the twin communities, but remained reluctant to act. In the back of their minds were the 1953 raid and two other events involving religious leaders that had ended in disaster. One was the 1970s mass suicide of over nine hundred people in Guyana, led by Reverend Jim Jones, who'd talked his flock into drinking poisonous Kool-Aid on their way to the grave. The other was the 1993 federal attempt to raid the Branch Davidian compound in Waco, Texas, ending the lives of scores of men, women, and children. The inferno at Waco was widely viewed as an FBI catastrophe, and it left a permanent stain on the distinguished career of U.S. Attorney General Janet Reno.

Arizona and Utah officials had long ago given up on prosecuting polygamy among consenting adults, but if the fundamentalists were aggressively promoting underage marriage or sexual abuse, that was another matter. In Arizona, coercing a woman under eighteen into marriage with an older man or performing that marriage was a felony known as "forcible rape." If crimes were being committed in Colorado City and Hildale, was there a better way to go after these religious practices than coming in with bulldozers roaring and guns blazing?

For years, people in and around Colorado City had talked how about the FLDS-run construction companies had stockpiled dynamite, automatic weapons, and tens of thousands of rounds of ammunition, squirreled away in a cave at the edge of town. Maybe these were only tall tales, meant to frighten outsiders or the authorities, but the last thing either state needed was another Jonestown or Waco, and the situation along the border was complex, volatile, and potentially tragic. Smith was suggesting a new approach. He sought a veteran investigator, somebody with a police background, under-cover experience, and plenty of guts and skills, along with something more intangible. This person had to be sensitive to the local issues and people, but not so sensitive that he couldn't put up with the insults and intimidation sure to come his way. Was there somebody willing to take on this extremely diffi-cult challenge—which didn't offer much job security or pay—who wouldn't cut and run when things got nasty?

Gary Engels walked with a permanent limp and with pain that had settled into the lower half of his body, a constant reminder of his years as a police officer. Early in his career, he'd been an undercover narcotics officer in Denver before relocating to Arizona. In 1988 in Bullhead City, he was called out to a domestic dispute and when he arrived on the scene, an armed man was in the act of assaulting his wife. The man suddenly opened fire and hit Engels in the hip, missing a fatal artery by one-sixteenth of an inch. Gary drew his weapon and fired back twice, killing the assailant.

After recovering from the wound, Engels rejoined the Bullhead City PD, where things were changing for the worse. He hated office politics, but the in-fighting inside the department had become too obvious to ignore. Police chiefs kept coming and going, a half dozen in about as many years, until they hired somebody whom Engels felt was playing favorites with certain officers at the expense of others, like himself. His boiling point was always several degrees lower than normal, and it wasn't in his nature to stay quiet or worry about taking guff from other cops who supported the current chief. When Engels spoke out against his superior and led an effort to form a police offi-cers' association, it cost the chief his job. Other cops started digging for dirt on Engels, who found himself spending too much time looking over his shoulder at work instead of pursuing criminals. In 1993, he took early retire-ment and began searching for something to do.

He tried relaxing, but was terrible at it. He tried welding and working on muscle cars, but these were just hobbies. He was born to practice law enforcement, but too old to dodge bullets or chase down offenders on the street, especially on a bum hip. He was too young to stop working, so when he heard about a company providing security at a power plant, he applied and was hired.

"The pay was good," he says, "but the job was incredibly boring. I was on the night shift and sometimes I thought the sun would never come up again."

Unable to retire *or* find the right job, Engels lasted a few years at the power plant before restlessness overtook him—he was a man who needed a mountain to scale. He'd once attended classes at the University of Phoenix in Bullhead City toward a degree in management, but had quit ten credits short of his goal. In the 1990s, he thought about pursuing business opportunities, but nothing was right. He wasn't interested in business. He was interested in investigating crimes and busting criminals. Engels partly conjured up the strong-armed Russell Crowe character in the movie *L.A. Confidential*—the cop who burns to help victims and stop the bad guys who've hurt people.

With a thick neck, a perfectly square red face, short whitish hair, and beefy shoulders, he had enough flesh on his torso to take all the slack out of his pressed and highly starched shirts. A martial arts expert, he resembled a smaller Mike Ditka, the most crazily intense player in the history of the National Football League. Engels could be extremely curt if necessary and gave the impression that at any moment he might blow. At times, he chafed at playing by the rules of American law, the U.S. Constitution, and due process, but he forced himself to because the legal system was there to restrain not just criminals but also those who went after them. Restraint would be critical in the next phase of his career.

In early 2004, when he received a call from Matt Smith about Colorado City, Engels was in a listening mood, and when he heard about the Ross Chatwin press conference he drove up to assess the situation for himself. Things on the border were extremely complex, he was entering hostile territory, and it would most likely be impossible to penetrate the FLDS or get anyone in the church to open up to him. But the conditions there stimulated him in a way nothing else had for a very long time. Potential crimes weren't being properly investigated, the local police weren't enforcing the laws against underage marriage, and victims trapped inside this religious community could use Engels's help. What chance did a young FLDS girl have if she was being forced into marriage—and motherhood—at fourteen or fifteen? What hope remained for a teenage boy who'd been thrown out of his school and hometown by a dictator who didn't want him competing with the Prophet for the young females?

He was interested in the position, he told Smith, but it would be months before his own vital role in the investigation would begin. The first person Engels and Smith contacted about investigating the FLDS was a woman who'd escaped from it. Like most other people, they found her to be a very mixed bag.

Raised in a Colorado City family with twenty-eight siblings, Flora Jessop had interacted with the Jeffs clan long before Warren became the new Prophet. What she remembered most about him were his soft voice and long, bony fingers.

"He liked to touch both boys and girls a lot," she says. "He was always trying to touch me, and when you've been molested as a child, you don't want people touching you."

At fourteen, she'd shocked her hometown by filing sex abuse charges against her polygamous father, but a local judge dismissed the case and for the next two years Flora was confined to a relative's home. The FLDS then gave her two options: she could either marry the older man they'd selected for her or be admitted to a mental hospital. She chose marriage, but at eighteen, with only a fifth-grade education, she ran away from Colorado City and fell into a life of hitchhiking, topless dancing, and cocaine addiction. Decades later, she was still bitter about her past.

"I ate out of garbage cans to survive," she says. "For years, the only emotions I had were hate and rage. I despised God with everything inside of me, but it wasn't God who did this to me. It was the church. God was sitting on my shoulder the whole time I was running or I'd never have made it out alive."

Flora eventually had a daughter whom she supported with her dancing, before meeting an ex-Marine and settling into marriage in Phoenix. By 2004, she was in her mid-thirties and had long ago gone public with her story of abuse and underage marriage, believing—or hoping—that she'd become visible enough to be protected from FLDS retaliation. Flora may have had a streak of paranoia, but she also had some actual enemies. When eating in restaurants, she carried a gun and insisted on facing the front door. She chain-smoked Camels and swigged coffee. It was difficult to imagine that her petite body had ever been clothed in the long cotton dresses and elaborate braids of an FLDS girl—she'd never forgiven those who'd made her look that way.

People across the Southwest knew her as the most outspoken female in the struggle against Warren Jeffs and his church, and she soon launched an organization to help women and children escape the FLDS. Her motivation for doing this came after one of her sisters—fourteen-year-old Ruby—had been forced into a marriage ceremony performed by Jeffs. On Ruby's wedding night, she'd been handled so harshly in bed that she'd hemorrhaged large amounts of blood. When Ruby tried to run away, FLDS members found her, brought her home, and hid her inside the secretive world of Colorado City. Because of Ruby, Flora vowed to assist other young people eager to break free of the FLDS. Creating a modern-day Underground Railroad, she began sneaking back into town under cover of darkness to rescue women and children—fifteen by her own count—and putting them up in safe houses around the West.

Utah and Arizona authorities viewed her activities as borderline violations of the law. When they told her to stop or face possible arrest, she was as defiant with them as she'd been with the leaders of her former church.

"Don't threaten me," she snapped back. "If you don't like what I'm doing, cuff me and put me in jail."

With an intimate knowledge of the region's back roads and alleys, she set up hidden meeting points and whisked people out of town before either the FLDS or the local police knew what hit them. Despite the threats and the danger to herself and those she was rescuing, it was worth the risk if she could get one more person away from the Prophet.

"Everybody else is afraid of being arrested," she says, "but I don't care about that. I'm not running anymore, from anyone, because this work has to be done. Religion is no excuse for child abuse or terrorism. Because I was born and grew up in Colorado City, I know how bad it is in there. The people who live there aren't doing what they do for sex or money, but for God. They're true believers, so they're unstoppable. And Warren thinks on a level that's much bigger than most people realize. He's always been extremely ambitious. He doesn't just want to control the FLDS, but to cleanse the North American continent to enable the Second Coming."

In early 2004, as Jeffs was excommunicating twenty-one men, a Phoenix

TV station sent a news crew with Flora as she traveled to a location near Colorado City and brought out two teenagers, Fawn Holm and Fawn Broadbent. The latter moved in with a family in Salt Lake City and did well in this environment, earning a scholarship to attend Weber State College, but Fawn Holm had a much harder time, eventually bolting from her new home. While Flora was certain she'd done the right thing with the girls, not everyone agreed. A Phoenix judge barred her from further contact with them and *New Times*, the Phoenix weekly that was usually deeply critical of FLDS practices, characterized her as a publicity-seeking "fanatic." Her demands "to have control over someone else's children are becoming eerily similar to the dictatorial attitude of her sworn nemesis, Warren Jeffs."

None of this fazed Flora.

"You have to understand," she says, "that I'm willing to die for these kids. These children are not children, but currency for the FLDS. If you think your religion gives you the right to rape children, then your religion needs to be burned to the ground."

Every revolution produced somebody like Flora Jessop: a flamethrower who jolted others into action. She had a knack for inspiring victimized women to come forward—and for turning off strong FLDS opponents and embarrassing the police or other authorities. In the absence of any organized effort to enforce the law along the border for the past several decades, Flora, like Laura Chapman before her, had stepped forward and done what others wouldn't. Nobody else had wanted to take the risks to help the men, women, boys, girls, and childhood victims of polygamy—least of all the Latter-day Saints church up in Salt Lake City.

At the start of the new millennium, the contrast between the radical vision of Joseph Smith and the conservative nature of the modern LDS religion had never been more striking. The church had fervently opposed the Equal Rights Amendment in the 1970s, had kept African American men from being LDS priests until the end of that decade, and then poured major financial and political resources into fighting gay marriage. In spite of the rise of Warren Jeffs and the growing human damage created by the "sacred principle" of polygamy, the official Mormon Church ignored these developments. It had charged into the twenty-first century and was spreading its own message with a missionary zeal, making it America's fastest-growing religion, with more than twelve million members. The LDS Church wanted nothing to do with its bastard cousin down in Dixie, even if the fundamentalists were living truer to Smith's ideas than were the faithful in Salt Lake City.

Instead of quietly going away, the FLDS was drawing more bad publicity to itself than ever before. The official church wasn't about to step into this quagmire, so cleaning up the mess had fallen to women who'd been personally hurt by the fundamentalists and were still trying to provoke the politicians and law enforcement into action. After years of private struggle, they were no longer alone.

21

IN 2002, ELAINE TYLER MOVED TO ST. GEORGE FROM DENVER, where she'd worked as a pharmaceutical company sales rep and been a member of the Junior League. Reared in Atlanta and with a trace of the South still on her tongue, she didn't bring to mind many Junior League images. Wearing colorful sandals, denim jackets, and long flowing skirts that echoed the 1960s, she seemed part earth mother and part unstoppable force. Elaine embodied both a tenderness and a toughness that were most evident when she ran into injustice. After moving to St. George, she began noticing women in very old-fashioned dresses walking around town or shopping in local stores. She thought they were Mennonites or part of an Amish community, but discovered they were Fundamentalist Mormons and began asking questions about them. She absorbed the history of Colorado City and heard stories about Warren Jeffs and his tyrannical rule—teenage girls forced into marriage, young men thrown out of the community, and families broken up with a few words from the pulpit. She was intrigued—and angered. Why wasn't someone doing something to stop Jeffs's madness? Why wasn't somebody helping his victims?

Like Gary Engels, she wasn't easily discouraged by a challenge. Both she and the former cop had left behind other careers with the vague notion of finding something better to do—or discovering some larger cause to commit themselves to. They'd been successful, but weren't fulfilled. Now both were moving toward the chance to lessen the misery growing right next door. The more Elaine learned about what was happening forty-five minutes away, the more determined she was to get involved. She was in a financial position to do some volunteer work, but had no idea how much volunteering would be needed.

Elaine continued the work of Flora Jessop in assisting women trying to escape the FLDS, founding the Hope Organization in March 2004 in Washington, Utah, just a mile from St. George. Three days a week, she went into a small office where she became the CEO, the secretary, and everything in between—a one-woman clearinghouse for all things related to Warren Jeffs and his church. She looked for more volunteers, wrote grants to raise money, and sought out donations, piecing funds together for material assistance and legal advice for females and children trying to get away from Colorado City. The Hope Organization didn't try to help people escape the FLDS the way that Flora did. But if they wanted to leave, Elaine provided food, transportation, clothing, shelter, pots, pans, furniture, and other items needed to live. As her role expanded, she became a victim advocate for women who'd been abused, making court appearances with them.

She offered financial advice to adult females who'd never had to handle money or make decisions about it until now. She assisted the Lost Boys streaming into St. George by the scores and then the hundreds, until there were estimates of nearly a thousand. She helped them with all the things they knew nothing about: health insurance, car registration, car insurance, making budgets, and paying cell phone bills. She dealt with the ever-increasing requests from media for information about the plight of former FLDS women, teenagers, and children, which streamed in from around the world. She posted articles and the latest developments on the Hope Organization Web site. If Utah and Arizona were still trying to decide what to do about the victims of polygamy, and if the LDS Church chose to ignore them, Elaine would look after them herself. She poured herself into the job, working harder than she had as a sales rep—and she was unpaid. You couldn't put a dollar figure on what her position was worth. Now that people knew there was someone out there to help them break loose from their past or escape the fear of the present, Elaine's phone never stopped ringing. One of the former-FLDS women who approached her had 428 siblings.

Out of curiosity and concern, Elaine began digging into the numbers surrounding the educational system inside the border towns. In 2000, Jeffs had commanded parents to pull their children from the public schools so they wouldn't have to associate with the apostates from Centennial Park. After hundreds of local youngsters had followed these orders, attendance had plunged, yet the schools had continued to apply for—and receive—major government funding. For the fiscal year 2002–03, expenditures for the Colorado City Unified School District were $14.6 million. During the same time, the comparable Littlefield, Arizona, Unified School District spent $3.9 million. The average annual expense for educating a single student in Colorado City was over $40,000, but just under $9,700 in Littlefield.

Despite the dramatic loss of enrollment and far less need for transportation, the monies doled out for school buses in Colorado City had *increased*, with 2002 expenses of $145,000 for the purchase and lease of two more such vehicles. The extra funds, according to those who'd left the church, had been used for family vacations for church members, private trips on airplanes, and other creative ways of "bleeding the beast." Elaine crunched the numbers and sent them off to Arizona Attorney General Terry Goddard. With the black and white figures staring them in the face, the authorities launched their own investigation.

Once again, a civilian had led the way in uncovering corruption. Others were jumping on board.

22

PRIVATE INVESTIGATOR SAM BROWER, who lived fifty miles north of St. George in Cedar City, Utah, was brought up as a mainstream Mormon in Southern California and studied at Riverside City College, where he initially majored in chemistry. While taking a genetics course at Riverside, he'd focused on the breeding habits of one small American community to see where bloodlines had overlapped and created higher tendencies for hemophilia.

Intellectual and soft-spoken, but with the powerful-looking chest and shoulders of a wrestler, Brower didn't match any stereotypical image of a gumshoe. When Sam was twenty-one, a close friend of his was shot to death in front of the victim's four-year-old stepson. After the funeral, Brower went out and got drunk, feeling the bitter loss of his buddy and thinking about his future life as a chemist. The murder had jarred something loose in him that until now had remained tucked away inside of Sam. Nobody had been arrested for the homicide and the Santa Ana Police Department didn't even have a suspect. This injustice bothered Brower so deeply that it took on the quality of a haunting, until he decided to act. He changed his major to a combination of criminal justice and criminalistics and became a PI.

He, his wife, and their three children eventually left Southern California to resettle in Cedar City. Over the years, Sam had drifted away from the Mormon faith and experimented with many different religions, including Hinduism, but he gradually returned to his roots. In Utah, he became a practicing Mormon again and worked as a private investigator and bounty hunter, still tormented by the death of his friend decades earlier. As part of his job, he educated himself about new forensic technology, wondering if it could be applied to that murder. In the late 1990s, he asked the Santa Ana PD if using digitally enhanced methods of uncovering old finger or palm prints might help solve this very cold case. They were skeptical, initially resisting his ideas. Sam had an easy smile and an ever-present sense of humor, but he was also tenacious; after much persuasion, the police decided to reopen the murder investigation, so old that the files were stashed away in cardboard boxes in a dusty corner of the department. The case was handed over to some retired Santa Ana detectives who received a lot of input from Brower.

Following his suggestions and employing the new technology, they found more prints and matched them to a suspect. They arrested the man as he was going to see his parole officer for another crime. The homicide went to trial, the jury hung, and the killer took a plea of eight years without parole for aggravated manslaughter. More than two and a half decades after his buddy's funeral, Sam felt at peace and vindicated. With that case finally solved, he needed a new challenge.

In the winter of 2004, when he heard about Ross Chatwin's public defiance of Warren Jeffs, Brower decided to drive to Colorado City and nose around. He was inside the city limits before realizing this was the place and these were the people he'd studied in that genetics class thirty years ago. On a whim, Brower pulled up in front of Chatwin's home and knocked on the door. To his surprise, Ross answered and was eager to share his recent experience with the FLDS. The longer Brower listened, the more he wanted to help this man and others hurt by Jeffs. When Chatwin floated the idea of hiring the PI to do some work for him, Sam laughed and said it would take a dollar to retain his services.

"I don't have a dollar," Ross replied.

At the moment, he was dead broke.

Reaching into his own pocket, Brower pulled out a buck and loaned it to the man so he could start investigating the church and its Prophet. Sam was now officially in Chatwin's employ, involved in both the search for potential criminal behavior inside the FLDS and the hunt for Warren Jeffs. If asked, the PI would say that being a Mormon had nothing to do with his participation in the case, but he seemed motivated by something more than money or adding to his professional reputation.

Another civilian had stepped forward to join the fight.

In the coming months, Brower began examining the Prophet's recorded words and behavior with the same determination he'd brought to solving his friend's murder. This as yet unpaid job required his skills as a private investigator, bounty hunter, criminal profiler, victim advocate, and mediator. By mid-2004, the state of Arizona, Mohave County, the state of Utah, Washington County, two attorney general's offices, and other law enforcement entities were all starting to weigh their options regarding Jeffs, his church, the UEP Trust, and FLDS followers. Brower would soon become the man in the middle of everything—the go-between in an investigative web growing larger and more complex by the week. He searched for Jeffs, shared information with various police agencies, talked to attorneys, communicated with the FBI, and began gathering stories from those harmed by the Prophet or his congregation.

The more Sam uncovered, the more he felt that an overall battle plan was going to be necessary. There was still foot-dragging on both sides of the border; nothing in the past had worked to stop the marital or sexual abuses in Colorado City, so why should anything be different now? This attitude only left Brower more committed to moving ahead. Maybe it would take another two and a half decades to get anything done in the twin communities, but it had to start somewhere, and he knew where that was.

The PI hooked up with a pair of Salt Lake City brothers and attorneys, Gregory and Roger Hoole, and on July 29, 2004, they filed a civil lawsuit against Jeffs, the UEP, and the FLDS on behalf of six Lost Boys who'd been banished from Colorado City, alleging that they'd been driven away to reduce the competition for plural wives. The six were Richard Ream, Tom Steed, Donald Fischer, Dean J. Barlow, Walter Scott Fischer, and Richard Gilbert. In a splash of publicity the legal team announced the suit from the steps of the state capitol building in Salt Lake City. The Lost Boys' attorney fees would be paid by ex-FLDS member Dan Fischer, who'd created the Diversity Foundation to help banned teens get schooling and life skills training and find jobs. This was a new and very visible step in the battle against Jeffs. Following the pronouncement and its widespread media coverage, the Prophet finally went underground for good, taking off from Colorado City and moving from one state to the next, resurfacing only to perform more "spiritual marriages."

As Jeffs had once watched Laura Chapman and her sister, Rena, from a distance, afraid these "daughters of perdition" might damage the FLDS, he now had many more enemies to keep track of. From the FLDS compounds in Texas, South Dakota, and other Southwestern locales, he heard reports of the Lost Boys' lawsuit, of Sam Brower's pursuit of him, and of the gradual movement of Utah and Arizona toward enforcing the laws they'd so long ignored. Jeffs's minions asked church followers for more money so he could go deeper into hiding. The Prophet made fewer trips back to the border towns and undertook them in greater secrecy, traveling at night and wearing disguises, transferring from one vehicle to the next along the way. He ventured farther from his home base, thinking he'd be safer, and made a swing through the Southeastern United States.

The longer he stayed on the run, and the more support his followers gave him, the more invulnerable he felt. He could wield power just as successfully from the back of a car, moving along the freeway at sixty miles an hour and talking on a disposable cell phone, as he could sitting in his father's old office in Hildale. He had a tight-knit group of leaders, some of them his brothers, who were totally loyal to the Prophet and committed to carrying out his orders. All he had to do was issue a directive and things got done. He could ban more boys from the community this way, or separate more families and reassign the women and children to other men, or relocate some of his key people to Texas. He had almost unlimited resources, he was smarter than those in law enforcement, and God was on his side. The Lord would protect him from his tormentors, as He always had before, and keep him from being caught.

Once the Lost Boys' suit had been filed, Jeffs and the other defendants were given the chance to respond in court, but they did nothing—nothing at all. It was an extraordinary legal strategy (or nonstrategy), ensuring that the plaintiffs would win by default. Jeffs's indifference to the suit confirmed the deepening sense that he'd given up on Colorado City and was now focused on carrying out his vision in Eldorado, Texas. For decades his father and earlier Prophets had preached that before Christ returned for the Second Coming, God would cleanse all of Babylon. More particularly, He'd wipe out the LDS temple in Salt Lake City with fire and death, preparing the way for true Mormons to reclaim their rightful position as the head of the faith. Once the Lord had purged the false temple, the restored Mormons would build their own great house of worship. Jeffs had grown tired of waiting for divine de-struction and had decided to preempt Jesus' return by constructing a temple in West Texas. What happened to those who stayed behind in Colorado City was no longer his concern, and neither was the Lost Boys' lawsuit.

Four weeks after its filing, on August 27, Maryland lawyer Joanne Suder, whose firm had successfully sued the Baltimore Catholic Diocese over child sexual abuse, launched another suit on behalf of Brent Jeffs, who alleged that decades earlier Warren and his brothers had sodomized the boy at Alta Acad-emy. The suit also charged them with covering up years of serial child mo-lestations by other FLDS leaders. Warren's brothers would eventually be dropped from the case, but not the Prophet himself. That same month Sam Brower traveled to Texas to serve legal papers on Jeffs's top aides, now living at the new 1,691-acre Eldorado community. The private investigator then vis-ited Jeffs's compound in Hildale to serve the Prophet personally with a sum-mons to appear in court for the Brent Jeffs case. Warren had long since disappeared. He was treating the Brent Jeffs civil action as he had the earlier one regarding the Lost Boys, pretending that neither it nor the American le-gal system existed.

By autumn 2004, as the lawsuits against Jeffs and the FLDS were mounting, Mohave County Attorney Matt Smith decided to formally hire Gary Engels. Funds for the job were limited and the veteran cop would be working on probation. If he could get something done in the first six months, the county might decide to pay him more and keep him on longer. If not, it would be just another law enforcement experiment on the border that had failed. As Engels waited for the bureaucratic wheels to grind, he read about the funda-mentalist Mormons and some of the violent episodes in their past, absorbing the concept of blood atonement. What kind of trouble was he walking into in the twin communities?

Since the early 1970s, Engels had been preparing himself for this kind of mission, and it would take all his inner resources to see it through. He was still capable of physical action if that was what the situation demanded, but he wasn't traveling north to dominate the citizens. He'd carry a gun in Col-orado City and had long ago proven that he had a deadly aim, but his firearm skills probably wouldn't be much good in these circumstances. Starting that November, Engels would be the lone frontline soldier in a new kind of battle against religious terrorism. The federal government had lately sent hundreds of thousands of military personnel overseas to combat Islamic extremism in Afghanistan and Iraq. By mid-decade the death toll for Americans abroad would be more than three thousand, with estimates of foreign fatalities climbing over half a million. The strategy on the border would be just the opposite.

Engels would attempt to confront and disarm the FLDS without force or hostility. Mohave County wasn't employing him to conduct a war on polygamy or Mormon fundamentalism. It wasn't going after the church as a cult. Engels had a single goal: to investigate, uncover, and help prosecute specific criminal behavior, much as the police had once successfully done against the Mafia. He would approach religious terrorism like any other crime, using the rule of law instead of muscle.

Both Arizona and Utah were trying hard to learn from past mistakes—and to avoid bloodshed. It would be a fight like no other.

IV

IN THE SHADOWS
OF ZION

23

As the crow flies, it's only about 150 miles from Bullhead City, Arizona, to Hildale, Utah, but by car it's more than twice as far across Nevada's vast stretch of high lonesome desert. It was a drive that Gary Engels would become familiar with over the next several years. He was used to investigating a single suspect or maybe a handful, but not ten or twenty or thirty thousand people, all of them convinced that their actions had been sanctioned by God.

"You can't reason religion into people," he liked to say, "and you can't reason it out of them."

Engels had an edgy personality, and as he drove north out of Las Vegas on Interstate 15 to start his new job, he was already filled with concerns. Some might have seemed minor. Gas was expensive and he had to pay for this long commute. He didn't know anyone on the border and was certain that nobody wanted to know him. If he got lonely, he couldn't bring his wife, Sheila, to town with him because she liked to speak her mind about women's issues; that was a problem in Colorado City. He hoped to lay low, at least at the start, and doubted he could accomplish much in six months.

He wasn't sure where he'd be living. He wouldn't be comfortable at Hildale's Mark Twain Inn after church members figured out who he was and what he was trying to accomplish. He might have to take a room over in Hurricane (pronounced "Hurricun"), about halfway between St. George and Colorado City. Hurricane wasn't much more than a main strip with gas stations, cheap motels, a historical museum, fast-food joints, and knickknack stores, but that was better than spending the night on the border. When darkness fell, the place had few streetlights and took on a bizarrely eerie and unwelcome quality for outsiders. One thing was for sure: Engels was the ultimate outsider.

Packing his bags and saying goodbye to his wife, he headed toward Utah without high expectations. He couldn't really know what he was walking into the first day he went to work in the triple-wide trailer on the edge of Colorado City, but it was better to attempt something difficult and fall short than do nothing, especially when families were being ripped apart and a scourge was on the loose. Despite his best efforts to go quietly about his work in the twin communities, he quickly stomped on some local toes.

Frank and Mary Anne Jessop were devoted followers of the Prophet—at least two of their daughters had already been married off to Warren, in fact. A third one, seventeen-year-old Janetta, had gone missing fifteen months earlier, and nobody seemed to know where she was. In November 2004, just as Engels was starting his new job, another Jessop daughter living in the area, Suzanne Jessop Johnson, received a frantic call from Janetta, begging to be rescued. She wouldn't say where she was and or what she needed to be rescued from, and she didn't want her parents to know that she'd contacted Suzanne. Before hanging up, she promised to give her older sister instructions for coming and getting her, but she never phoned back.

The call was deeply disturbing to Suzanne, and when she heard about the new Mohave County investigator working out of the big silver trailer by the city limits, she contacted Engels and told him about Janetta. He was reluctant to jump into this conflict, but didn't want to ignore Suzanne. This was as good a place as any to start his investigation, yet the complexities facing him were beyond anything he'd confronted in the past.

Before coming north, he and Matt Smith had decided that Engels should have no interaction with the hometown cops because they were loyal to Warren Jeffs. Information shared with them could result in a family getting evicted or someone being tossed out of the community. If Engels hoped to develop reliable local sources, he'd have to find people who didn't trust the police; if they saw him working with the Colorado City marshals, they wouldn't feel comfortable telling him their secrets. Fortunately, he had a few other allies and had assembled a small team for this mission.

Along with Suzanne, Cedar City private investigator Sam Brower, a caseworker from Arizona Child Protective Services, and a Mohave County sheriff's deputy, Engels began the search for Janetta by driving over to the Jessop home. At the house, Suzanne saw a white van approaching with her mother, Mary Anne, behind the wheel and Janetta in the passenger seat. When Mary Anne spotted the sheriff deputy's car parked at her residence, she swerved away and hit the accelerator, speeding across town. The deputy leaped into his vehicle and chased after her with the others close behind, a string of cars blowing through the quiet streets of Colorado City, tires grinding on gravel roads and red dust swirling everywhere. When the officer caught up with Mary Anne, he pulled her over and asked Janetta to identify herself. As the others poured out of their cars and surrounded the mother and daughter, Janetta gave her name, was separated from Mary Anne, and transported to the Children's Justice Center in St. George.

Engels and the caseworker tried to interview the young woman, but she wouldn't talk. Mary Anne wouldn't, either. Engels wasn't long on patience, but was trying to be careful and restrained in order to make a good first impression on the locals. The only thing Janetta told them was that she'd called Suzanne for help and had apparently returned to her parents' residence in the past several days. The authorities couldn't determine if she was married to Jeffs or where she'd been staying for the past fifteen months. She was defiantly, maddeningly quiet and nobody could persuade her to answer questions.

As Engels attempted to pry information out of her, the story of the sheriff's deputy running down Mary Anne in his car and taking away her daughter quickly spread through Colorado City and made an immediate stir. Somebody alerted the regional media, who shot over to the border towns to cover the story, creating even more action on the normally quiet streets.

Engels had never cared much for journalists and had spent most of his career avoiding them.

"Every time I talk to a reporter," he once explained, "something bad happens."

Part of his new job involved adjusting this attitude and being friendly to the press. The more media exposure of the problems in Colorado City, his superiors down in Kingman believed, the better for law enforcement. With all that in mind, Engels spoke about Janetta Jessop to Nancy Perkins of the *Deseret Morning News*, who then wrote an article indicating that the young woman *had* addressed questions about being married to Warren Jeffs. The Associated

Press picked up the story and put it on its wire service. This was now national and international news.

When Engels learned about what he saw as misreporting of the facts of the case, he was furious at Perkins, worried that she'd put his investigation in jeopardy before he could even get started. Janetta was under extreme pressure not to say anything about Jeffs to the authorities—or anything about her marital status. If she revealed something she shouldn't and it became public, her family could be punished by the Prophet, the police, or both. Her parents could be excommunicated or even jailed; they could lose their home and children. Everything in these circumstances had needed to be handled with great delicacy, but it was too late for that. A possible witness against Jeffs and his church would never feel comfortable divulging more information now, and Engels's efforts to do the right thing and cooperate with the press had only made the situation worse.

So much for good first impressions.

This was his first taste of dealing with FLDS victims and their relatives, and he'd never encountered such a strong code of silence or so many dead ends. He couldn't follow all the routes a criminal investigator regularly takes—couldn't interview Janetta's mother, father, siblings, friends, or neighbors, because they wouldn't speak to him. He didn't have access to her health records because the local medical clinic wouldn't share information with outsiders. The local cops were beyond worthless, downright hostile to his efforts, and when he saw them in town every day, he had to pretend they didn't exist, which only made them angrier.

After Engels's attempts to speak to Janetta, she was taken to the St. George Children's Justice Center in Washington County, but they couldn't hold her indefinitely. Law enforcement had no choice but to return her to her parents' home, and Engels could do nothing more than occasionally drop by the Jessop household to see if she was all right. She seemed to be fine and he was relieved—a small victory for the investigator—but the Colorado City cops didn't see things that way. Hoping to squelch Engels before he tried anything else, they began communicating with his superiors in Kingman, saying that he'd overstepped his boundaries by interfering in church, family, and police business, and he needed to be reprimanded or worse.

The first showdown had come, and the investigator wondered how Matt Smith, along with the Washington County authorities and the Arizona

Attorney General's office, would respond. He was completely alone in Colorado City, trying to do a very difficult job. Did anyone out there have his back?

Engels was enormously grateful when his boss and the other authorities refused to criticize him for his role in the Janetta Jessop episode, and offered him their support. He had help, even if it was hundreds of miles away.

The ice had been shattered on the border and everyone now understood that a new legal weapon was in town, camped out in that ugly trailer on the outskirts of Colorado City and carrying an edge of toughness and swagger the town hadn't seen in decades. He was only one man, but his aura and attitude were powerful enough to conjure up tremors and distant fears of the raid of 1953. Until the Janetta Jessop incident, he'd only been disliked by a handful of people, but that was about to change. Locals would soon detest the sight of him driving around town in his Jeep, walking into their stores to buy a few supplies or pulling up in front of their homes. If they spotted him coming, they grabbed their kids, ran inside, locked the doors, and lowered the shades. When he rang the bell, nobody answered.

That was bad enough, but he had more pressing problems.

24

IT WAS NOW CLEARLY UNSAFE FOR ENGELS to spend the night in the border towns. Anyone could break into his room at the Mark Twain Inn or trash his Jeep in the parking lot. His only choice was to drive the twenty-two dark, crowded miles—with speeding trucks and cars bearing down on him—back to Hurricane. He tried one motel there for a while, then another, and then another. Money was an issue, because he was paying for his food and lodging, but he was also dealing with more intangible problems. Motel rooms were unfamiliar and lonely, no matter how long he stayed in them: just a bed, a couple of tacky paintings on the walls, and a free bar of soap. Working all day in an outwardly hostile environment and then coming back to a small empty room, in a town where he didn't know anybody, was nothing to look forward to, but what else could he do? Engels had signed on for six months, and isolation was something he'd just have to get used to.

At least the surroundings were magnificent. On chilly winter mornings, he'd rise early and ride back to Colorado City through the mist hanging so low on the southern end of Zion National Park that it nearly touched the road and created the impression of driving through veils of smoke. Snow sat on the red rocks of the desert, and swatches of black and blue clouds were stacked above the giant sandstone formations of Zion, a word meaning "heaven on earth." Fingers of sunlight poked through the cloud cover and illuminated the surrounding mesas, glowing in the distance like pale fires. In good weather or bad, the ever-shifting beauty of the sky and the landscape produced a feeling of humility and awe, so that even a nonbeliever had a difficult time dismissing the majesty of southern Utah.

It was a steady climb from the floor of Hurricane Valley to the mile-high elevation of Hildale, and the ascent carried with it the feeling of moving into another reality. Engels never knew what he'd find when he pulled up in front of the trailer, whose exterior sign read: "MOHAVE COUNTY, STATE OF ARIZONA, MULTI-USE FACILITY, STATE ATTORNEY GENERAL, CHILD PROTECTION SERVICES, COUNTY SHERIFF, COUNTY ATTORNEY VICTIM WITNESS PROGRAM." In a community that many saw as unruly, the trailer represented law and order for the county, state, attorney general, and Sheriff's Department, making it a natural target for vandalism. Parking on the orangish dirt by the trailer's entrance, Engels always wondered if his tiny office had been burglarized during the night or if someone had sneaked in and planted bugs in the walls.

If anybody had broken in, there wasn't much to steal. At the beginning, he didn't have a phone, desk, or chairs; the only decoration was a map of the border towns tacked to a wall. He'd relocated himself several hundred miles from home to do something daunting—"to make legal history with these people," he once said—but how was he supposed to do that without the required tools? He pinched a couple of chairs from the conference room down the hall and went to work. It wasn't long before he sensed the presence of strangers.

Two months after Engels took the job, Kim Nuttall moved into another small space inside the trailer. A native of Moccasin, Arizona, about twenty miles from Colorado City, she'd grown up a nonfundamentalist Mormon and earned a bachelor's degree in criminal justice before earning another degree in psychology. In early 2005, she was hired as a victim advocate for the Mohave County victim/witness program, specifically designed to serve the local FLDS community. Part of her duties was to clean up the recent image problems of her office: the woman holding the position before her had lasted only twenty-eight days. She didn't fit in well in an environment where skin was supposed to be covered from head to foot whenever a female left the house.

"This lady believed that your body should be shown off at all times," says Nuttall. "She came to work in miniskirts and tank tops. She'd had breast augmentation and was proud of it and wanted everyone to know that. This didn't go over really well in this town.

"When I started working here, I came into my office three or four times in the morning and found the door open. I thought the cleaning lady had done this, but she never left it unlocked. We didn't have a security system back then and somebody had broken in and left muddy footprints all over the floor. We did a bug sweep but didn't find any bugs. I felt the locals were listening to my phone calls because I'd hear a click on the line, but that eventually stopped. After we put in the security system, my door was no longer left ajar in the morning."

Because Nuttall had been raised near Colorado City, she was familiar with many of its tales, legends, and hidden tragedies.

"I grew up listening to all these horror stories about the FLDS," she says, "and how they used to kill their babies if they were deformed or had Down's Syndrome. Then I came here and talked to people and found out this had really happened. The baby graveyard in the middle of town is far too big to just have the normal numbers of infants buried there. One lady I know married her first cousin, after he raped her, and she got two severely retarded children and one had head trauma. Her husband beat the child when it was an infant and it died mysteriously. She has three other boys who are normal with the same man, so it doesn't always turn out bad."

The first time a local called Nuttall an "apostate or" a "gentile" it shocked her; she'd grown up Mormon and considered herself inside their circle of faith.

"There are people in Colorado City," she says, "who don't pray to the Heavenly Father or to Jesus Christ, but to Warren Jeffs. They think he's the greatest person in human history—even greater than Joseph Smith. Now that's pretty freaky."

As a student of both criminal behavior and human psychology, Nuttall speculated on the influences of the closed FLDS community that had turned Jeffs into the adult he became.

"Who molested *him*?" she says. "That's what I want to know. Was it his dad? Or it could have been an uncle or other relative. It stands to reason that he was also a victim of this kind of abuse, because these things are cyclical and in this culture they tell boys that doing this stuff, or having it done to them, is what prepares them for the priesthood."

Nuttall's professional training involved working with crime victims, with witnesses subpoenaed to appear in court, and with victim compensation. When she took the new job, her hope was that if local women suffering from spousal abuse or women who were aware that their sons or daughters were being mistreated came in to see her, they'd drop by Engels's cubicle and also share information with him. That never happened. Very few people would talk to Nuttall about their problems, and nobody wanted to speak to the investigator. He was shunned everywhere.

"Gary is so paranoid, " Kim once said about her colleague up the hall, "but it's justified. These people just don't like him."

If he didn't have any friends in town, at least Engels had a plan.

25

B Y LATE 2004, NEARLY A YEAR HAD PASSED since Richard Holm had been excommunicated by the FLDS, Isaac Wyler had been kicked out of the church, and Ross Chatwin had stood on his lawn on a winter morning and defied the Prophet by refusing to give up his wife. More than twenty other local men were in similar positions to Holm or Wyler, and they'd had plenty of time to realize they were never going to reclaim what had once been theirs—not without a legal fight. They were bitterly hurt and angry over how Jeffs had not only driven them away, but fooled them into thinking they could confess theirs sins to him, repent, be forgiven, and come back home. They were quietly seething, but no one except their most intimate friends had ever taken the time to listen to their stories or try to understand what they'd been through. No one had tapped into the rawness of their emotions or asked them to express their rage.

These were, after all, rural men, many of whom were middle-aged. They weren't supposed to be depressed or heartbroken, let alone vent their feelings in front of others, especially others outside their own faith and hometown. Engels put together a list of the excommunicated and wondered if a few might be ready to open up. When he first approached them, they resisted, mistrusting his motives, but he was persistent and persuasive. And he had an extra motivation for asking them to talk to him about Jeffs and the secrets of the FLDS: he was looking for companionship to alleviate his own loneliness.

That winter he decided to move out of the Hurricane motel rooms where he'd been staying and live in the trailer (or "fifth wheel") he often pulled behind his Jeep on long road trips. Hurricane had a sizable RV parking lot, just off the main drag, where he rented trailer space, and each night after work he drove there for a quiet evening. It was smaller than a motel room but more familiar and comfortable, almost like having a piece of Bullhead City to come home to.

Both Engels and Jeffs were now living out of vehicles. The Prophet was using his to traverse the western half of the United States, up to South Dakota to check out the property near Pringle; down to Texas to stay in the new limestone temple and perform ceremonies; through eastern Utah and over to Mancos in western Colorado, where loyal followers were ready to give him food and shelter for a few days before he took off again; and all the way to Florida, where he visited Disney World and bought some contact lenses. At each stop, his flock lavished him with money and adoration, with cell phones, prepaid credit cards, police scanners, and other pieces of technology to assist him in eluding the law. Jeffs was spiritual royalty, and they trusted him with the simple conviction that because he was their Prophet, he would not lead them into disaster. He'd become an underground hero—an old-fashioned Western outlaw too clever to be caught. Or perhaps he'd turn into another Mormon martyr, like Joseph Smith, who'd gone down resisting the gentiles.

Engels, by contrast, was sleeping alone in the back of a small trailer, making a modest salary and missing his wife, struggling with doubts over his mission and scorned by the population he was trying to help. As his first months on the job passed, he wondered if he was accomplishing anything except making more and more enemies. For a while, he'd felt comfortable enough to eat lunch in the border towns, but it had become too dangerous for that, so he bypassed the noonday meal. He ate breakfast and dinner in Hurricane.

Engels knew there was investigative gold inside the minds and hearts of the men who'd been tossed out of the church—if he could just get to it. Richard Holm had lived in Colorado City since 1952 and knew everyone, not to mention where the skeletons were lurking. He'd done business with FLDS members and was aware of who'd married whom and what age the partners had been at the time of the wedding. Engels started inviting Holm to dinner so they could sit down and relax together, away from Gary's minuscule office. By now Engels knew that many Fundamentalist Mormons, despite their strict adherence to the original principles of Joseph Smith, were fond of alcohol (by far the biggest problem for teens in the border towns, according to victim advocate Kim Nuttall, was alcohol abuse, as young people finagled adults into buying them booze at a roadside liquor store and then got drunk in the desert).

Engels hoped to have a couple of glasses of wine with Holm, and gradually loosen up the conversation. At first, Richard was reluctant even to meet with the investigator, but Gary kept working him until he finally said yes. Richard was lonely, too. Once he began to trust Engels, he was as willing to spill his secrets as the other man was to listen.

In early 2005, Holm began laying out for Engels the inner workings of the church, the power players, the highly complicated local family trees, the marriage rituals, the politics, and the money of Colorado City. He wasn't just an encyclopedia of factual history; he was hungry for revenge. As he talked, Engels sketched out a mental road map of the FLDS and the community. Deep into the night they bantered, joking about the Prophet, bonding and piecing together information about underage spiritual marriages (which left no paper trail or other documentation), sexual abuse, and other potential crimes. As Richard felt more at ease sharing with Engels, he encouraged other banished husbands and fathers to share as well. Maybe Gary could help them get their families and homes back—and put some of these criminals in jail. One man came forward, then another, pouring out more anger and more stories, as Engels's map of the situation continued to expand. He didn't believe everything he heard, convinced that each individual he spoke to had an agenda, so he constantly needed to sift fact from the fiction. But he'd found the leak in this closed society and intended to drain it.

Every two or three weeks he'd start to feel so cut off from his previous life that he'd climb into his Jeep and head back to Bullhead City to see his wife and decompress. After decades of marriage, Sheila understood her husband better than anyone and offered him a lot of support for the assignment he'd taken on. If she knew how isolated and difficult his job was, she also knew that he was much happier when he was working. He was getting the chance to employ his tenacity, intelligence, and moral indignation to bore through the walls of silence that for generations had sealed off the border towns from the laws of Arizona, Utah, and the United States of America. It was too early to say if he was making progress, but he didn't regret volunteering for this tough mission—which would only get tougher.

FLDS members didn't hate him right away because they didn't really know what he was up to. Even if they had known, they'd have assumed he was like all the rest who'd come to town before him. Since the 1920s, Arizona and Utah authorities had been sending PIs, outside police forces, and other intruders into the community to clean things up and stop polygamy, but none had lasted. The locals, like many engaged in long-term religious conflict around the world, counted on being able to grind the foreigners down, and it had always worked in the past. Why bother trying to change a mind-set so self-righteous and deeply entrenched? Why waste the time and resources? Unlike Engels, the earlier lawmen had lacked the hide of a mule. He was singlehandedly trying to infiltrate and perhaps break apart a fundamentalist religion. No wonder he got lonely.

26

ON APRIL 1, 2004, nineteen-year-old Wendell Musser had received an unexpected call from the Prophet, who said that he'd be married within the next few hours. A Short Creek native, Musser was the great-grandson of Joseph W. Musser, an early community leader, and the grandson of Rulon Jeffs. Musser was in favor with the church power structure and felt blessed to be receiving a wife, although he didn't know who Jeffs had picked for him. Wendell learned her identity after a driver picked him up from home that evening and stopped by the house of seventeen-year-old Vivian Barlow, who got in the car with them. Wendell recognized her face but barely knew her name. The couple was transported to a Holiday Inn Express in Kanab, Utah, where they were hustled through a back door and escorted to a lower-level room. The Prophet, his brother Lyle Jeffs, Bishop William Timpson Jeffs, and a bishop's counselor, Nathan Jessop, greeted them, and Warren asked the teenagers if they felt all right about marrying each other. They answered yes and were joined in matrimony. Following the ceremony, the Prophet told them not to talk about these events because law enforcement was after him for performing secret marriages. The next day, Wendell and Vivian were assigned a home in Hildale and she was soon pregnant. Their son, Levi, was born on July 30, 2005.

Their lives were routine until that November, when Musser got another call from the Prophet, who informed Wendell that he was about to be given a special mission as a "caretaker." Jeffs told the young man to prepare to leave his job as an installer for Redstone Surfaces and be ready for his family to go underground. Wendell wasn't supposed to let his wife know any of this. He

IN THE SHADOWS OF ZION

had enough faith in the FLDS leader that he didn't question his mission, but he did tell Vivian about the call. Like her husband, she was eager to obey the Prophet, but worried about raising their child on the run.

A month later, Jeffs phoned again and said that Wendell had been chosen to look after the Prophet's family. He, Vivian, and Levi would depart the border towns immediately, but Warren didn't say where they were headed. At 2:00 A.M., a pair of FLDS "high priests," Nephi Allred and Tom Cox, loaded the family into a car and drove them nineteen hours to Williamsburg, Colorado, population 753, about thirty miles west of Pueblo. The Mussers' new home was isolated and unfurnished, with only a couple of beds. As soon as the three men had dropped off Vivian and Levi at this "safe house," they went shopping at a Wal-Mart in nearby Cañon City, buying a handful of prepaid cell phones and passing the numbers along to the Prophet. The next day Jeffs called Musser and said that a group of his wives would be arriving soon. Wendell and Vivian were to prepare this home for them, along with two others, purchase groceries, and tend to the women's needs, and Musser was to act like a father to his wives while Jeffs was gone. Musser felt overwhelmed by his duties but was committed to serving the Prophet. Everything would be paid for by church money. Wendell learned that he was only one of the men assigned to this kind of mission. The Prophet had similar safe houses tucked around the western United States, with wives installed in each one. Jeffs was now "spiritually married" to as many as 180 women, many of whom had once been "sealed" to his father.

The morning after Jeffs's last call, nine of his wives arrived in Williamsburg, all in their late twenties and traveling without their children. During the next few months, more wives and several of Jeffs's daughters stayed at the three houses Musser was in charge of. All the females traveled very light, as if they were used to being quickly moved from one location to the next. Their lives on the road were highly repetitive and quiet—some would say dull. In Williamsburg, everyone awoke at 6:00 A.M. and studied the sermons of Leroy Johnson. Jeffs had instructed Musser to have the women go into their rooms every hour and pray for God to protect Jeffs from harm. They spent the remainder of the day reading the Bible or hand-sewing the ankle-to-wrist undergarments worn by the FLDS faithful. There was no television or other entertainment, no contact with the outside world. Musser tried to come up with household chores to keep the women busy, letting them exercise in the yard, but keeping them concealed behind a fence. Only he was allowed to leave the property, and then just briefly. Keeping the women physically active was easy compared to keeping them peaceful and calm. The stress of their lifestyle showed on many of the wives, who were struggling with depression. Small eruptions between the women were common, and it was all Wendell and Vivian could do to hold the group together without the conflicts escalating.

A couple of weeks after the Mussers settled into Williamsburg, Jeffs and his brother Issac came by unannounced. Wendell was taken aback by the Prophet's new look and his behavior. Warren wasn't wearing the dark suits he'd favored in Colorado City but the street clothes popular outside the FLDS. He resembled the outsiders he constantly railed against. Whiskers covered his cheeks, and before going into town, he donned a wig and sunglasses or crammed a ball cap over his forehead. Wendell was dedicated to following all of Jeffs's orders, but balked when the Prophet told him that Vivian had to wear the pastel pioneer look common to Colorado City—exactly as his own wives did. Vivian already felt disrespected by some of the wives, who believed they were more spiritually elevated than her because of their connection to Jeffs. The clothing demand didn't sit well with the Mussers, but after a minor protest they gave in.

During his visits, Jeffs liked to have intimate private time with one or another of his wives. Then he'd bring them all together, along with Wendell and Vivian, and unleash sermons of such fierceness that they frightened the Mussers. The Prophet said that the devil was raging all around them now—in the form of those trying to bring him down—and that Christ's return was imminent. All of his wives should repent while they still could and be ready to join Rulon Jeffs in a "sacred place." Wendell observed that Warren's behavior had grown much more alarming since he'd gone on the run, but Musser didn't want to confront the question lurking in the back of his mind: was it possible that their church leader was not merely unstable or deluded, but mentally ill? Like so many before him, Wendell felt that something was deeply wrong with the situation but didn't question or resist. Warren might ravage the lives of others, but not those of his closest allies.

After staying with his wives for just a few hours and getting a fresh supply of money or food for the road, Jeffs and his brother vanished without a hint of where they were going or when they'd return. The longer the men remained on the run, the more their attitude shifted from confidence to arrogance. The Prophet liked to tell Wendell and his wives that "the Lord would sweep the wicked off the Earth before he was caught."

27

WHILE GARY ENGELS WAS MAKING MORE ENEMIES in the border towns, he was also finding allies. As loathed outsiders in Colorado City, he and Sam Brower naturally gravitated toward each other, sharing information and investigative strategies about Jeffs and the FLDS. They were roughly the same age and had a passion for their work that went beyond money, and a sense of adventure, as if they'd been seeking this kind of quest without quite knowing it. When either man began feeling overwhelmed or discouraged, the other provided a sounding board and built him back up. They had strikingly different personalities, different strengths and weaknesses. Engels was perfect at acting like the bad cop, but Brower had a softer presence and a more empathetic feeling for the local church members, probably because his own great-grandfather had gone to prison twice for polygamy.

"Gary gets a little cynical sometimes," Sam has said. "He's more of the bold police type and when he gets mad, he's really scary. I believe more in gentle persuasion. I like to work with *everybody* and bring different groups together. Gary's much more high-strung than I am and has a tendency to turn his work into his life. At times, I have to tone him down."

"Sam," Engels says, "is one of the very few people I could ever count on for anything in this job—usually the only one. I could always call him and this at least gave me somebody to talk to. Most of the time, the only people who were really out there looking for Warren Jeffs were Sam and myself. We've been through some stuff together."

Both men packed guns and looked like retired linebackers. They had an air of commitment and seriousness that nobody could ignore, and it wasn't long before folks in Colorado City noticed them riding together, searching for new leads and representing a kind of united force the church had never seen before. Instead of just a lone troublemaker in town, now two of them needed to be taught a lesson.

One day Brower was driving around the community with a video camera and taking footage of FLDS-run businesses. He'd parked his truck alongside the road and cars kept blowing past him, speeding up and slowing down, getting closer with each pass and throwing dust and dirt in his face. He yelled at them to stop, but they just kept coming and shouting back at him, closer now, buzzing him and hurling insults. He drove to another location on the outskirts of town, stepped out, and began snapping more photos. They'd followed him and shot by his truck again—one man mooning Brower from an open window. Sam grabbed his camera to get visual evidence of this, but it was too late, and the vehicle sped off down the road. Jumping into his truck, Brower gunned the accelerator and gave chase, tailing them all the way out to Apple Valley on Highway 59, nearly halfway to Hurricane, but couldn't get a better look at the culprits. He reported the incident to local police and was surprised when they identified the offenders and gave Sam their names. The mooning stopped.

Brower continued his surveillance and in April 2005, he went down to Texas to check out the new YFZ Ranch. The FLDS celebrated April 6 as Jesus' birthday, so Brower expected increased activity at the new compound. For months he'd been attempting to track Jeffs across the western United States and was convinced the Prophet was now holed up in Eldorado. On the evening of April 5, Brower drove out to the ranch's fenced-in perimeter, getting as close as he could to the compound and its huge white limestone temple. Hiding alongside the road in some bushes and using night-vision binoculars, he could see inside the house of worship, where lights burned everywhere and people were feverishly working. Sam couldn't be sure, but one of those busy figures walking around in the temple might have been the tall, spindly Prophet.

At midnight, everything in the temple suddenly shut down. Brower saw no movement and then the lights went dark. He waited a while to see if anyone left the ranch or switched the lights back on, but when nothing changed he drove away. The next night he was back in the bushes in his truck at 10:00 P.M. and he had Engels on the phone. The temple lights were on and there was a lot of action inside. He trained his binoculars to see if he could spot Jeffs. As he was trying to get a better look, a couple of trucks came roaring out of the compound, turning onto the road he was parked on and heading straight toward him. The closer they got, the farther down he slid in the driver's seat, until his head was almost even with the wheel. Warren must have been preparing to depart the ranch and the trucks were out looking for intruders, clearing the way for his exit.

Sam still had Gary on the line, in case things turned bad.

"The trucks hauled ass right by me," Brower says, "but then one slammed on its brakes, backing up slowly and looking in the bushes. They spotted my truck and were coming nearer, twenty yards away, ten. I'd been talking to Gary, but I had to whisper now. The truck stopped right in front of me and I leaned as far down in the seat as I could so they couldn't see my face. They shined a bright light on my vehicle and I lowered my hand to my pistol, a .45 Colt Defender, ready for anything. I ducked down some more but they must have seen me because one guy leaned out of the truck window and screamed, 'What are you doing?' I didn't make a sound."

The men took off in their four-wheel pickup and scattered gravel all over the road. Sam didn't move and held his silence, but his cell phone was still connected to Engels.

"Gary started talking again," he says, "telling me to stay down and be careful. I sat there a while longer, till after midnight, because I kept thinking Warren might come out in another car, but I never saw anyone else leave the compound."

Brower's investigation took him far beyond Arizona, Utah, and Texas, but this was probably as close to the Prophet as he ever got.

One day he received a call from a reporter friend at a paper in the Lone Star State about some construction up near Pringle, in the Black Hills of South Dakota. Sam quickly learned that FLDS member David Allred had bought 100 acres near Pringle and another 120 by Mancos, in far western Colorado. Sam was in communication with Flora Jessop nearly every day about these developments, while trying to keep them away from the rest of the world. The PI hoped to uncover more about these new FLDS outposts or to find Jeffs hiding out in one of them before the media or anyone else got wind of this, but the press was now snooping around everywhere, trying to pick up the Prophet's trail.

"Mike Watkiss [a TV reporter in Arizona and one of the leading investigative journalists on the case] blew it for me," Brower says. "I'd asked him not to broadcast this information about Pringle until I'd had a chance to go there and scope it out and see if Warren was up there. I thought maybe I was closing in on him. Mike agreed to this plan but then went ahead and put it on the air."

After pausing for emphasis, Sam adds, "Sonofabitch."

28

NOW THAT HE WAS OPENLY ASSOCIATING with apostates and excommunicated church members like Richard Holm, Gary Engels had also begun attracting more heat. He was followed and harassed nearly every time he left his office, stuck out in that cramped, dull-looking, triple-wide trailer on a flat stretch of rust-colored dirt at the edge of town, with only jackrabbits, coyotes, and lizards for company. When the desert wind gathered speed and swept across the Arizona Strip, orange dust devils rose up and swirled beside the trailer, dancing on their tails and evaporating in the scorching sunlight. From Engels's perspective, they weren't the only devils lurking near the trailer. A whole caravan of local men was devoted to making him miserable whenever he went for a ride. One hostile vehicle stayed on his rear bumper before handing him off to another and then another, in an effort to intimidate or frighten him. When that didn't work, they tried to run him off the road. When that failed, they flipped him the finger, threw rocks at his Jeep, yelled slurs, tapped his phone, stole his belongings, and said things that he didn't believe the Chosen People of God were supposed to say to anyone.

Engels heard that members of the congregation were getting together and praying for his destruction, either through illness or accident or some other nasty twist of fate. Because of this, he was determined to appear strong and healthy around them, even when he didn't feel well. He was trying hard to stay calm, although it was his nature to let out whatever he was feeling. If he blew up, or if he stopped his Jeep and got out and confronted the men who were hounding him just once, it could ruin everything he hoped to accomplish on the border. He'd never been tested like this before.

Engels used to exercise regularly in Bullhead City, but those days were gone. He gained five pounds and then five more. He had no place to work out now and he couldn't even take a walk around town—walking didn't feel safe. He was driving far too much, twice a day between Colorado City and Hurricane, and sitting for too long in his office. He'd gain fifteen to twenty pounds during the coming year, but that was easier to handle than the other challenges.

"In this place," he once said, "I've got to deal with everybody else's stuff, plus my own."

He was too proud and too private a man to reveal what his own "stuff" was, but spending this much time alone—away from Sheila, under constant pressure, and with money issues chewing away at him—was bound to catch up with him. The deeper he moved into the job, the more edgy and irritable he looked, his face redder than usual, his sentences short and choppy. Tension had settled into his jaw and defensiveness had taken root in his eyes, as if he expected everyone he met to say or do something against him. It was an obvious effort for Engels to try to be polite. Over the years, the investigator and his wife had developed a fondness for wine, planning their vacations around exploring this passion in California vineyards. While collecting stories from ex-FLDS members, Engels was encouraged to discover that several of his new acquaintances had this same taste for excellent grapes and weren't shy about pursuing it. Drinking had opened doors with Richard Holm, and it was about to open some more. Engel had finally found common ground with the locals and began visiting their homes and sharing bottles of wine. It was not only a good release from all the stress, but helped free up tongues. There were all kinds of ways to investigate criminal behavior, besides paying snitches or strong-arming people or doing undercover surveillance. With each empty glass, Engels was picking up more information from those who now feared or hated Warren Jeffs.

After returning to Hurricane at night, Gary tried watching TV but was quickly bored. With his eyes closed to help him concentrate more fully, he lay in bed and listened to tapes of Jeffs's sermons or absorbed music the Prophet had written and recorded, looking for clues to the man's personality and leadership style. The preaching and singing were delivered in Jeffs's trademark hypnotic tone, designed to lull people into submission. Engels was worried that the sounds would cause him to drift off to sleep, and the Prophet's message would sink into his subconscious.

"I didn't want that crap in my brain," he joked.

Laboring sixteen-hour days and well into the night, he was slowly making headway, but he needed something more.

At Richard Holm's residence he met a young woman named Tammy Shapley who blurted out that her sister, Candi, was in an underage marriage to Randy Barlow. Stifling his excitement, Engels gently prodded Tammy to reveal more. It was the first time somebody in Colorado City with direct knowledge of a young local girl marrying an older man had confirmed such an arrangement for the investigator.

Would Tammy, Engels wondered aloud, mind asking her sister if she'd speak with him?

Not at all, she said.

Tammy introduced the two of them, and Candi didn't hold back. She'd recently been kicked out of the FLDS for disobedience, was no longer married to Barlow, and was more than ready to talk. After months of legwork, Engels was closing in on what he'd been looking for—a live female witness eager to go into court and testify about her ex and FLDS marital practices. He also had something else: information from Candi that he could verify through the birth certificates of the young woman and her former husband, establishing that she had in fact been married to Barlow as an underage teenager. The only problem was that those certificates were stored in the birthing clinic in Hildale and the investigator wasn't allowed on the premises. And there was one further complication: Hildale was in Utah and Engels was employed by prosecutor Matt Smith of Mohave County, Arizona.

Engels had built up resentment against Utah, feeling that it was doing virtually nothing to assist him. After consulting with Smith, he approached Utah Attorney General Mark Shurtleff and asked for help in getting access to the documents in the birthing clinic. When Shurtleff came through, it was the break Engels needed.

He gathered more information from Candi about underage marriages besides her own, digging into other local records and birth certificates. If any of the girls he was investigating were under eighteen at the time of their weddings, their marriages were illegal. Through speaking with Candi and his own widening investigation, Engels was able to piece together seven such marriages. Then he uncovered an eighth in which the bride had been just fifteen. He was starting to make real headway—and to create more opposition.

Another former FLDS wife, Carolyn Jessop, had been married to a high-ranking church member, Merrill Jessop, but their union had ended in an ugly divorce. She'd taken the children and moved to Salt Lake City, while her husband had been picked by Jeffs to go down to Texas and run the YFZ Ranch. He and the Prophet were intimately linked. One of Merrill's daughters, Naomie Jeffs, was seventeen when she married Rulon Jeffs, then almost ninety. After his death, Naomie and her sister Paula became the first of Rulon's widows to marry Warren. He was currently married to as many as ten of Merrill's offspring.

Whenever Jessop wanted to see his and Carolyn's young daughters, he'd send one of his sons up to Salt Lake to get them, ignoring his and his ex-wife's custody arrangement. In the winter of 2005, the daughters were transported, against their mother's will, from her home to Merrill's residence in Colorado City. Carolyn called Engels about this and on a chilly night, he drove over to the Jessop household. When a pair of teenage girls matching the description of Carolyn's daughters answered the door, Engels introduced himself and asked to speak to an adult. They slammed the door and locked it.

He walked around the house, peeked through a side window, and saw the girls and several adults, but when they spotted him, they shut the drapes. He called the deputy police chief, an FLDS member in good standing named Jonathan Roundy, who called his father, Sam, the police chief and an important figure in the church and community. When Sam arrived at the Jessop address and knocked on the front door, nobody answered, which was good enough for the top law enforcement official in town. Since there was obviously nothing more Sam could do in this situation, he announced that the matter was resolved and he was going home.

Engels erupted, months of frustration with the local cops finally rushing to the surface.

"I'm gonna get a search warrant," he yelled at Roundy, "and I'm gonna get those girls out of there—now!"

The chief of police was unmoved.

As Engels started in again, one of Merrill Jessop's sons, who lived across the street, walked over to say that his father was on the phone and wanted to have a word with the investigator. Merrill was used to getting his way in Colorado City, especially when it came to dealing with the authorities, and a little conversation would clear all this up.

Engels grabbed the receiver and things got stormy fast, Jessop refusing to hand over his daughters and Engels threatening to go in and get them out.

"If you don't release them from the house," he snapped, "you can be charged with kidnapping."

Merrill hesitated; this wasn't what he'd expected. Something in the man's tone told him that the investigator wasn't backing down.

Jessop asked if the girls could spend the night in his home before being returned to their mother the next day.

Engels agreed to this plan and Merrill kept his word, his daughters safely making their way back to Salt Lake City.

The conflict had been peaceably resolved, but Sam and Jonathan Roundy felt that Engels had again overstepped his boundaries and needed to be reined in, reprimanded, or fired by his bosses in Kingman. Intervening in the Janetta Jessop episode had been his first offense against the local cops; this was his second. They wanted Mohave County to get rid of him now, before there was a third.

Again, Matt Smith and his colleagues in Kingman stood behind Engels's work. The investigator hadn't really intended to go inside Merrill's house in the middle of the night, alone, and search the darkened rooms for the girls. Nor was he able to charge Jessop with kidnapping, but his bluff had worked. He knew how to lean on people when necessary, but dealing with the population of Colorado City and Hildale was teaching the veteran cop to improvise.

29

O N THE RUN, the Prophet was also learning to improvise. He'd adjusted to controlling the FLDS from afar, but for the women he'd hidden throughout the countryside adapting was much more difficult. The longer his spiritual wives—who waited around in cabins for his occasional drive-by visits—were away from their homes, the more discouraged they became about their own futures and ever seeing their children again. Wendell Musser was in charge of some of them, in rural Colorado, and he was also having trouble coping. As they tried to fight off overcrowding, boredom, and bad moods, he could barely keep them placated. Wendell was the only male around for them to talk to and the demands on his time and emotions were draining, both to him and his marriage. If he tried to phone Jeffs about these problems, the Prophet ignored him or claimed that from the grave Rulon had spoken to him, revealing that Warren should not talk to the women until their attitudes had improved.

One day when Jeffs stopped by the home in Williamsburg without warning, he ordered Musser to move everyone into an eight-bedroom house in the town of Florence, Colorado, near the top-security federal prison known as Supermax. It housed some of the nation's most high-profile criminals. On several occasions, the Prophet told Wendell to meet him in the Wal-Mart parking lot in Colorado Springs, and each time they rendezvoused, Jeffs had a brand-new BMW, Chevy Suburban, or SUV. (Before the car he was riding in could be identified, he had an associate buy a new one.) In the Wal-Mart lot, Warren gave Musser another set of clandestine missions: transporting envelopes filled with cash and Jeffs's sermons over to Utah or up to Wyoming. Wendell carefully followed orders, and every trip was successful.

After only a month in Florence, the Prophet told Musser to move all the women once more, this time to Westcliffe, Colorado, at the edge of the Sangre de Cristo Mountains. They took up residence in a cramped unfinished cabin, and during the next three months Jeffs showed up three more times, his visits filled with more bedroom excursions with his wives and more hellfire sermons. Every time Wendell saw Jeffs, he became more alarmed at the man's behavior and apparent instability.

Month after month, Musser fulfilled the Prophet's demands without complaint and tried to handle the growing stress inside the cabin, but everything was getting harder. He looked forward to his time away from the women. Once, when he was driving back home after dropping off envelopes and sewing machines to other safe houses in Utah and Wyoming, he stopped in Colorado Springs to unwind in a bar. As Musser left the tavern, his driving was impaired enough for a policeman to pull him over. He was thrown in jail and booked, and his vehicle searched. Colorado authorities knew of the FBI's hunt for Jeffs and noticed Wendell's Hildale, Utah, home address and his GPS equipment. They grilled him about having connections to the Prophet, but he remained loyal to Jeffs and gave the police nothing. Two days later, he got out of jail and called "High Priest" Nephi Allred, who told him to ditch his phones and avoid Westcliffe until he felt it was safe to go back to the cabin.

When he returned there, everyone he'd brought to Westcliffe was gone, including his wife and son. The stranger now living in the cabin said they'd moved without leaving a forwarding address. It was a rainy day and Musser—who suddenly realized that Jeffs was punishing him in the deepest way possible for his drunk-driving charge—fell to his knees in the mud in pain, feeling both rage and dread. He knew what Jeffs was capable of. He began calling FLDS members, who told him to drive to Hildale, write up a list of all his sins, and give it to the Prophet. In one of these phone conversations, Warren's brother Lyle said to Wendell that Vivian and Levi now belonged to someone else. Musser felt bitterly betrayed and humiliated, yet still believed that his best hope for recovering his wife and son was to do what he'd been told, so he wrote up his transgressions and sent them to the Prophet. That accomplished nothing, so he set out in search of his family.

30

WHILE HUNTING FOR JEFFS, Sam Brower put an estimated hundred thousand miles on his vehicle and logged another 100,000 in the air, never making direct contact with the fugitive. During the tedious driving trips or sitting on a plane, Sam had plenty of time to think about the man he was chasing and to use his intelligence, educational background, spirituality, and bounty hunter/criminal justice instincts to try to understand the FLDS leader. On occasion, Brower felt he was getting hauntingly near to the Prophet, both physically and otherwise.

"A couple of times," he says, "I was just a heartbeat away from Warren or perhaps we were in the same place at the same time, but what could I do? I couldn't go kick in his door, couldn't arrest him. There were a lot of valid concerns that if someone found him and tried to bring him in, there could be violence. We didn't want to storm his Texas compound and have people drinking the Kool-Aid or re-creating what had happened at Waco, so it was very complex. I just kept traveling and looking, and traveling some more."

The longer Sam searched, the more he tried to penetrate Jeffs's mind.

"His psychology," the investigator says, "is that of a narcissistic sociopath. He can only get along in a closed society where he can control everything— kind of like how a sociopath operates inside of a prison. He never really worked in his life, never ventured out beyond his father's circle, never tested himself in the larger world, so his ideas about people and society are very limited. His experience is limited, too, but he understands certain things extremely well."

When he started as an instructor at Alta at age seventeen, Jeffs wanted to see how far he could go in punishing children, in turning family members against one another, and in using sex to dominate and terrify kids. He found that nobody really challenged him or his teaching methods. If he could do this to children, could he do the same thing to adults? Could he pick and choose who got married and had babies? If he tore grown men away from their families and assigned their wives and kids to other men, would they fall in line with his plans? Could he do this to his own brothers? Would these people repent and confess their sins to him, begging to be let back into the community and church? And if he carried out all these plans, would his followers keep worshipping him and giving him their money? Were they so willing to believe in his authority that he could basically do *anything?*

"He learned," Brower says, "that the answer to every question was yes."

The more Brower dogged Jeffs across the Southwest, the more the Prophet became aware of his pursuer and the more Sam himself became a target. One evening, he was driving through the streets of Colorado City with Gary Engels when they found themselves being tailed by several cars. Brower kept trying to ditch the vehicles, but he couldn't lose them. He was chased along Main Street and down the side roads, around dark corners and into back alleys, the intimidation growing more reckless with each block—tires screeching, brakes whining, and gravel flying into the air. Taunts, insults, and fists flew from the open windows, clouds of dust spun in their wake. Brower didn't want to be forced into leaving town, but he wasn't sure what to do. The harassment had never gone on this long or been this dangerous, and he was running out of options. He headed back to the trailer where Engels worked, in the hope that it would be safe there. As he pulled into the small parking lot and cut the engine, their tormentors roared in behind them, blocking the exit.

Sam and Gary were trapped.

For months they'd tried to avoid a violent confrontation with the local men, but that was no longer possible. They had to make a show of force tonight and take their chances. Glancing at one another, they reached down for their guns and flung open the doors.

"Dirty bastards!" Sam shouted as they charged at their antagonists, hands on hips and ready to draw.

When the men saw them coming with firearms exposed, they turned and jumped into their vehicles, screeching out of the parking lot and disappearing into the night.

31

JEFFS AND HIS MINIONS COULD INTIMIDATE INDIVIDUALS, but the American legal system, which they detested, was steadily grinding against the Prophet and the FLDS. In the winter of 2005, the Lost Boys' civil suit made its way to Third District Judge Denise Lindberg. As Lindberg considered its merits, the Utah attorney general's office became concerned that the church would start liquidating its assets to prepare for an unfavorable ruling and the seizure of FLDS property. The UEP trust was conservatively valued at $107 million, Jeffs always needed more money to maintain his life on the run, and there was evidence that a sell-off had already begun. When Sam Brower saw work crews dismantling sections of an eighteen-thousand-square-foot UEP building and breaking down equipment and fixtures from a high-tech potato processing plant, he assumed they'd be peddled to raise cash.

On May 27, 2005, another Third District judge, Robert Adkins, issued a temporary restraining order suspending the authority of UEP trustees. Jeffs and the others on the board—James Zitting, Winston Blackmore, Truman Barlow, William E. Jessop (AKA William Timpson), and Leroy Jeffs—were given three weeks to file court papers opposing their permanent removal as overseers of the United Effort Plan. Following the Prophet's lead in the Lost Boys case, they ignored the judge's ruling, lending even more creedence to the notion that Jeffs was abandoning the border towns. Then Judge Denise Lindberg announced a separate decision and placed the UEP under the control of Bruce Wisan, a Salt Lake City certified public accountant. A new front had been opened against the FLDS, with money as the major weapon. For the first time ever, the church's assets had been transferred into an outsider's hands, the sixty-three-year-old trust essentially broken. Wisan began the vastly entangled task of trying to collect taxes on the property while deciding what to do with the communal real estate. One option was allowing local citizens to have outright ownership of their homes—a radical departure from the past and calculated to end the FLDS's financial strangehold on the community.

In the spring of 2005, Utah Attorney General Mark Shurtleff and Arizona AG Terry Goddard met in St. George to publicly display their unity and muscle. They gave Jeffs and the church one more chance to cooperate and change their pattern of forcing girls into underage marriage, but the warnings were again dismissed. After years of prodding from civilians, authorities in both states were at last starting to confront the abuses. Their strategy for undermining the FLDS was comprehensive and multidimensional, as Brower had been pushing for, and by mid-2005 it was being unleashed from all sides.

That spring Gary Engels passed his six-month probation, accomplishing more than enough to justify staying on the Mohave County payroll. Throughout the past winter, he'd constantly gathered information from birth certificates, other documents, and interviews, feeding it back to prosecutor Matt Smith. Since meeting Richard Holm, Isaac Wyler, Candi Shapley, and other former church members, Engels had been building criminal cases against men in underage marriages, one or two at first, then a handful more, until he had enough for eight potential indictments. They weren't the strongest cases, because he couldn't rely on any firsthand testimony besides Candi's, but he'd come to town last November with nothing. The late nights with Holm, the wine-drinking with the locals, the gradual loosening of the tongues, the talks with Candi, and his old-fashioned legwork had paid off. Engels was eager to push forward against the eight men, but knew the risks associated with this kind of prosecution in Arizona. His also knew that his boss had never dodged a difficult legal challenge.

A ninth case, also based on Candi's information, was about to become public. On June 9, 2005, Matt Smith indicted Jeffs on two Class Six felonies, accusing him of sexual conduct with a minor and a second count of conspiracy to commit sexual conduct with a minor. For the first time, the Prophet had been charged with a crime. Engels was relieved and gratified, but the charges wouldn't mean anything until they could find Jeffs and get him in front of a jury.

The following month, Smith brought criminal indictments against the eight other men: Kelly Fischer, 39; Dale Evans Barlow, 48; Rodney H. Holm, 39; Donald R. Barlow, 49; Vergel Bryce Jessop, 46; Terry D. Barlow, 24; Randolph J. Barlow, 33; and David R. Bateman, 49. Each had been charged by a Mohave County grand jury based upon testimony from Richard Holm, from Engels himself, and from Candi Shapley, who at sixteen had been "spiritually married" to Randy Barlow. Candi's testimony had been crucial in getting these indictments and would be just as important at Randy Barlow's trial and in trying to build a broader case against Jeffs. Each of the eight men was charged with one count of sexual conduct with a minor and another count of conspiracy to commit sexual conduct with a minor. In Arizona, it was a Class Six felony to engage in sexual activity with anyone under eighteen, unless that person was a legal spouse, and conviction carried a sentence of probation to two years in prison. The investigation was gathering momentum.

Some mornings Engels ate breakfast in Hurricane with Richard Holm. One day they were sitting together in a café when a friendly-looking young man with reddish hair walked in and waved to Holm. Richard called him over and introduced him to Gary: his name was Lamont Barlow. Because Engels was with Holm, Barlow felt comfortable joining them and opening up about his knowledge of the FLDS and his wife. She was Elissa Wall—the girl Jeffs had secretly married to her first cousin at the Caliente Hot Springs Motel in April 2001, when she was fourteen. Elissa had had two painful miscarriages with her first husband, Allen Steed, but she was now pregnant with Lamont's child and their baby would be born later in the year. Through Richard and Lamont, Engels was able to meet the young woman and thought she'd make a good witness against the Prophet.

"She was just a sweet girl who seemed very credible," he said, but would she be willing to talk?

It was a delicate situation. Gary didn't want to push her into a criminal prosecution unless and until she was ready to go through what any woman could confront when bringing sexual charges against a powerful man. In the late 1990s, Elissa had seen her own father kicked out of the FLDS and stripped of his family, so she knew what kind of pressure and force the church could use against people who created problems or *were* turncoats. Engels took it slowly, socializing with her for months and getting to know Elissa while avoiding the subject of her underage marriage. He couldn't avoid it for too long, however, because the four-year statute of limitations in Utah for this offense was running out. Finally, she was ready to tell him her story.

Before the deadline expired, Engels notified officials in Washington County, where the alleged crime had taken place at Fred Jessop's home in Hildale. Elissa was about to do something that no woman had ever done before—in an environment that was beyond hostile. She'd agreed to this only after Washington County had promised not to reveal her identity.

For years, the cops in Colorado City had operated under their own rules and with no regard for outside authorities. They didn't follow the normal procedure of handling calls on police radios, but were dispatched to trouble spots via their cell phones, so that other law enforcement agencies couldn't pick up these messages on scanners. They didn't want anyone beyond the border towns to know their business, but instead meted out punishment as they saw fit. Compared to the police in other towns, they dramatically underreported crimes, especially sex crimes, letting the FLDS handle offenders without the intrusion of the legal system of Washington or Mohave County.

Jeffs himself was judge and jury, imposing his own arbitrary sentences. Sometimes he banished men for transgressions, other times he temporarily separated them from their wives and children—even when he was traveling. He called this discipline an "adjustment" and declared that because he'd dealt harshly with the guilty in this life, they wouldn't have to pay for their sins after death. According to the Utah Department of Public Safety, Hildale listed a *total* of three crimes—two burglaries and a larceny—for the entirety of 2004. The numbers were so clearly skewed that Arizona finally decided to take action. Officer Rodney Holm had earlier been decertified for his conviction for bigamy and sexual conduct with a minor. Then two more local policemen were decertified: Vance Barlow for practicing bigamy and Sam Roundy for bigamy and failing to report child sex abuse cases to the state. In 2007, another pair was decertified when Fred L. Barlow and Preston L. Barlow were stripped of their powers, and later resigned.

In the summer of 2005, Attorneys General Shurtleff and Goddard stepped up the hunt for Jeffs, offering a $10,000 reward for information leading to his arrest. Sam Brower, using his experience as a bounty hunter, pushed for widening the search for Warren and raising the profile of the case by bringing in the FBI. Brower and Gary Engels asked for the issuance of a federal UFAP (Unlawful Flight to Avoid Prosecution) warrant for the Prophet. When a fugitive had been charged with a felony and then fled the state, regional law enforcement often contacted the FBI because of the Bureau's far greater resources and visibility. In mid-2005, Engels and Brower were the only two people seriously looking for Jeffs, and neither had the power to make an arrest. The FBI, by contrast, had twelve thousand agents and countless connections. At Brower's prompting, the feds obtained a UFAP warrant for the Prophet, then chipped in an additional $40,000 to bump the reward for Jeff's capture up to $50,000.

As the FBI joined the investigation, an Arizona grand jury began studying the financial activities of FLDS construction companies doing business in the desert. One entity, Paragon Contractors Corporation, would eventually be fined more than $10,000 by the U.S. Department of Labor for employing kids twelve, thirteen, and fifteen, and then not paying them to work. Another front had been opened against Jeffs and his church.

And then another, as Arizona finally turned its attention to the Colorado City public school system, which had been bilking the state for years. Using statistics generated by Elaine Tyler of the Hope Organization, Arizona investigated public funding for local schools and found massive misspending. The educational system, headed by Alvin Barlow, had allegedly fudged reports on how it had spent hundreds of thousands of dollars in 2003 alone. Tyler also gathered anecdotal evidence of school monies spent on private vacations and other financial abuses. Despite all the suspect numbers she'd uncovered, she still had difficulty selling the severity of the problems to the authorities. At that point, she turned to Plan B.

"After talking about it and talking about it," Elaine says, "I started screaming at [Arizona Attorney General] Terry Goddard to do something about the school system in Colorado City. I guess that worked. They investigated what I was telling them and then took action."

The Arizona Board of Education threatened to withhold 10 percent of the local school district's assistance until a proper report was filed. Faced with mounting pressure to conform to state law, Barlow retired and the schools went into receivership. As the Arizona grand jury expanded its investigation, virtually all the district school officials resigned and the entire system would go through a shakeup before starting over with new leadership. Less than a year after Engels had come to town, virtually no aspect of life inside the twin communities was free from assault by county, state, or federal government. And with each new development, more and more media descended on the border with microphones and cameras in hand, further aggravating the FLDS.

The Arizona and Utah attorneys general, coming at the church from yet another angle, applied for a grant from the U.S. Department of Justice's Office of Violence Against Women. The grant was specifically intended to help victims of abuse in polygamist families. Seven hundred thousand dollars were awarded to provide food, shelter, transportation, counseling, and case management services for those who'd escaped the plural marriage lifestyle. The "Safe Passage Grant" was managed by John Larsen of Utah's Department of Human Services, a Mormon who worked near Hurricane and had spent the past three decades dealing with domestic problems inside the FLDS. As part of the grant's outreach, Larsen conducted a series of "Safety Net" meetings held around the region for former FLDS members or those who might be ready to leave the church.

The grant's parameters did not allow it to provide financial help to minors, like the Lost Boys, but Utah was starting to recognize the crisis Jeffs had unleashed by banishing all these young men from his community. The state had begun working to pass legislation allowing sixteen- and seventeen-year-olds to petition the juvenile courts for emancipation from their parents; if they won this right, they'd gain access to social service resources. While the LDS church in Salt Lake City was content to ignore or deny the FLDS refugees and the growing human cost along the border, Utah's government was trying to make amends.

The Safe Passage Grant funded a bimonthly newsletter placed inside every post office box in the twin towns. Spreading the word about the availability of federal monies, victim counseling, and Safety Net meetings, the letter was intended to "reduce isolation, secrecy, abuses of power and crime . . . All services coordinated and provided through this model will seek to be: Personalized, accessible, accountable, and comprehensive. Coordinated across systems. Culturally responsive."

The official message now being sent to the polygamists in Dixie was a distant cry from the invasion of Colorado City in the summer of 1953. Half a century later, the authorities had learned something about the long-term effects of attacking people's lifestyle and religion from the perch of moral superiority. Larsen himself was an excellent choice to head up the grant, and not just because of his long experience with the FLDS. A friendly man with a gentle smile and a quick sense of humor, he embodied the light touch and the heart that had been missing from the earlier approach to the renegade church.

"The change we're trying to bring in Colorado City is painful but necessary," he says, "and we're finally moving in the right direction. The raid of '53 was done wrong, so we're trying community relations instead. I don't think we'll see positive results right away because it's very hard to change their mind-set and habits, but we're making progress. One person coming to grips with domestic violence is success."

With the help of people like Elaine Tyler, Larsen, and others, a few women were continuing to leave the church, while a number of the Lost Boys were successfully moving on from their painful pasts and were now either employed or going to school, or both. In a symbolic shift, they put aside the old-fashioned attire of the FLDS in favor of ultramodern clothes, dyed hair, and the tattoos and jewelry of their generation. The boys met regularly in St. George, and police officers came in to talk to them about the dangers of street drugs, like cocaine laced with rat poison. The federal government agency Job Corps actively recruited among them for education and training in different fields. Some boys had trouble understanding that the American government, which they'd been taught to fear and hate, would offer them an opportunity to live and study for free for two years, then help them find work. On the whole, they seemed very bright and quick to adapt to the external world.

"We have some awesome young men in this group," says Shannon Price of the Diversity Foundation, which helped the Lost Boys find employment and deal with drug issues. "We want the communities they're living in to know how hard they're trying to get beyond their backgrounds. Their progress is amazing."

In the mid-1980s, the American government had brought down the neo-Nazi group known as the Order by using the RICO (Racketeer Influenced and Corrupt Organizations) statute, a 1970 federal law enforcement weapon designed to prosecute organized crime outfits. The combined governments of Arizona, Utah, and the United States were now employing a similar set of legal tools in Colorado City and Hildale, investigating the FLDS and treating it as a kind of religious Mafia, headed by a fugitive don.

It might have been the result of using a more intelligent and restrained strategy this time around—or it might have been sheer dumb luck—but the authorities were about to catch a break. It wouldn't be their last.

32

O N THE NIGHT OF OCTOBER 28, 2005, Seth Steed Jeffs, one of Warren's many half-brothers, was riding in a Ford Excursion on I-25 in southern Colorado, about two hours south of Denver, with Colorado City native Nathaniel Steed Allred. When a driver spotted the Ford weaving from lane to lane, he called the police to report a DUI. A Pueblo County sheriff's officer stopped the Excursion and questioned Allred, who told law enforcement that Seth had hired him for "sexual companionship" and paid him $5,000. The thirty-two-year-old Seth—tall, pale, extremely thin, and with distant eyes—bore a strong resemblance to Warren, conveying the same air of self-righteousness and defiance of authority. He'd also been living a similar itinerant lifestyle. Inside the Ford were illegal narcotics, a laptop computer, a Palm Pilot, a GPS system, FLDS sermons, sealed envelopes addressed to Warren Jeffs or the "Prophet," $142,000 in cash, $7,000 worth of prepaid credit cards, and seven untraceable prepaid cell phones—the communication device of choice for modern-day criminals and terrorists.

With bravado, Seth told his interrogators that he was an FLDS "messenger" on his way to Texas to deliver materials to the Eldorado compound. He insisted that he didn't know where his infamous half-brother was and that even if he did, he'd never inform the cops of Warren's whereabouts; under the First Amendment, he and his family had the unconditional right to practice their faith as they chose to.

"Prophets are often persecuted," he said to his captors, indicating that he'd go to prison for as long as necessary before informing on his spiritual leader. "It would be stupid to tell anyone where he is because he would get caught."

Seth was arrested on suspicion of harboring a fugitive and confronted with the difficult options presented to him by the American legal system. He could either remain defiant and keep proclaiming his innocence, which would lead to an expensive trial, a possible conviction by jury, and a potentially lengthy prison sentence—or do what about 90 percent of those charged with crimes do and cut a deal. Jail got his attention and he took the second option, pleading guilty to one count of harboring and concealing a fugitive. By the time he was sentenced in a federal court in Denver in mid-2006, he didn't sound nearly so brave or indifferent to authority.

"I've had a lot of time to think about what I did," he meekly told U.S. District count Judge Robert Blackburn. "I know what I did was wrong while I was doing it . . . I never want to find myself in a courtroom again. I just want to get on with my life."

The judge, who found Seth convincing, addressed the defendant and said, "I must not and will not visit the sins of your fugitive brother on you."

Judge Blackburn gave him three years' probation and ordered him to pay a $2,500 fine, an extremely lenient sentence in the eyes of many. The courtroom was filled with rumors that in exchange for this leniency, Seth had given up useful information to help locate his half-brother. That wouldn't prove to be the case, but he'd inadvertently provided insight into the FLDS under Warren Jeffs.

One item seized from the Ford Excursion was a long, obsequious letter the new Hildale/Colorado City Police Chief Fred Barlow had recently written to the Prophet, later published in the *Salt Lake Tribune*. It was to be delivered to Jeffs and left no doubt that while on the run he still controlled the faithful in the border towns—starting with the police department. Filled with misspellings, the letter began:

> *"Dear Uncle Warren,*
>
> *I would first like to acknowledge you as the one man that was and is called of God to stand at the head of his priesthood and the Kingdom of God on the earth in this day and time. I rejoice in the peace that comes over me when I follow the directives that you have sent to me through Uncle William Timpson. I have felt a unity between the peace officers. They have all stated to me their desire to follow the directives that are placed before us. . . .*
>
> *I fill [sic] that without priesthood I am nothing. The community has been getting harassed by many news reporters. They are asking us why no one will talk to them. As law*

enforcement we get many calls and I have explained to them that the media have never told the truth about this people and that the people are not trying to justify themselves to the world . . .

"I am praying for you to be protected and yearn to be with you again. . . . I rejoice in the tests and hope and pray that I will not offend God. . . . I hope to hear any directives that you have for me. I know that I still have thing [sic] to purge out of my life and have bee [sic] striving to get them out. . . . I love you and acknowledge you as my priesthood head. And I know that you have the right to rule in all aspects of my life. I yearn to hear from you."

By late 2005, the FLDS was gaining more and more exposure—southern Utah convenience stores were selling T-shirts that read, "Polygamous Beer: Take a Six-Pack Home to the Wives." The media deluge along the border had become a constant burden to the locals and if that weren't enough, in early 2006 HBO was debuting a new fictional series called *Big Love.* The show chronicled a polygamous family in suburban Salt Lake City with ties to a strange fundamentalist Mormon sect out in the countryside, whose assets were under the control of something called the UEB; it was headed by an aging tyrant who was being challenged for power by his dangerous son. Even Hollywood was piling on.

A year after Gary Engels had come to town, Colorado City was under siege by county attorney detectives and law enforcement officers in two states; by a CPA-turned-tax-collector who'd assumed control of the church's $100,000,000-plus in property and was about to start evicting those who wouldn't pay up; by an Arizona grand jury taking testimony on FLDS schools, welfare scams, police corruption, and illicit construction projects; by FBI agents looking for Jeffs from Mexico to Canada; by the investigative efforts of Sam Brower and Elaine Tyler; by eight unfolding criminal cases in Kingman; by regional, national, and international media who flocked to the border to hound the locals for interviews; by a growing number of sightseers who drove along Main Street gawking at the outdated clothing and hairstyles; and by women who'd escaped the FLDS and were assisting others trying to do the same.

The community was on edge and first-time visitors were given strict guidelines by Elaine Tyler and others before entering the city limits: "Don't break any minor laws over there. Don't speed. Use your turn signal at every corner. Stop at all stop signs. Don't litter. Make sure your brake lights are working. Don't point at anyone. Don't even stare. Don't loiter. People will be watching you and the cops will follow you everywhere in unmarked cars. You won't know who they are. They're all working for Warren and they're just looking for a reason to pull you over. And whatever you do, don't take any pictures of the locals. They hate that."

Nobody knew how church members would respond to the gathering tension, which had become palpable on the streets and inside the stores.

"The people in Colorado City have never felt this kind of scrutiny before," Elaine said. "It's hitting them from every angle and they're increasingly afraid. Anything could happen now."

33

THE $142,000 THE POLICE HAD CONFISCATED from Seth Jeffs's Ford Excursion on the night of his arrest never reached the Prophet, who constantly demanded more money from his congregation. While the faithful in Colorado City and Hildale were living under increasing pressure—some of it financial—Warren was moving around the western United States in secrecy and style.

On the final day of 2005, a grain elevator suddenly and mysteriously disappeared from Four Square Mill in Colorado City. When Bruce Wisan, the court-appointed accountant overseeing the UEP trust, heard about the missing elevator, he protested that this was community property and now under his control; it couldn't just be sold off for cash to be funneled to Warren Jeffs. Town officials countered by telling Wisan and his lawyer, Zachary Shields, that the elevator was private property—the owners could do anything they wanted with it. Wisan demanded that the elevator be found and reconstructed, and he got his way. The building went back up almost as fast as it had come down, and this was more money that never made its way to the Prophet.

The CPA had a face that conjured up Daddy Warbucks of the comic strip *Little Orphan Annie*. Stocky, bald, and square-shouldered, he seemed as solid professionally as physically, rarely raising his voice or showing much emotion in public. Patient but not infinitely so, he was committed to doing what Utah had hired him to do—figure out a way to redistribute the local real estate assets—no matter how difficult. He very quickly made enemies in town who nicknamed him "Bruce Almighty," "Uncle Bruce," "Wisepants," and the "State Ordained Bishop," or "SOB."

In February 2006, Wisan and attorney Zachary Shields interrogated police chief Fred Barlow about the recent dismantling of the grain elevator. The previous October, Barlow had promised in his later-publicized letter to the Prophet that even under pressure he wouldn't buckle to the powers that were trying to undermine Colorado City. He kept his word to Jeffs, maintaining that the elevator wasn't subject to Wisan's rule, while protecting the identity of those who'd torn it down. As the dialogue between the two sides almost comically revealed, the CPA and his lawyer were as hard-headed as the people whose lives they were now in charge of changing:

> SHIELDS: "Do you recognize Bruce Wisan as the one who has the authority to control the UEP land, to manage the UEP land?"

For a full two minutes, an excruciatingly long time, Barlow refused to respond. Dead silence, until the attorney spoke again.

> SHIELDS: "Did you tell Wisan, 'I will send an officer to check it [the elevator] out?'"
> BARLOW: "Yes, I did."
> SHIELDS: "Who did you send?"
> BARLOW: "I don't remember the officer . . ."
> SHIELDS: "What happened next?"
> BARLOW: "A few minutes later the officer called me and said that he had gone over there and asked the workers to stop and they agreed to stop."
> SHIELDS: "Who is they? Who was there?"
> BARLOW: "I don't know. I didn't go . . ."

The next several questions were met with more silence.

> SHIELDS: "So what have you done to investigate this theft after Bruce Wisan called two or three days later and said it's gone?"
> BARLOW: "You would have to talk to Jonathan Roundy, the deputy who investigated the missing equipment."
> SHIELDS: "So you've done nothing?"

BARLOW: "I personally have not . . ."
SHIELDS: "You haven't even asked him for a report of his findings?"
BARLOW: "I did not ask him for a report . . ."

Shields asked Barlow about the tearing down of the Cozy Log Home building one day after Wisan had assumed control of the UEP Trust. Did the police chief know who took that structure apart?

BARLOW: "I can't even think of one person that I can say I remember
being there . . ."
SHIELDS: "You can't remember one person who was there dismantling
this building?"
BARLOW: "Not right off the top of my head."

Police Chief Barlow was already under scrutiny for communicating with
a known fugitive. Half a dozen other local cops would soon be investigated
and face possible decertification as the community's power structure went
through a sustained shakeup. In mid-March 2006, following a quarter-
century as Hildale's Justice Court judge, Walter K. Steed was dismissed by
the Utah Supreme Court after it ruled that he'd violated state law by
openly living with three wives. Within days, Hildale's mayor, Richard
Allred, and his son, town clerk Joseph Allred, resigned, offering no explanation for their actions. In early April, deputy town marshal Mica Barlow
disregarded a subpoena to testify before a federal grand jury in Phoenix
and U.S. District Judge Susan Bolton issued a warrant for his arrest. On
April 6, Barlow surrendered to authorities and was jailed at the Central Arizona Detention Facility in Florence, where they threatened to hold him until he started talking.

A week later, after a Colorado City town council meeting, Bruce Wisan,
an attorney named Jeffrey Shields (different from Zachary Shields of the
Barlow hearing), and Isaac Wyler were standing outside town hall chatting
on a pleasant spring night. Wyler had become the CPA's assistant in managing the UEP trust, and part of his job was handing out subpoenas to residents on the accountant's behalf. If Isaac had been unpopular with FLDS
members before taking this position, he'd now become an open target for

abuse. As the group talked that evening, a white pickup full of young men drove by and snapped pictures of them. A few hours later, Wyler's home and horse trailer were splattered with yellow and orange paintballs, while Ross Chatwin's house was struck by vandals, leaving behind broken windows and shattered glass.

34

In the spring of 2006, as the FLDS foundation and financial assets came under increasing attack, the feds decided to ratchet up the publicity in their hunt for Jeffs. On May 6, the FBI placed him on its Ten Most Wanted List and the reward for his capture was doubled to $100,000 (Sam Brower had not only pushed for this move, but encouraged the federal government to widen its investigation to include charges of "white slavery" against the Prophet for forcing underage girls into marriage).

Gary Engels, for one, was very pleased that Jeffs had made the FBI's list.

"He's on there right alongside Osama bin Laden," the investigator said that June, "which is right where he belongs."

Since the feds had created the Top Ten list in 1950, 94 percent of those placed on it had been caught, and it didn't take long for the new strategy to produce a response.

On May 10, police in Lakewood, Colorado, received an anonymous tip that Jeffs had been spotted at a home in this Denver suburb, just a couple of hours north of the safe houses holding his wives near Pueblo. The Lakewood Police Department, Jefferson County officers, and the FBI rushed to the address and scoured the neighborhood, but the fugitive wasn't there.

Ten days later, on May 20, Bruce Wisan turned up the pressure on his front. A month after he'd targeted some of the community's largest homes for delinquent property tax payments, only $100,000 had come in out of $800,000 owed, plus penalties and interest. Hundreds of other houses were being posted for past due taxes, the notices demanding that occupants pay up now or find new places to live. Warren had sent word back to his followers in Colorado City not to cooperate with Wisan and his tax strategy. If questioned by authorities, the faithful were specifically to "answer them nothing"—Jeffs echoing Jesus when he'd been interrogated by Pontius Pilate. Many locals were obeying the Prophet's orders, and when Isaac Wyler showed up to post a notice on their home, they ran inside and locked the door or stood their ground and told him to go away. Wyler refused to leave until the notice was up.

"Isaac," Engels said about his friend and ally, "has guts."

At night, church members retraced Wyler's footsteps, going through the community removing or changing the numbers on the houses to confuse Wisan and make Isaac's job harder.

Five days after they began posting tax notices, Engels and sixteen Mohave County sheriff's deputies and detectives made their boldest move in a year. At 8:00 A.M., a fleet of police vehicles drove across Colorado City in a line before five of them broke off and pulled up in front of a home on Richard Street belonging to David Bateman, one of the eight men charged with sexual conduct with a minor. In August 2002, when Bateman was forty-four, he'd impregnated an unidentified seventeen-year-old girl and been named as the father on the birth certificate. In July 2005, he'd been indicted and this morning, two hours after parking in front of Bateman's address, Engels walked out of the residence carrying a cardboard box full of additional potential evidence.

The law enforcement team entered three other local homes with search warrants supporting further investigation for the indictments. Each of the eight cases involved an older man and various girls between fifteen and seventeen who'd become pregnant from December 1998 to March 2002. All the men had pleaded not guilty and were facing trials scheduled to start in the summer of 2006. Authorities were looking for more facts or forensics, and—much to Engels's annoyance—a Colorado City town marshal had been allowed to come along on this morning's mission. The investigator believed that the marshal had tipped off suspects that a raid was coming and helped some of their relatives escape.

"I got into it with this guy," Engels said, "because he interfered with me during the execution of a search warrant. He wouldn't cooperate and he wouldn't talk to me. We were inside one of the houses and I asked him if he recognized any of the people in the pictures on the wall. I was trying to figure out who they were and what their connection was to the men we were investigating. He said, 'Maybe.' I said who do you know and he said, 'Nobody.' He was lying to get me off his back."

Once inside the houses, Engels and the others gathered up letters, bills, bank statements, photographs, tax information, genealogy charts, and Social Security cards—anything that might bolster their prosecution, as the Mohave County Attorney's office had a severe lack of witnesses. When the county had tried to serve them with subpoenas, they'd run away, gone into hiding, changed location, or simply refused to answer the door. In those instances where the victim or her family wasn't cooperating with the investigation, the police collected saliva samples from men, women, and children for DNA tests to prove paternity. All the cases fit that category except one. Only Candi Shapley had come forward to the grand jury and testified about her relationship with Randy Barlow and offered more information about Warren Jeffs. She'd emerged as the star female witness in the series of legal proceedings set to kick off in Kingman in early July. Engels couldn't count on much when it came to firsthand victim testimony, but he was counting heavily on Candi.

Within hours of Engels's arrival at David Bateman's home, the news spread across town that the Mohave County investigator working out of that triple-wide trailer was heading up a raid on the community. Inevitably, people began comparing this to the 1953 invasion by Governor Pyle and the state of Arizona, with Engels playing the role of storm trooper. The anger toward him in Colorado City, which had been gathering for the past eighteen months, only intensified.

He hunkered down inside his tiny workspace, which looked more lived-in than when he'd started the job. It not only had several chairs now, but five pictures of Jeffs and a photo of John Wayne dressed as a cowboy, with the Stars and Stripes waving behind him. A plaque honored Engels for his recent efforts with the polygamist community and a wall hanging came from a children's home in Calcutta, encouraging the reader to love people even if they were "unreasonable, illogical, and self-centered." One of Jeffs's images depicted him as the male figure standing next to his wife and holding a pitchfork in the famous Grant Wood painting *American Gothic*. In bad times, this mock work of art gave Engels's sense of humor a needed lift.

On May 25, the day the search warrants were executed, Bruce Wisan filed a lawsuit accusing the former UEP trustees, including Warren Jeffs, of failing to protect the trust's assets and of unjustly enriching themselves. Among other charges were breach of trust, breach of fiduciary duty, civil conspiracy, and profits arising from administration of the trust. The next evening, Washington County deputies and Colorado City deputy marshal Helaman Barlow showed up at a town council meeting and arrested Colorado City mayor Terrill Johnson. He was facing allegations of fraudulent vehicle registration, a second-degree felony. By evening he'd made the $5,000 bail and was released.

As May ended, the FLDS was being hit with a new legal or financial problem almost every twenty-four hours.

35

IN THE FIRST WEEK OF JUNE, FBI Director Robert Mueller held a press conference in Salt Lake City to talk about the latest addition to the Ten Most Wanted List. In recent weeks, the feds had come under sharp criticism from Arizona Attorney General Terry Goddard, who felt the FBI wasn't using state and local investigators enough in its manhunt for the Prophet. Goddard had asked for a task force to manage the search for the fugitive, but his request had been denied. Mueller had traveled to Utah in part to stifle the carping.

"We are looking for Mr. Jeffs on a nationwide basis," Mueller said in Salt Lake City. "Identifying, locating, and arresting those who are predators—child predators—is among the top priorities of the Bureau. We *will* catch him."

Two thousand miles to the east in Washington, D.C., a Mormon Apostle named Elder Russell Nelson, a member of the Quorum of the Twelve Apostles of the LDS Church, stood next to President Bush and urged Congress to amend the U.S. Constitution to ban gay (and plural) marriage.

"While those of us here today represent a broad spectrum of religious diversity," Nelson had said earlier to the media, "we are firmly united in our declaration that marriage of a man and a woman is ordained of God."

Not since the Equal Rights Amendment battle of the 1970s had leaders of the Church of Jesus Christ of Latter-day Saints been so openly involved in a political fight. The more publicity Jeffs had brought to the fundamentalist Mormons in southern Utah, the more aggressively the LDS church had scrambled to distance itself from the FLDS, taking their campaign all the way to the White House.

Later that week, a group of bikers made their own push against the Prophet as sixty Harley-Davidson motorcycles thundered into Colorado City and Hildale. The ponytailed, tattooed men, clad in black leather and chaps, represented Utah's chapter of Bikers Against Child Abuse and were on a poker run to raise awareness and funds for area kids who were victims of violence or sexual molestation. At each of five stops along Highway 59, they drew a card and the rider with the best hand won a prize.

Bruce Wisan, meanwhile, had started serving eviction notices on the homes of William Shapley—a Colorado City town council member and the father of Candi Shapley—and James Zitting, a former trustee of the UEP. They had exactly five days to pay up or move out. Wisan himself was now going door-to-door to persuade residents to settle their past-due property taxes—or else. Four days after receiving their notices, Zitting and Shapley arrived at the Mohave County treasurer's office and wrote checks totaling nearly $7,000. Isaac Wyler, undiscouraged by the daily harassment from locals and the recent paintballing of his home and horse trailer, stayed busy posting tax notices on 240 other homes in Hildale and 500 more in Colorado City.

As Jeffs moved from safe house to safe house in new cars to meet with his wives, tension in the twin communities continued to rise.

"These people," Elaine Tyler said of those living in the border towns, "have been put in a terrible position. Bruce is telling them to pay their taxes or get evicted and Warren is telling them to ignore him. They're caught in the middle and Jeffs doesn't care how much they suffer. What are they supposed to do?"

Despite distant orders from the Prophet to disregard the tax notices, some residents were deciding to be practical. They'd begun zigzagging through the streets of Hildale with wheelbarrows, running up to front doors and collecting handfuls of cash from houses (many locals had never used a checking account). They gathered up about $17,000 in this manner and dropped it off at the Washington County Treasurer's Office, nearly paying off their debt before the deadline.

Eviction wasn't the only way Wisan was squeezing the community. One of its largest businesses, Western Precision Inc., employed nearly a hundred people and made the components used in blood pumps, bicycles, and military aircraft. In 2002, Western Precision had relocated from Salt Lake City down to the border, following the FLDS prediction that catastrophic destruction would hit northern Utah during the Winter Olympics. More than two years later, after the Lost Boys' suit was filed in the summer of 2004, UEP trustees shed some church assets by selling the 55,266-square-foot Western Precision facility and the 3.3 acres it set on to the company for a mere $25,000—the price was so low because the UEP badly wanted to keep the business in town. Book value for these properties was in the neighborhood of $5 million. When Wisan took over the UEP, he accused the trustees of having had no right to unload these assets, and certainly not for $25,000. He filed a suit alleging that the building and land did not belong to Western Precision, but were now under his control.

According to affidavits in the case, the business had also channeled as much as $100,000 to the FLDS church and to Warren Jeffs. While Western Precision lawyers disputed the last charge, this was more trouble than the company needed. In late June 2006, it delivered harsh news to the local economy by announcing it was transferring its business to Las Vegas. It changed its name to New Era Manufacturing Inc. and settled with Wisan by turning over its former facility to the UEP Trust. Eight months later, the accountant sold the building at public auction to Tom Davis of Northwest Land Company for $1.65 million. As part of Wisan's overall plan to bring private enterprise and new jobs to the border towns, Davis had plans to lease the structure to Champion Safe, which intended to hire seventy-five to one hundred workers to make gun safes in the plant at $15 to $18 an hour.

In the summer of 2006, a judge ordered the trust to pay just under $48,000 to Wisan's accounting firm for its work during the past year and just over $270,000 to the attorneys now managing the UEP. Four years earlier, when Sam Barlow had passionately addressed the FLDS congregation about the legal and monetary battle they were facing, he'd been absolutely right about one thing: lawyers are expensive.

Progress was being made on every front except in the hunt for Jeffs. As the authorities' combined strategy—of prosecuting local men for crimes against minors and draining the FLDS financially—took hold, fear and anger spread throughout the community. One man felt it most.

In June 2006, Gary Engels drove alongside a small park that lay in the shade of Canaan Mountain, towering above the border. Sunlight flooded the late afternoon and a young mother, clothed in a full-length pink cotton dress, sat on a blanket as four young children romped around her. The woman on the grass looked serene until Engels's Jeep startled her and she recoiled. Even the sight of it disturbed the locals.

"Dammit," Engels said, glancing behind him and goosing the gas pedal.

He was being tailed again, as he was each time he left the office now. One van followed him for a while before passing him off to another. They got right up on his bumper and stared in his back window.

His cell phone rang and he took a call from Sam Brower, who gave him a lead to pursue. Reaching for a pen, with one elbow steering the wheel, Engels scribbled a license plate number on his palm while keeping an eye on the rearview mirror. The person connected to the license plate was named "Moroni"—the name of the angel Joseph Smith claimed had appeared to him more than 180 years ago in upstate New York. It was Moroni who'd told Smith about the golden plates filled with hieroglyphic-like writing, and about the two stones wrapped in silver bows used to decipher the words, which had become the Book of Mormon. A number of people in the FLDS were still being named after the angel.

Engels took a hard left turn onto a red dirt path. After driving a few yards in the opposite direction, he pulled the Jeep back onto the main road and was now tailing the vehicle that had just been tailing him.

"How do you like that?" he said to the other driver. "How does that feel?"

He rode the bumper in front of him until the vehicle accelerated and exited out of the park.

Engels gave a satisfied laugh.

Heading back into Colorado City, he scoured the streets for anyone else who might harass him.

He pulled up in front of the address of Richard Holm, which was set on Richard Street, named for Holm when he was still in favor in town. Two white vans had begun shadowing Engels and now parked across from him. Both drivers were staring at the investigator and talking on cell phones. Engels kept glancing over at the menacing vehicles. Holm came outside and greeted his friend warmly, asking if he wanted to have dinner tonight at Ted and Allen's sports bar in Hurricane. Engels looked delighted with the offer.

Holm had been fighting to get back his fifteen-thousand-square-foot house, which he'd lost when banned from the FLDS. After a two-and-a-half-year absence from the community, the businessman had won visitation rights with his children and was able to return to his home after agreeing to pay property taxes on it. He'd recently purchased a seven-acre parcel of land and a metal warehouse on Highway 59 for $130,000, and was making plans to develop office space. He wanted to be part of the economic development Bruce Wisan was promoting.

As Engels got out of his Jeep and the men stood together in the early evening sun, the drivers of the vans glared at both of them. They tried to ignore the hostility and laughed about the rumor that the Prophet had built a crematorium down at the YFZ Ranch in Texas capable of reaching a temperature of 2,700°F.

"The locals say there's plenty of room in that oven for you, Richard." Gary chuckled.

"And for you, too," Holm said.

They exchanged goodbyes and Engels drove off to look for Moroni.

One evening the investigator was alerted through a police bulletin that Jeffs was traveling through southern Utah in a car that had just been identified by its license plate. Because stories were always circulating that the Prophet was in or near Colorado City to perform underage marriages, Engels wasn't completely surprised when he spotted the vehicle passing through town. He followed it up and down the dirt side roads, keeping his distance, but coming close enough to make the ID. What should he do? He had no authority to pull the car over and make an arrest—if Jeffs was even still inside. Engels was armed and assumed the men he was tailing were, too, but he didn't want a bloody confrontation. He needed backup but was unable to call on the local police department, while the officers on duty in St. George or Kingman were hours away. He could do nothing but mutter at the darkness as the car disappeared into the night, another opportunity missed.

36

ON THE AFTERNOON OF JUNE 30, officers from the Cedar City, Utah, police department, the Utah Highway Patrol, and the Iron County Sheriff's Office and a SWAT team descended en masse on a home in the Black Rock subdivision of Cedar City, after receiving a tip that the Prophet was holed up inside. Police dogs were assembled and the FBI was notified, one regional agent heading straight for this address. With the house surrounded and the cops loudly announcing their presence, a man and woman came out of the residence but refused to let the officers in. After some discussion, they changed their minds. As a search of the home unfolded, as many as ten more women and children wandered out from inside and gathered on the street. Nearby houses were also evacuated, and two vehicles were searched for financial documents connected to the FLDS. Nobody was taken into custody, but the police did locate the man whom the tipster had falsely believed was Warren Jeffs.

The searched home belonged to Willie Jessop, a known bodyguard for the Prophet, and it was believed to be a safe house for the fugitive. Jessop was one of ten people who'd recently been subpoenaed to testify before an Arizona grand jury about monetary issues surrounding FLDS construction projects.

Well before the police were notified to come to this address, Sam Brower, who lived in Cedar City, had been conducting his own surveillance on the place. He knew of Jessop's connection to Jeffs and had been feeding information about both Jessop and Jeffs back to law enforcement. On June 30, Brower was in town when the tip came in. His phone immediately rang, and he learned that the arrival of the police at Jessop's had caused a great stir in the neighborhood.

"The FBI called and asked me to see what was going on over at Willie's," Brower says. "Ten minutes later I was there and cops were everywhere with shotguns and M-16s on full display. They were supposed to keep this thing low-key but believe me, they didn't. When I drove up, they were doing barrel rolls over the hoods of cars as a show of force. Then they charged into the house like bulls in a china shop. Things inside the house got messed up and broken.

"I didn't go in myself until an FBI agent got there and started apologizing to the people for what the local cops had done. He was picking up pieces of smashed glass and vacuuming the floor, trying to clean the place while making jokes to calm everything down. I like the FBI touch."

Six days after the dry run in Cedar City, Engels and Mohave County attorney Matt Smith, along with their two key witnesses, Richard Holm and Isaac Wyler, gathered in Kingman for the start of the Kelly Fischer trial, the first of eight scheduled for that summer. When he was thirty-three, Fischer had fathered a child with a sixteen-year-old, and Engels came to court with the birth certificates to prove this. Holm and Wyler delivered testimony about the FLDS culture of secret marriages. Because Smith hadn't been able to get the victim on the witness stand, he was relying on this trio of men to make his case. If convicted, Fischer faced up to two years in prison, but as the trial approached, Engels felt it would be difficult to win without a firsthand account of the crime.

Holm described to the jury his own two plural marriages and how Rulon Jeffs had personally "blessed" these unions and "sealed" him to his two wives a few hours later. As part of the prosecution's legal strategy, Holm was asked to repress the anger and hurt he felt toward the FLDS; he made a point of calling Fischer an "honorable man." Wyler, who was a horse trainer, told the jurors that in his religion neither courtship nor affectionate displays were allowed prior to marriage. He'd seen Fischer and the teenage girl riding horses together and spotted her next to the man in a pickup, sitting between Fischer and his legal spouse. It was a clue to their relationship. Inside the FLDS, if a man sat next to a woman in a vehicle, she was usually not only his wife, but the one currently most in favor. At a later date, Wyler noticed that the teenager was pregnant.

Because there was so little direct evidence, the presentation of testimony lasted only a day.

"Sex with underage girls would be condoned up there . . ." Smith told jurors in his closing arguments. "But keep in mind that doesn't make it okay . . . This is, in effect, sex with [Fischer's] stepdaughter . . . You're her voice. You get to speak for the victim in this case. Don't let him get away with it."

Fischer's lawyer, Bruce Griffen, contended that the words of Holm and Wyler should be discounted because they were disgruntled ex–church members. The allegations had no substance because the prosecutor didn't know when or where Fischer and the girl had had sex—it could have taken place outside of Arizona, voiding the charges. Griffen asked the jurors to put aside their feelings about polygamy and the FLDS faith so they could "give a Colorado City fundamentalist a fair trial."

As Judge Steven Conn sent the jury into deliberation, Engels was anxious. His work during the past twenty months was about to be validated or invalidated by a group of strangers who only had a portion of the facts. His bosses had given him a strong vote of confidence by extending his job for almost two years now, but if Fischer were acquitted, it would set a bad precedent for the other seven trials. The media later reported that the investigator was too nervous to be in the courtroom during the reading of the verdict, but Engels denied this. He disliked listening to the legalese surrounding the end of the trial and he didn't—regardless of the outcome—want to deal with any more journalists at the moment.

An hour after the jury began deliberating, a guilty verdict came in.

Engels didn't show as much relief and excitement as he felt, but a newspaper camera caught him smiling broadly on a street in Kingman. Matt Smith had taken on another tough mission and won; the county attorney had gone into court without a victim's testimony and gotten a conviction. A good precedent had been set for possible future victories. Engels and Smith relaxed only briefly before preparing for the upcoming August trial of forty-three-year-old Don Barlow, charged with having sex with Laree Steed when she was sixteen.

A week after the verdict, two more members of Jeffs's inner circle joined former town marshal Mica Barlow and assistant postmaster James Allred at the Central Arizona Detention Center in Florence after refusing to testify about the FLDS before a federal grand jury. One was Leroy B. Timpson, who owned Spectrum Kitchen & Bath and was closely aligned with the Prophet's core strategists. The other was Leroy Jeffs, Warren's older brother and an accountant in charge of church finances, property records, and marriage and birth records. All were being held on contempt charges, and by the end of the month, a fifth man, Benjamin Jeffs Nielsen, twenty-five, had joined them in jail.

In late July, Winston Blackmore, the rival Canadian church leader whom Jeffs had excommunicated during his climb to power, showed up in Colorado City to dedicate a slab of rock at the entrance to Cottonwood Park—a new monument to those who'd lived through the 1953 raid. Exactly three years earlier, Jeffs had destroyed a similar monument erected without his approval, before making his exodus from the border towns under the pretense that they'd been defiled by the monument. Blackmore's actions in midsummer of 2006 were a direct affront and challenge to Jeffs's reign. With the Prophet in hiding and many of his cohorts behind bars, rebellion against him was building within the FLDS, but still the community remained filled with his supporters. Three months later, vandals attacked and defaced the new monument, smearing it with oil and tar.

Regardless of who was visibly in control of the church, sooner or later the FLDS would have to contend with Bruce Wisan. In August the UEP Trust, which had defined property rights in town since the early 1940s, was dissolved, signaling the end of communal living. It would gradually be replaced by private home ownership. The restructured trust allowed residents to receive property through deeds or "spendthrift trusts"—the latter designed to prevent homes from passing into the hands of those still loyal to Jeffs and then selling them back to the Prophet for next to nothing. A seven-member board, led by Wisan himself, would manage the new trust and oversee a variety of new economic and educational opportunities in the community. Basic American property rights and free enterprise were coming to Colorado City, while Jeffs continued shifting operations and key people down to the Texas compound.

As the summer progressed, the hunt for one of the FBI's Top Ten fugitives became an almost nightly talk show topic on cable TV. The Prophet's face was plastered on wanted posters all over the Southwest, and everybody had a strong opinion about where he had gone. The leading media pundits believed that Jeffs was holed up at the YFZ Ranch, where he was protected from arrest on enclosed FLDS land. And the new arrivals seemed to have developed a cozy relationship with the local authorities: cops in Eldorado had good things to say about the FLDS. The transplanted church members paid their taxes on time, generally behaving very well since their appearance in the Lone Star State. Given all this, talking heads on CNN, MSNBC, Fox, and elsewhere suggested that Jeffs would most likely never be caught. He'd found a safe haven inside the grand limestone temple at the ranch, money was rolling in from all over the Southwest to support his lifestyle, and he was hunkered down for the foreseeable future. No one in power had any thoughts about storming this compound and creating another public relations disaster. The transition out of Colorado City was complete; he could stay in Texas forever without facing arrest.

While July and August unfolded amidst endless speculation about the Prophet, a new war broke out in the Middle East between Lebanon and Israel, and within weeks hundreds were dead and a million people had been removed from their homes by the fighting. The Lebanese suffered the most casualties, but both sides were pounded by daily bombing and destruction, and with the heat of the season intensifying and adding to the human suffering, trees in northern Israel caught fire during a shelling, so much smoke and flames filling the desert sky that it blotted out the sun. In America, fundamentalist Christian groups claimed the war was the fulfillment of Biblical prophecy—a sure sign that the End Times were drawing near and God's chosen people were about to be called up to heaven.

37

LAINE TYLER FELL naturally into the role of mother for anyone
who'd been harmed by the FLDS or Warren Jeffs. Fierce in her protective tendencies and just as fierce in her advocacy for victims, she'd
become a magnet for those trying to escape Colorado City and start a new
life. A steady flow of refugees walked into her cramped office at the Hope
Organization in Washington, Utah, asking for help with education, counseling, material goods, legal advice, financial aid, or just coping in the outside
world. In 2006, she'd gone into the border towns to assist a woman fleeing an
abusive marriage and trying to resettle in another location. Like others who
formed the heart of the resistance against the FLDS, Elaine had put herself at
risk and was now concerned about being identified as an enemy of the
church. She refused to have her picture taken or displayed anywhere in connection with her work, and wasn't seeking public acclaim.

"If I can help a single woman or child live in less fear," she said, "that's
enough for me."

As the head of the Hope Organization, Elaine always had far too much to
do and too few resources, putting in 40- to 60-hour weeks without pay. She
ran on a mixture of passion, compassion, and indignation.

"The faithful in the FLDS," she said in the summer of 2006, "just keep do-
nating money to Warren to support his life on the run. He has an extremely lavish
lifestyle—the best food, the best technology, the best of everything. The people
who believe in him are living on welfare and giving him any extra money they have
so he can live in luxury. It really makes me angry. I don't care about polygamy one
way or another, but I don't like how these people are being treated . . .

"The women are constantly told to 'keep sweet,' 'keep sweet,' 'keep sweet,' so they feel they have to be that way. I'll tell you how they 'keep sweet.' They 'keep sweet' by taking Xanax and Prozac."

She turned away no one, even if all she could offer was encouragement, but sometimes she offered much more.

One morning in early August, a tall, strapping visitor came into Elaine's office and sat down in front of her crowded desk. At the moment, she was multitasking on the phone and the Internet simultaneously: raising money, dealing with media inquiries, confirming court dates, and completing her plans to get married later in the week. As she finished up her call, the young man looked around at some photos of Warren Jeffs, at a wanted poster of the man being circulated by the FBI, and at some pamphlets on polygamy and abuse. He'd grown up in one of Colorado City's most prominent families but had left the community years ago because of conflict with his father. Now twenty-one, he lived in St. George and worked construction in the area, and had heard of the Hope Organization through his connection to the Lost Boys. His face was sunburned, his hair cropped short. His hands were huge and rough, and he had the unvarnished, rawboned look of country boys from coast to coast. He wore a white T-shirt that exposed sunburned muscles, blue jeans, and a wide black belt emblazoned with the silver silhouetted girls usually seen on the mud flaps of pickup trucks.

He was proud of certain parts of his upbringing, convinced things had been much better in town before the rise of the Jeffs clan. Although he'd left the border and the FLDS behind, he retained some of the church's attitudes toward the government. Because he'd been employed and paying taxes for several years, he felt entitled to public financial aid to further his education. He'd ventured into this office with the desire to learn how to use computers so he could get a more lucrative job. While Elaine talked on the phone, he picked up a flyer about the Hope Organization and intently studied the front and back, moving his lips as he tried to form the words into a sentence.

Hanging up, Elaine warmly welcomed him to her office. She'd been expecting him this morning and knew why he was coming to see her, but she also understood much more about his background than he realized. She knew that his father had beaten him severely when he was a youngster, which was why he'd left home early. For a few minutes, she listened to his request for money for more schooling, but she wanted to address other things first.

"You have a problem," she said, "with violence."

He shifted his long legs in front of him, one of his knees bumping against her desk.

"We need to talk about this," she said.

He fidgeted and glanced away from the woman, whose eyes were probing his face.

"Tell me about it."

"You don't . . ." His sunburned cheeks had turned redder.

"I don't what?"

"You don't know me," he stammered. "You don't know who I am. You just know the things people have said about me."

"I've read the reports on you. I know what's in there."

"But you don't know *me*." His hands had rolled into fists that he was pounding on his thighs.

"But I've—"

"All the stuff in those reports came from my wife. She just likes to talk. That's all that is. You don't know who I am."

"What I know is that you've got violence issues with women and children. I think you need an anger management class."

His lips were trembling and his gaze had fallen to the floor.

"She just likes to talk about me," he said.

Elaine nodded, wanting him to keep talking.

"My biggest problem in life," he said, "is not anger. It's school. I never finished high school. I can only read at a third-grade level. I just want to learn how to read and write and do math."

He paused and cleared his throat and said, "I just want to be able to read."

"I can help you with all that, but you need to get these other things under control."

"I'm not a bad person but—"

His voice cracked and his big hand rose to cover his face. Tears slipped through his fingers and he slumped over in the chair.

"I just don't—want to hurt—anyone."

Elaine stood and walked around the desk.

She reached down and touched his shoulder as he came up out of the chair, looming above her, his long arms dangling at his sides. She hugged him and he returned the embrace, the two of them standing together and crying in the middle of the office.

Grabbing the box of Kleenex she always kept on hand when young men or women dropped by, Elaine took one and gave him a couple, and they dabbed at their eyes. She gave him a huge smile and he returned it, nodding a thank-you. The room felt different, as if something in the air had popped open—and Elaine could now help him with his reading, writing, and math. Before leaving that morning, he agreed to attend an anger management class.

38

O N MONDAY, AUGUST 28, Elaine dropped by the small local FBI office in St. George and spoke to the special agents about the search for Warren Jeffs. Almost four months earlier, the FBI had dramatically raised the fugitive's profile by placing him on the Ten Most Wanted List, but now the effort to find him seemed limited or haphazard. Like many others, Elaine questioned the authorities' motives and didn't feel the police or the feds were doing all they could to find the Prophet. In her work with those who'd left the FLDS, she'd heard many stories and rumors about where Jeffs was and how his life on the run was being financed. She wasn't shy about sharing her feelings with law enforcement—or passing along to them what she'd been told. On this visit to the FBI office, she prodded the St. George agents to look for Jeffs in Nevada. More particularly, she said to search for him near Henderson, outside of Las Vegas, or over in Mesquite, the site of numerous FLDS construction projects that generated a lot of money. Maybe Warren was making stops at those sites for infusions of cash. The agents patiently listened to Elaine, thanked her for her input, and said goodbye.

By late August Gary Engels's frustrations were rising, too. The long summer of tension in Colorado City was coming to an end, with no break in the hostility directed at him and no hint that the feds were any closer to catching Jeffs. While Kelly Fischer had been convicted in July in the first trial in Kingman, he'd received a prison term of only 45 days—a minor deterrent for committing a crime and a bad precedent for the other seven upcoming cases. The sentence had surprised Matt Smith and upset Engels. In turn, Engels angered Fischer and his lawyer by insisting the defendant be put on a registered sex offenders list for the rest of his life.

"In my probation report on Mr. Fischer," the investigator said, "I wrote that he had no remorse and would do all this again. The defense responded by saying that Fischer didn't consider anyone his enemy, except for Mr. Engels. I'm so used to being hated by the people around here that I don't think about it anymore, but I have to be careful. After that trial, people followed me around town even more than usual, two or three cars, and one time I pinned a guy in and confronted him. I asked if he needed to speak to me and he said no."

Engels's mood didn't lighten when the subject turned to the search for Warren Jeffs. Asked if the FBI was looking hard enough for him, he responded, "If I answer that, I'll just get in trouble."

In spite of potential recent sightings of the fugitive in suburban Denver and Cedar City, the growing feeling throughout the region was that the feds weren't searching hard enough for the Prophet. Many theories about this neglect existed: The FBI was fearful that if they found him, there would be a shootout or FLDS followers would unleash a wave of violence against all of Jeffs's perceived enemies. The government didn't want to arrest him, march him into court, and give him a huge platform, through national and international media coverage of a trial, to spread his message. There was a fairly strong Mormon presence in the FBI in the Southwest and agents shied away from the FLDS issue because it spilled over onto the LDS Church in ugly ways. Besides, everyone knew that Jeffs was hiding down in Texas, so there was no reason to commit resources to looking for him in Utah, Arizona, Nevada, or other states. He'd found his new promised land and would rule from inside the ranch perimeter for years to come. The feds were fighting a massive war on terror throughout the U.S. and abroad—they could hardly be expected to focus on finding this one man. And if they weren't that concerned, why should local or regional law enforcement put out much effort trying to bring the fugitive to justice?

There was constant grumbling about this in St. George, Mesquite, Hurricane, and among the apostates in Hildale and Colorado City. In Engels's mind, only three people in the world were seriously looking for Jeffs: Sam Brower; Arizona-based FBI special agent Rob Foster, whose jurisdiction included the extremely busy Navajo Reservation; and himself.

But there were several things investigators didn't realize: the Prophet had been monitoring the hunt for himself as much as those who wanted him caught. While he'd banned TV in Colorado City, along with newspapers and magazines, he watched television programs about his status as a fugitive, read media accounts, and knew all about Gary Engels and his ongoing infiltration of the FLDS. Jeffs was aware that the authorities had taken a soft approach to finding him—they hadn't set up roadblocks around the border towns or other FLDS enclaves, hadn't gone house to house seeking him or his closest allies. After generating an initial wave of national publicity by putting him on the FBI's Ten Most Wanted List, the government's attitude had been relatively lax. They'd told everyone they were looking for him, then sat back and waited for him to surface or make a mistake. As a result of this policy, Jeffs had also grown more relaxed about being on the lam. He didn't always travel late at night, and sometimes he didn't wear a disguise, let his whiskers grow, or pull a ball cap down over his forehead. He let himself appear exactly like the man on the FBI poster.

39

A T 9:04 ON THE NIGHT OF AUGUST 28, just a few hours after Elaine Tyler had stopped by the FBI office in St. George, Nevada, state trooper Eddie Dutchover noticed the new red Cadillac Escalade going north out of Las Vegas on I-15. Because the vehicle's temporary license tag was partially obscured by a rear plate holder, Dutchover followed the car and then pulled it over to the shoulder of the road.

Glancing in the driver's window, the trooper saw a man at the wheel and another man and woman in the back seat. Sitting right behind the driver was a very lean figure whose downcast eyes caught the attention of the officer. Dutchover also spotted a Global Positioning Unit and a radar detector on the dashboard, which suggested that the trio could be involved in either money laundering or drug dealing.

"Can I see your license and registration?" he asked the driver.

With shaking hands, the man produced some curious documents. He had a Utah license identifying him as Issac Steed Jeffs, but the Escalade was registered in Iowa and had a temporary Colorado plate (the Cadillac had recently been purchased in suburban Denver and was registered to a John C. Wayman, who worked for New Era Manufacturing of Las Vegas). Issac told the patrolman that he was employed at New Era as a supervisor, and that he and his companions were on a one-week vacation; they'd gone out to San Francisco to see the ocean and were returning to Utah. The trooper took a second look at the man in the rear of the Escalade, who was poking at a fast-food salad with a plastic fork.

"What's your name?" Dutchover asked.

The answer was muffled, as the man stared straight ahead.

"Who are you?"

"It doesn't matter," the passenger replied, taking another bite.

This wasn't the response Dutchover had been expecting. Then he saw something startling: the carotid artery in the man's neck was pulsating so hard it was visible in the semidarkness of the car's interior.

"Is everything okay?" the trooper asked.

The man kept eating.

"You're making me nervous."

He shrugged and picked at the salad.

Twelve minutes had passed since the officer had stopped the Escalade. Enough had already happened to raise Dutchover's antennae. He walked over to his car and tried to run a check on the registration and license plate, but the dispatch computers were down. Under other circumstances, he might have let the minor license plate violation pass with just a warning and sent the trio on their way, but something felt wrong. He went back to the Cadillac and asked Isaac Jeffs if he was transporting weapons or drugs. The driver said no and then signed a consent form to allow a search of the vehicle, which began at 9:30 P.M. It quickly turned up letters to "the president" and "WSJ," along with a pair of envelopes crammed with hundred-dollar bills in the lining of a suitcase. The more the trooper discovered inside the car, the more suspicious he became. He called in for backup and minutes later two other patrolmen, Rosell Owens and Shawn Martin, parked on the shoulder of I-15, beside the luxury SUV.

They stepped out and helped Dutchover sort through the Cadillac's contents: some suitcases and pillows, sixteen cell phones and two iPods, nearly $60,000 in cash, a $2,000 check, ten pairs of sunglasses and eight sets of car keys, a radar detector, a Global Positioning System unit, a police scanner, four laptops, three wigs in shades of blond, black, and brown, a handful of knives, a black briefcase containing thirteen religious books, including the Bible and the Book of Mormon, a black duffle bag, a photograph of the man in the back seat and an older man who somewhat resembled him, plus debit cards totaling $10,000. The officers found a box containg CDs, a backpack, and workout weights. They found a list of addresses from the western United States, with the names of people who'd offered safe houses for the travelers to stay in. They found an envelope addressed to "President Warren Jeffs."

A couple of weeks earlier, Troopers Owens and Martin had pulled over a car holding FLDS members. Owens recognized the name on the envelope and motioned for the other officers to move away from the Cadillac; they huddled among themselves and walked back to the driver, still sitting at the wheel.

"What's the name of your passenger?" Martin said, nodding toward the man behind him.

"John Findley," Issac replied.

Owens ignored this response and asked the man himself for identification, but he refused to comply.

Martin reached into his pocket and took out an FBI business card he'd been given that afternoon. He dialed the number of the special agent on the card; then they stood around and waited. The agent quickly arrived from Las Vegas, and after briefly consulting with the other officers he approached the Cadillac.

"What's your name?" he asked the male passenger.

For the first time since the Escalade had been pulled over, the figure eating the salad looked at the person who was questioning him. His eyes were filled with quiet alarm and his neck was still pulsating. He stared at the agent, and the silence inside the car became overwhelming.

"Warren Steed Jeffs," he finally said.

As the words floated through the quiet desert night air and reached the four officers, they were met with expressions of amazement, then shock, and then smiles of congratulation. It took a few moments for the reality to settle in: Nevada law enforcement had just stumbled across and captured one of the FBI's Ten Most Wanted fugitives.

Dutchover asked Jeffs to get out of the Escalade, cuffed him, and made him stand alongside Highway 15 in the darkness as one of the others snapped his picture. Staring vacantly into the camera, he tried to maintain the calm exterior and firm posture he was known for, but he looked humbled and stunned, nothing at all like the revered and feared godlike dictator he'd become during the past decade. He wore long, baggy olive-green shorts that accentuated his pale bowed legs and a white T-shirt with a slogan on the front (he didn't allow his flock to dress in either shorts or T-shirts and had severely punished people for doing so; he'd been arrested riding in a red vehicle, a color he'd long ago banned from the FLDS; there were lottery tickets inside the Cadillac, another violation of church rules; and he'd railed against materialism, but the vehicle was filled with high-tech gadgets and money). To complete his outfit, Jeffs had on black socks and black shoes. He resembled a befuddled camp counselor or a poorly dressed tourist just awakened from a deep sleep.

With all three suspects handcuffed and under control, the arresting officers surmised that the trio had just made a one-day stop in Las Vegas to replenish their cash supply. As the patrolmen continued rummaging through the Escalade, they found a decree from Jeffs, written in near-Biblical language, ordering his followers at the safe houses not to give up any information to outsiders: "So I have to be hiding in my travels, not let anyone know. And when I come to a land of refuge, you must not reveal where I am in your phone calls and your letters."

The troopers transferred Jeffs into a patrol car and drove him to the Las Vegas county jail, where he was booked, while Issac Jeffs and the woman in the Escalade, Naomie Jeffs, were questioned and released. Later that night, Steve Martinez, the FBI special agent in charge of the region, announced the arrest and underscored that the fear of bloodshed by either Jeffs or his worshippers had been an ongoing concern for the feds. Martinez spelled out the relief all law enforcement felt after bringing the man in "without violence." So far, the special agent was also pleased to report, the ex-fugitive was being cooperative.

It didn't take long for the news to reach those who'd pursued Jeffs the longest and hardest.

Just before midnight on August 28, Sam Brower received a call from an FBI contact who'd heard about the capture at 11:23 P.M. and informed the private investigator that the Prophet had been taken into custody.

"You're shitting me!" Brower said.

"I wouldn't call you at midnight if I was shitting you."

Brower was shocked not just by the fact that Jeffs had been caught, but by where he'd been picked up.

"My first thought was: What was Warren doing in Las Vegas?" Sam later recalled. "What could he have been thinking? He was safe at the compound in Texas because the police never bothered the FLDS members in there. The FBI didn't want to invade the compound as they had at Waco and risk a disaster. Warren could have stayed there indefinitely. Then I stopped and told myself that I was looking at this like a rational person, not like Warren Jeffs. He had to keep feeding his ego and pushing the envelope by taking more and more risks."

On the night of August 28, Gary Engels was in Bullhead City awaiting the start of the Randy Barlow trial in Kingman the following day. He was excited and hopeful at the prospect of his first witness, Candi Shapley, taking the stand to testify against the defendant. Because he wanted to get plenty of sleep and be fresh for court, and because he wanted to avoid any calls from the media about the Barlow case, he'd turned off his cell phone, but a Mohave County deputy sheriff knew how to reach him at home. Engels got the call about Jeffs after midnight and initially had a subdued reaction, preoccupied with getting a conviction at the Barlow trial. At the moment, all he wanted to do was go back to bed.

At dawn on August 29, former FLDS member Sara Hammon, who'd escaped from the sect as a teenager and now worked in real estate in Mesquite, was sound asleep when her phone rang.

"This better be good," she told her girlfriend on the other end of the line.

"It is," the woman said.

"It was good!" Sara said a few weeks after the arrest. "It was very, very good."

She then phoned Elaine Tyler.

"My first thought," Elaine has said, "was hallelujah! Then it was—*Hall-e-lujah!* I wasn't planning on coming into work that day but I thought somebody better be here to handle the calls from reporters. It was flat-out crazy in the office. I had calls from all over the world."

Remembering her visit to the FBI office the day before, she was tempted to phone the agents in St. George now and remind them of what she'd told them within the past 24 hours.

"When I'd gone in to talk to them that Monday," she said, "I just felt Warren was in the area. After I heard the news, I thought about asking the FBI for that $100,000 reward."

Laura Chapman learned of the arrest on the morning of August 29 and then heard from a friend in the International Cult Studies Association. The woman told her that Laura was very fortunate because most people who'd managed to escape cults never got to see their former leader arrested or put on trial. As Laura thought about Jeffs sitting in jail in Las Vegas, she felt a special satisfaction—even joy. Warren was so used to being waited on by everyone and to giving orders, so accustomed to the good life and all the perks of power—but not anymore. "Sweet poetic justice," she told herself.

She wondered how he would adjust to life behind bars and the intimidation from other inmates sure to come his way. How would *he* deal with being despised and threatened by dangerous people? For the past few years Laura had kept a low profile, but she was now invigorated to rejoin the fight against religious and sexual abuse.

One evening a week, Elaine Tyler oversaw a dinner for a handful of the Lost Boys in St. George, but two days after the arrest she made lasagna for a much larger group of thirty. News of Jeffs's capture had brought in far more teenagers. Many inside this "*Lord of the Flies*" society, as Elaine had dubbed it, were astounded that the police had actually found the Prophet and locked him up. A few were outwardly happy about it, but a number were oddly saddened. Despite what Jeffs had done to them and their families, they still looked at him as he viewed himself—above the rules of the law—and his incarceration seemed to contradict this perception. They brought up fonder memories of Warren as a teacher and a preacher, recalling his sense of humor and his skills as a softball player. They worried that his arrest might bring harm to their parents, who remained inside the FLDS.

"We shouldn't be focused just on Warren Jeffs," one boy said after the Prophet was caught, "but on fighting religious terrorism as a whole. You can't change everything all at once. There's no fix-it pill for this problem. But what you can do is talk to the person on your right and to the person on your left and help them understand. Reach out to them, one heart and one individual at a time. We have the experience to tell them what we went though with Warren and the dangers of giving your power away to fanatical leaders who use religion to manipulate people. Just talk to them and then listen."

One Short Creek native was anything but subdued about the arrest. Local historian Ben Bistline was thrilled to learn that Jeffs was sitting in a cell in Las Vegas.

Bistline's entire life echoed the tumultuous saga of the FLDS. Ben was eighteen in 1953 when the police raided Short Creek. As one of the fortunate men who wasn't jailed or relocated, Bistline stayed behind in The Crick, got a

job in a sawmill, and was soon married. He hoped to enter into the polygamous lifestyle, but when church elders denied his request for another spouse
he became convinced that family connections were more important than
faith.

In the 1980s, he broke with the Colorado City establishment after it had
evicted his brother from his home on UEP land. Ben's children were taunted
by other kids and called names on the playground, while schoolteachers dis-
criminated against them in the classroom. Bistline's mother, Jennie Johnson
Bistline, had captured some of the early years at Short Creek in her self-
published memoir, *Jennie*, and her son would now follow in her steps. It took
Ben ten years to finish and bring out his first work, *The Polygamists: A History of
Colorado City, Arizona*, which sold five hundred handmade copies. While writing it, he and a score of others sued the FLDS and claimed ownership of the
houses they'd built in the town. A decade later, after spending nearly $1 mil-
lion on this legal battle, the group won the right to occupy their homes or ne-
gotiate a buyout with UEP trustees. Ben settled this dispute when the trust
sold him a mobile home at a bargain price and his family moved down the
road a few miles to Cane Beds. The Bistlines now lived in a rundown, isolated
spot far removed from almost every trace of civilization—but were ecstatic
to have a home of their own and to have escaped the FLDS.

On a flat stretch of high desert, Ben and his wife, Annie, settled into a
cramped single-wide trailer filled with ancient magazines, a potbellied stove
that hissed in cold weather, and pictures on the walls that were slightly askew.
In their front yard, a vegetable garden filled with corn stalks separated the
trailer from a bumpy red clay road, while stray dogs roamed around outside
and barked at every sound. Like Short Creek in the 1920s, Cane Beds was being built from scratch on the Arizona Strip by another generation of religious
renegades.

When Ben had worked in a sawmill, a wood trimmer had clipped off the
end of his right index finger, making it harder for him to type, but that hadn't
stopped him from pecking out the letters for his book. In recent years, he'd
gone blind and been forced to dictate into a computer. Then a heart attack
had slowed him down a little more, but he'd continued hammering out chapter after chapter about the FLDS, becoming its most authentic and notable
historian. In his seventies, the barrel-chested, crew-cut author spent his days
sitting in an oversized chair, attached to a breathing hose that was connected

to a small oxygen tank. As he spoke, his eyes popped open and almost seemed to be watching, but they were blank—a haunting sight.

Despite his joy upon hearing that Jeffs had been taken into custody, Bistline remained cautious about predicting that the ex-fugitive was finished as the Prophet.

"I don't think these local prosecutors will stand a chance in court against Warren," he said soon after the arrest. "He's gonna hire some of these damned high-priced lawyers out of Salt Lake City and they're gonna come down here and do a snow job on the Washington County attorneys. All we got are rookies in that courthouse. I don't know if this thing will even get to trial. Warren will probably make a deal and be out of jail in a couple of years.

"These big-city lawyers like Jeffs will hire are some of the lowest, meanest, dirtiest people on earth. If they get this girl making the allegations up there on the stand, they're gonna go into all the lewd crap that was done to her and she probably won't be able to deal with it. If she caves in or refuses to testify, they won't have any case at all. They better get that girl and hide her away and keep her there or this whole thing's gonna fall apart. Anyone who thinks convicting Warren will be easy is a damn fool."

4 0

GARY ENGELS HAD NO TIME TO CELEBRATE THE ARREST. As reports of it broke throughout the country, the investigator found himself in court for the opening of Randy Barlow's trial. With twenty-year-old Candi Shapley taking the stand to testify about being forced into a polygamous marriage at age sixteen, Engels was unusually optimistic about the prospects for a conviction. A landmark moment had arrived in the prosecution of the eight men Matt Smith had indicted in July 2005. For the first time, the prosecutor had come into court with a female witness who'd agreed to help convict one of the accused. Because of Candi's willingness to participate in the trial, the charges against Barlow had been expanded to include sexual assault.

But after being sworn in, the young woman confounded the prosecution by refusing to answer any questions. For months she'd been speaking openly about her legal situation in the press, including interviews on *Good Morning America* and CNN, yet this morning she went silent, offering no explanation for her actions. Smith was confused and Engels angry, but there was nothing they could do to force her to testify—they could only wait for her to change her mind. The case was postponed indefinitely.

The immediate speculation was that Jeffs's arrest the night before had affected Candi's choice to testify, but that was only part of the answer. Before the trial began, Shapley had written a pointed letter to Judge Steven Conn, which was later published by the *Kingman Daily Miner*. It described how she'd felt mistreated by Mohave County attorney Matt Smith and his investigative team. Over her protests the previous June, she'd been flown from Salt Lake

City to Kingman to deliver grand jury testimony—at the same time that her baby was scheduled to have brain surgery. Distracted and upset, she'd told the grand jury "whatever they wanted me to say" so she could get back to her child as soon as possible. Following her grand jury appearance, her name was released to the press, and against her wishes she was now a public figure.

"I was very harassed [by the media], thanks to Matt [Smith] and his cronies," Shapley wrote the judge.

By the time the trial started in late August, she'd decided not to cooperate at all, but hadn't bothered sharing this with the county attorney. This was a double blow to the prosecution—in the Randy Barlow case and because two of the four counts pending against Warren Jeffs in Arizona were based on what Candi had told the grand jury. Now that Jeffs was in custody, her testimony had become even more important for his future prosecution. That, too, was suddenly in jeopardy.

According to Candi's attorney, Mik Jordahl, the young woman had failed to deliver in court because she believed that Arizona's legal system had victimized her. In her letter, she took on the Mohave County authorities, but singled out Engels for her sharpest criticism.

"He said that he did not care how I felt or anyone else, that he was going to bring Warren Jeffs down," she wrote. "So this was really about Warren Jeffs. They don't care about me or me being a supposed victim."

She claimed that the prosecutors had threatened her and her parents with arrest if she didn't testify—hinting that her mother and father had told her not to open up on the witness stand out of loyalty to the Prophet.

"I certainly don't feel like I have been justly dealt with," the letter said. "I am the supposed victim. I didn't feel too bad about testifying when this began. But now I am angry. I have been treated like someone with no feelings."

Matt Smith responded to the letter by acknowledging that while aspects of Candi's circumstances could have been handled better, her accusations were exaggerated and the likely result of influence from both the FLDS and her parents. Smith still hoped she'd be available to testify against Barlow at some later date. The county attorney and the region's law enforcement establishment had been given a bitter lesson when trying to prosecute church members based on the testimony of female victims: it was a very shaky way to build criminal cases.

After Candi shut down on the stand, Judge Conn found her in contempt and ordered her held in a battered woman's shelter until she was prepared to testify, or for thirty days. She served only two weeks of the sentence and was released from the shelter at the request of Matt Smith, who'd intervened on her behalf. If Smith was polite and guarded about the debacle, Engels was not.

"Candi got on the witness stand that morning and just stopped talking," he later said. "This happened right after her mother jumped up and moved to the other side of the courtroom, so she could have direct eye contact with Candi. Her mother was now sitting on the *defendant's* side of the room, staring right at her daughter, while Candi was supposed to be testifying against Randy Barlow. We later learned that her mother had already taken her to see the defense attorneys in order to sabotage our case.

"Candi wants to blame me for everything, but I only did what any aggressive investigator would have done. Nothing more. For the first time in my career, I've been put in a position of maybe having to call my own witness a liar. I've never worked that way before and I doubt I ever will again. Candi was high-maintenance. She wore me out."

The real source of the problem, Engels was convinced, lay elsewhere. Candi's father, William Shapley, a prominent Colorado City town council member, had recently been kicked out of the FLDS because his daughter had agreed to testify against Barlow. When she refused to do so, he was reinstated into the church.

"Dealing with these people," Engels said, "is like running full-speed into a brick wall. They count on one thing—that you will get discouraged and quit, because that's what always happened in the past. Not this time. Not me. I'm not gonna quit or stop investigating them. If I can't keep giving 110 percent to this job, I should walk away from it."

Candi's collapse was devastating to law enforcement, but by the summer of 2006 she wasn't the only female witness against Jeffs. After much inner debate and hestitation, Elissa Wall had laid out for Washington County officials the details of her secret April 2001 wedding to her first cousin, Allen Steed, at the Caliente Hot Springs Motel in Nevada. She described her initiation into sex at fourteen, and how Jeffs had repeatedly encouraged her to stay in the marriage and obey her husband. Her allegations raised fundamental legal questions that had yet to be answered. Did advising a young teenage girl to enter into wedlock, sexual intercourse, and continuing submission to her husband, constitute criminal behavior? Or were Jeffs's actions protected by the First Amendment? Could his guilt be proven in these circumstances, beyond a reasonable doubt?

In April 2006, Utah authorities decided to confront these questions head-on in front of a jury, filing two accomplice-to-rape charges against the Prophet. Elissa Wall was ready to testify against Jeffs, but she still had relatives, including her mother, who were in the FLDS and had at least some ongoing loyalty to the Prophet. Law enforcement had learned a hard lesson from Candi Shapley's courtroom silence, and decided to relocate Elissa, her husband, and their new child, putting them in hiding until the Jeffs case could begin.

"I'll tell you one thing," Engels said in the early fall of 2006. "We've got Warren in custody now and he's going to court. *This* witness will not have any contact with the FLDS or anyone in Colorado City before she testifies against him at his preliminary hearing. This will not happen again and you can count on that."

With the Barlow case on hold, Smith asked Engels to go up to Las Vegas and speak with Jeffs while he was in holding. The investigator left immediately in hopes of getting to the prisoner when his arrest was fresh and he might be looking for someone to talk to. Engels planned to have a casual discussion with the Prophet and, with any luck, get him to reveal more than he'd intended.

They sat together in a small room at the jail, studying each other at close quarters, with one thing in common: both were equally curious about the person across from him. If Engels had been trying to track Jeffs's underground movements for nearly two years, the Prophet had been monitoring the investigator's actions as well, as he'd moved into Colorado City and begun gathering evidence. He'd once hoped that his followers could intimidate the man enough to drive him out of town. A few minutes in Engels's presence would have indicated to most people that that wasn't likely to happen.

For months the investigator had kept pictures of Jeffs on his office wall to remind him of the enemy's face, but now that they were in the same room together, that face wasn't quite what he'd anticipated. It was so pale, the left side slightly caved in. Jeffs's arms were pitifully thin and his body looked fragile. At six-feet-five and 150 pounds, he conjured up a scarecrow or a rotting tree.

Engels had expected a stronger presence—not this empty figure sitting in front of him. Did any of Warren's wives, Gary couldn't help wondering, find him appealing? A thousand worshippers in the FLDS ready to take up arms and kill or die for *him?* Still, Engels couldn't deny feeling a strange presence in the room.

With cuffs on his hands and shackles on his ankles, the Prophet looked both shocked and detached, almost indifferent to his arrest. Fundamentalist Mormon leaders, after all, had been getting arrested for more than a century and a half. Jeffs himself had openly talked about becoming a martyr for his faith.

He didn't have a lawyer present, and Engels hadn't reminded him of his Miranda rights. If the investigator did anything that Jeffs perceived was out of line, this could come back to haunt the legal team that hoped to convict the ex-fugitive.

"Do you know who I am?" Engels asked.

"Yes," the prisoner said, giving a trace of a smile and speaking in a flat voice. "You're Gary."

"That's right."

Engels started to say more, but checked himself, wanting the inmate to give up something about his thoughts on his arrest or his years on the run.

Jeffs held his silence and the former cop couldn't stop glancing at the man's chalky arms, certain he could wrap his thumb and index finger around the Prophet's bicep. He was just as certain that Jeffs had never done a day's worth of physical labor in his life.

Softly, and with hesitation, the prisoner said that during his time on the lam he'd watched a lot of media coverage about his case and had seen Gary talking about him on television. Because of this, he almost felt as if he knew the investigator.

Engels nodded, and was now able to identify the peculiar feeling he'd sensed upon entering the room. It wasn't so much a feeling as a lack of one. Jeffs didn't convey any emotion whatsoever: neither anger nor fear nor bitterness, neither contempt for authority nor even relief at no longer being a fugitive. He was so removed from everything that it gave the space around him a chill. It had meant nothing to him, Engels sensed, that several of those he'd thrown out of the FLDS had committed suicide or had nervous breakdowns. (Another longtime church member, Louis Barlow, had recently suffered a heart attack and died after being driven from the flock). Had Jeffs had any remorse over ripping fathers from their families and reassigning their wives and children to other men?

Looking right at the investigator, the Prophet said, "I forgive you, Gary, for what you've done to me."

Engels shifted in his chair, momentarily flustered. His cheeks, always red, had turned crimson. A dozen things flashed through his mind and rushed toward his lips. This pasty-looking man, this pathetic stick figure in cuffs and shackles, this self-proclaimed spiritual leader, was forgiving *him*—for what? Enforcing the laws of Arizona and the United States of America? Trying to protect men, women, sons, and daughters from the FLDS and its Prophet?

Engels swallowed hard.

"Geez," he said sarcastically, "thanks."

They stared at each other, Jeffs expressionless and the investigator fumbling for words.

The Prophet announced that he was "at peace" in jail, and then said he didn't want to talk anymore without an attorney by his side.

Engels thought about pressing him for more information, but stood up instead. The men exchanged goodbyes and the investigator quietly left the room, a cold, hollow feeling remaining with him.

41

WITH JEFFS FINALLY IN CUSTODY, Arizona and Utah law enforcement had to produce a legal strategy. Utah decided to try him first and a week after the arrest, on September 5, amidst great drama and media coverage, he was transported via helicopter from Las Vegas to the Purgatory Correctional Facility halfway between St. George and Hurricane. The prison lies in a wide dirt valley constantly under construction and now scorched by the late summer, high hot winds blowing down from the mesas and sweeping across the landscape. While moving Jeffs into Purgatory, the police made a huge show of force, the helicopter kicking up dust and armed guards surrounding the prison to let everyone know that security around the Prophet was ironclad and interference by his congregation or anyone else would be futile. His arrest had brought no visible reaction from the border towns; the local scuttlebutt was that since Jeffs had been able to control the community while in hiding several states away, he could easily do the same from 30 miles down the road in Purgatory. His initial stance from inside his cell was one of defiance, but that would change.

"He's still running the show from jail," Engels said, "even though he's very carefully monitored."

Jeffs first hired attorney Richard Wright of Las Vegas, who went into U.S. District Court and filed an emergency motion demanding the return of the Prophet's "sacred" papers, taken from the Escalade right after the arrest. The defense would contend that if Nevada's dispatch computers had not been down on the night of August 28, Trooper Dutchover would have briefly questioned the trio in the Cadillac and let them go. He wouldn't have taken the time to search the vehicle or find these papers, which contained marriage records, confessions, priesthood blessings, teachings, revelations, testimonies of faith, the Prophet's spiritual guidance, and tithing records. The officer wouldn't have called in the backup that led to the identification of Warren Jeffs. The computer glitch had slowed everything down and opened the door for these discoveries.

Richard Wright, known for his defense of high-profile Las Vegas clients charged with corruption or tax violation, argued that Jeffs's writings, along with information on the seized laptops and recording devices, were "privileged communication" between a spiritual leader and his congregation. As such, they were all protected under the First Amendment. So were the list of safe houses where he'd stayed and the names of those who'd offered him shelter. While the legality of the August 28 search was being fought in court, Bruce Wisan filed motions giving him access to the same materials. He was looking for correspondence between Jeffs, other suspended trustees of the UEP, and businesses on UEP property; for occupancy or property use agreements involving the Trust; and for information about current FLDS lawsuits that described the UEP's organization, structure, and ownership.

After hiring Wright out of Las Vegas, Jeffs quickly brought in two more urban attorneys: Walter Bugden and Tara Issacson of Salt Lake City. They were sophisticated, media-savvy, nattily dressed lawyers with impressive résumés. In the past half-decade, Bugden had won twenty-two of twenty-seven trials in cases ranging from rape to assault, manslaughter, forcible sexual abuse, negligent homicide, and drunk driving. Since the mid-1990s, Isaacson had won fifteen jury trials. On September 27, Jeffs made his initial and uneventful appearance with his new attorneys at the Fifth District Courthouse in downtown St. George. The prisoner wore a dark suit and tie and a white shirt, not to mention a bulletproof vest. Eight armed officers guarded Judge James Shumate's chambers, while others roamed the perimeter outside and flashed their weapons.

When not in court, Jeffs was kept in lockdown twenty-three hours a day, with an allowance for visitors for one hour three times a week; the visits would play an unexpected and important role in the evolution of the case. The Prophet's younger brother and personal secretary, Nephi Jeffs, came to see him on ten occasions and for eight of these was accompanied by FLDS security force member Lindsay Barlow. Warren was allowed to make calls to his followers, so in Colorado City they gathered around a speakerphone to conduct church services, pray with the inmate, sing hymns together, and listen to his teachings. Those who traveled to Purgatory in person took messages back to the community about how Jeffs wanted town officials to conduct their business in his absence. In mid-September, the local city council chose not to include non-FLDS members to fill open seats; it rejected two outsiders and brought in hard-line church members instead. One was Philip Barlow, who worked for Streamline Automotive, and the other was Edson Holm, Richard Holm's estranged brother and owner of a prefab home building business. Their arrival on the council meant that the FLDS would be in control of this ruling body at least through 2008. But another crisis loomed for the church.

A partial payment of $609,128 was due on FLDS property in Colorado City on October 31, with Hildale's taxes coming due a month later. Jeffs ordered the faithful not to pay any of this money to Bruce Wisan and commanded them to resist the accountant's efforts to break up the UEP trust. When asked about church real estate, they were again to "answer them nothing."

"Do not sign your name," Jeffs said in an edict from prison, "to any document for property that has already been consecrated to God."

After Wisan became aware of this directive, he sent Jeffs a personal letter in Purgatory, urging him to tell his congregation to pay the taxes and avoid the tedious and expensive door-to-door posting the CPA and Isaac Wyler had been forced to carry out the year before. The Prophet dismissed the request.

Jeffs then repeated a demand from the summer of 2000, telling parents to pull their children out of the local schools and instructing the women to teach their kids at home. Many boys and girls stopped attending classes, and the private Jeffs Academy, along with the Barlow and Holm family school buildings, now stood empty. Wives and mothers who'd already felt burdened by raising a number of small children had just been handed an added responsibility.

"If these poor women weren't confused and overworked enough," Elaine Tyler said, "they now get to run the local education system. How many of them do you think are qualified to teach American history, science, and math?"

Jeffs had taken this step in the hope of bringing less attention to the town's schools and its children, but the effect was the opposite, with the media monitoring and reporting on his every move. The FLDS church and its imprisoned leader had become not just national, but international news. As the press notoriety grew, so did the government's response to what it had tried for so long to ignore.

Nearly a decade earlier, Laura Chapman and three other women had stood in front of the state capitol building in Salt Lake City and tried to persuade Utah governor Mike Leavitt to investigate and file charges against those breaking the law in Colorado City. Their efforts were resisted, and with the rise of Warren Jeffs, conditions along the border had only grown worse. By the autumn of 2006, things had dramatically evolved. Nevada's Democratic Senator Harry Reid was a practicing mainstream Mormon and the minority leader in the U.S. Senate. Following Democratic victories in the midterm elections that November, he became the Senate majority leader, the most top-ranking position ever held by a member of the LDS Church (another Mormon, former Massachusetts governor Mitt Romney, was about to launch his run for the presidency of the United States). A few weeks after Jeffs's capture, Reid called on the U.S. Department of Justice to help prosecute polygamists who committed crimes against women and children. His letter to the Justice Department and Attorney General Alberto Gonzales read in part:

> *I write to urge that the Department of Justice provide all necessary assistance to state prosecutors in the case of polygamist sect leader Warren Steed Jeffs. More generally, the federal government should work with state officials to address the broader pattern of serious criminal conduct by all those who use multiple marriages to abuse women and children . . . In addition, I suggest that you consider the establishment of a federal task force to investigate the interstate activity of the larger polygamist community in the western United States . . . For too long, this outrageous activity has been masked in the guise of religious freedom. But child abuse and human servitude have nothing to do with religious freedom and must not be tolerated. Individuals who force minors into adult relationships and marriage must be brought to justice . . .*

Reid concluded by calling this FLDS behavior "immoral, wrong and vile."

In mid-October, as Jeffs and his lawyers got ready for the November 21 preliminary hearing, Third District Judge Denise Lindberg prepared to sign the documents privatizing UEP Trust land so that beneficiaries could begin claiming property for themselves. As those details were being worked out, it came time for David Romaine Bateman's trial in Kingman for having sex with a seventeen-year-old girl. Matt Smith used a birth certificate in his prosecution, plus documents and photos Gary Engels had gathered in his search of Bateman's Colorado City home the previous May. After only 40 minutes of deliberation, the jury handed down a conviction, the second win in a row for Smith, not including the case involving Candi Shapely. Bateman received a 9-month prison sentence, even after his wife asked the judge for leniency. That fall the third of the eight men facing charges, Donald Barlow, was acquitted when the prosecution failed to prove that the alleged crime occured in Arizona, and Mohave County subsequently dropped its case against Terry D. Barlow, who established that his marriage had taken place in Canada. Vergel Jessop received three years' probation after his conviction, so by late autumn charges were pending against three remaining defendants: Rodney Holm, Dale Barlow, and Randy Barlow. In February 2007, Candi Shapley would again fail to testify against Randy Barlow and his case would be dismissed. Six months later, Dale Barlow was sentenced to forty-five days in jail for his no-contest plea to conspiracy to commit sexual conduct with a minor. He also had to register as a sex offender for the three years of his probation. For their loyalty to Jeffs, Fred and Preston Barlow were eventually decertified as Colorado City town marshals.

Smith and Engels had scored several recent victories, and the investigator seemed more relaxed since Jeffs's arrest, more at peace with his work on the border. It was easier to put up with the frustration and abuse if he had something to look forward to, and now he did. He couldn't wait to see the Prophet in court at the preliminary hearing, facing Elissa Wall's testimony.

The inmate, on the other hand, who'd adapted rather easily to life on the run, was having difficulty adjusting to prison. For a few weeks after entering Purgatory, he'd tried to act the part of Prophet around other inmates and administrative personnel, but quickly learned that no one inside the facility had any use for his beliefs or his sense of entitlement. He hadn't developed any skills for coping in the outside world, and for the first time in his life, he was beyond the protection of his father or his church followers. His exposure was sudden and raw. He'd come into jail with a lot of publicity and notoriety, which was bad enough, but the allegations against him included participating in the rape of a teenage girl and civil charges involving sodomizing a young boy. He wasn't at risk in prison just because he was famous, but because he'd been accused of being a child molester. It wasn't just the physical challenges that were overwhelming; his sense of reality was being stripped away from him day by day.

Other inmates taunted and threatened him, mocking his role as the Prophet and letting him know that they were better at scaring people than he'd ever been. The naked harshness of prison tested everyone, and nothing had prepared Jeffs for living behind bars. In his cell, throughout the long frightening days and loud endless nights at Purgatory, he got down on the cement floor and prayed so long and hard that he developed ulcers on his knees.

42

AT THE NOVEMBER 21 PRELIMINARY HEARING, Judge Shumate would have to decide if there was enough evidence for Jeffs to stand trial for the first-degree felony of rape as an accomplice. If there was, and if the defendant was convicted, he faced a prison term of five years to life. For the event, police muscle would be on display everywhere. Two weeks earlier, the St. George bomb squad had been put on high alert, and a few days before the hearing a strange-looking item was spotted at the courthouse. It turned out to be a duffle bag crammed with construction tools, but clearly the city was maintaining the utmost caution. For the hearing itself, police would block off the street in front of the courthouse as firearms specialists patrolled the mesas that formed a ring above St. George. A SWAT team was in place outside the building, with seven armed guards stationed inside the courtroom. There were more policemen and policewomen surrounding the judge than lawyers.

Washington County was as committed to hiding the identity of its star witness, Elissa Wall, as it was to protecting the safety of the defendant. It had taken more than two years of searching, and a combination of county, state, and federal resources, plus a computer glitch and a dose of luck, to get the Prophet into custody. The authorities couldn't risk that Elissa would be discouraged from testifying by intimidation or anger at the media. The press had never been allowed to contact, describe, name, photograph, videotape, draw, or depict Elissa or any of her immediate family members. For the hearing, cell phones would be banned not just from the courtroom but the entire courthouse so that no digital pictures of her could be snapped. Judge Shumate's court was quite small, with only three rows of seats for spectators. One row had been preassigned to Jeffs's relatives and church members who'd be attending the hearing to offer support to the Prophet. Regional, national, and international media got another row to themselves, and any leftover seats were for the regular folks, all of whom needed a special pass to sit in the gallery. It would be an extremely tight fit.

The Washington County prosecutors, led by county attorney Brock Belnap, had reached out to Utah Attorney General Mark Shurtleff for help with the case. The AG's office was trying to conduct its own organized crime investigation into Jeffs and his church, while the federal government was considering an indictment on UFAP (Unlawful Flight to Avoid Prosecution) charges. In Washington County, Jeffs was not being charged with the crime of performing an underage marriage—which struck many observers as peculiar—but with being an accomplice to rape. Craig Barlow, head of Utah's children's justice division, would be assisting Belnap, but it was a tough case to make.

Jeffs's lawyers were expected to assert that under the First Amendment the defendant had the right to practice his religion, and that in giving Elissa advice on how to conduct herself both before and after marriage, he was merely doing that. Other spiritual counselors in other faiths, his attorneys would argue, had being doing the same for centuries without facing criminal accusations. Interestingly, Elissa's ex-husband, who was also unnamed, wasn't being charged with a sexual crime. This raised even more sticky legal questions. How could Jeffs be an accomplice to rape if nobody was being accused of the rape itself? The Prophet's lead attorney, Walter Bugden, had already outlined his legal strategy by claiming that the case was about nothing more than the religious persecution of his client and promising to mount a strong defense.

Summing up his own feelings about the charges, Bugden declared, "Shame on the state of Utah."

The evening before the preliminary hearing, back in Hildale, Bruce Wisan held a public meeting at City Hall for those interested in how UEP Trust assets would be parceled out to individuals and families. Because both Hildale and Colorado City officials had stonewalled his efforts to conduct a survey of UEP property—a necessary first step before it could be sold off to private parties—Wisan was going straight to the local citizens. He laid out the ongoing obstacles to getting the town's government to cooperate with him, especially with Jeffs ordering church members from jail to ignore the accountant's efforts. Information about the trust mailed out to the congregation had been thrown on the post office floor and "used as a carpet." When Wisan or Isaac Wyler had posted flyers about their work, FLDS members had torn them down. Since regular city council meetings had been canceled to avoid discussing the property survey, Wisan had been forced to find other ways to resolve the issues legally. In Arizona, Mohave County could act to get this done, but that might take another eighteen months. In Utah, Wisan would likely have to go to court and sue the local powers, stretching the process out even further. Nobody but a bulldog would have taken on such a mission, and several things about the solid-bodied, tough-looking Wisan conjured up that animal.

One purpose of the property survey was to figure out who lived where and for how long. In most towns, that would have been easy, but Jeffs had commanded the faithful to start moving from home to home in the middle of the night—men, women, and children packing up and scurrying from address to address—just to keep Wisan off balance and confused. To make things harder still, in the accountant's opinion, the town marshals weren't protecting trust property from theft and were resistant when he and his staff tried to enforce court orders.

At the November 20 City Hall meeting, Wisan and his colleague, attorney Jeffrey Shields, spelled out these problems and the mind-numbing challenge of dividing up and re-allocating around $100,000,000 worth of real estate to people who'd never owned land or homes. One highly unpopular way of distributing the assets called for those getting the deeds to hand over $20,000 to help cover administrative expenses. Many attending the event felt that they'd already paid for their land and houses through labor and donations. Ben Bistline was sharply critical of this plan and wondered if most of the money would go to pay Wisan's salary. The accountant was unmoved by such questions.

He had a surprisingly light touch, pointing out to the standing-room-only crowd that he was just a boring CPA, with no sense of humor, trying to do an impossible job in hopeless circumstances. This got a laugh from an audience filled with people who had sleepy eyes and twangy country voices, many of whom looked eerily similar to one another. A heckler in the front row kept hurling insults at the accountant, but Wisan deftly sidestepped or deflected them with a joke and a smile. He wasn't there to make things perfect—that was the Prophet's mission on earth. The CPA was just trying to make them better and to jump-start the local economy through free enterprise and commercial development on the Arizona Strip. Jeffs had refused to allow exiles to visit the Colorado City cemetery, even when their loved ones were being buried. After taking over the trust, Wisan had declared the cemetery community property and made it open to all. Most of those at City Hall understood that the CPA was offering them far more than Jeffs ever had, and were strongly behind him. The patient and intelligent design behind the approach the authorities had taken with the FLDS this time was continuing to pay off.

Polygamy, Wisan kept repeating, would not be a factor in selecting who got a home and who didn't. Like Gary Engels, the CPA hadn't come to Hildale to discuss theology or plural marriage, but to make progress toward private ownership of real estate, nothing more. Utah had used financial leverage by strong-arming the community to pay taxes and was now using it to reward those willing to defy Jeffs and make a break with church leadership. In front of this crowd, which included men in bib overalls and many women who still wore ankle-length cotton dresses and long, braided hair that hadn't been cut for decades, it wasn't a hard sell. Virtually everyone in the room had already been booted out of the FLDS and labeled an apostate for speaking with Wisan or other outside officials. Many jokingly referred to themselves as "heathen" and acted as if they no longer feared the Prophet or his minions. Their side was growing in numbers every day, while the faithful were making a gradual exodus out of town. A dozen local homes, including a mansion with twenty-three bedrooms and three kitchens, had lately been abandoned, the occupants disappearing without a trace. As soon as the houses were empty, Wisan seized control of the property, one more victory against those currently running the church.

The accountant's speech at City Hall wasn't riveting, but it represented the dismantling of a way of life in the community and spread hope of more opportunity and freedom on the Strip. And also stood for something more: it showed that there were other ways to fight tyranny and religious terrorism besides direct force. It took time to convince people that they had alternatives and could learn to act in their own self-interest instead of following orders from a dictator, but many were eventually ready to listen and change. Wisan concluded by saying that he intended to see his difficult mission through, no matter how long it took, and that he wouldn't hesitate to bring the hammer down if necessary.

In December 2006, the Hildale City Council voted to "abstain" from any action on Wisan's scheme to divide parcels of land into individual lots intended for specific families. It was the town's way of stalling the accountant, but his patience had finally run out. The following month, he went to court and sued the council to demand its approval of his plan.

43

THE PALM TREES OF ST. GEORGE occasionally look out of place hundreds of miles from a beach or an ocean, but the three small ones in front of the split-level Fifth District Courthouse were a perfect fit for Dixie's late autumn weather in November 2006. The 21st was a spectacular day in this corner of Utah, with huge open skies, light that seemed bright enough to crack open the red and orange landscape and let out more colors, and a temperature nudging toward seventy degrees. Sunshine splashed across the face of the big white "D" (for Dixie) built into the side of a mesa rising above the city and illuminated both the white cupola of the LDS temple in the heart of town and all the white buildings surrounding it. Men who greeted church members at the temple's front door—no gentiles were allowed inside—were dressed in all-white suits, white shirts, and white ties, looking like attendants at the gates of heaven.

The courthouse sat on a steep hillside just off the town's main street. Well before dawn, police cars had encircled the building and were patrolling every movement at the scene. When the hearing began at 8:30 A.M., snipers and the SWAT team were at their stations. Across the street from the courthouse were the police department, a mobile command post observing all activity, and City Hall, decorated with a large wreath for the coming holiday season. St. George is a thoroughly modern town, with countless fast-food restaurants, motels, and constant construction, but a few blocks away from the judge's chambers is a pioneer museum, where a female guide clad in nineteenth-century clothing proudly takes visitors through each room, recounting the hardships and losses of early Mormon history. She reminds listeners that six out of ten babies born in this region in the 1800s did not see their first birthday, so there had been a great need for the settlers to "be fruitful and multiply." Polygamy was in part an outgrowth of that need.

A century and a half after those pioneers, led by Brigham Young, had arrived in Utah Territory, a man was due in court this morning to face charges of forcing a community to adhere strictly to the original Mormon principles. Nine satellite news trucks ringed the courthouse, preparing to send live reports from the hearing around the nation and across the planet. The case had brought in reporters from England, Canada, and the Far East, along with a group of FLDS men who were lined up outside the courthouse before the doors opened at eight o'clock. The men moved as a pack, sticking closely together and refusing to make eye contact with strangers. They had the thick, stained hands of those who labored for a living. They had awkward postures and choppy haircuts, wore ill-fitting dark suits, cowboy boots, or heavy black shoes, and spoke to no one beyond their own tight circle. When journalists approached, they smiled nervously and said they had no opinion about anything that was taking place today in the courthouse. Their shyness and air of silent anger said they only wanted to be left alone.

In the gallery, too many spectators had shown up for the proceeding; there wasn't enough room to accommodate Jeffs's family members, the media, and those given a public pass. Nobody volunteered to leave, so a heavily armed, muscular, redheaded female guard paced up and down the courtroom studying the overflow crowd—no one was willing to meet her withering gaze. She made her decision and booted out the unfortunate few. As the Prophet came into the courtroom, his supporters stood as one in the back row, their expressions reverent, hands folded in front of their belts. Everyone else rose when the judge walked in and took his place on the bench.

Jeffs sat down beside his two lawyers, the bow-tied Walter Bugden and the tall, blonde, short-haired Tara Issacson. The defendant was even more gaunt than usual. In prison, he'd tried to maintain his vegan, no-sugar diet, but he'd clearly been losing weight. His bones were getting closer to the surface. His skin looked more pocked, his cheeks more sunken. His eyes showed no depth. Though alert, his expression remained unchanged.

After meeting the Prophet in the Las Vegas jail, Gary Engels had described him as a blank and emotionless man. This same feeling, or lack of feeling, accompanied him in the courtroom. He reacted visibly to nothing in the proceedings. If his brethren in the back row were obviously unsettled at finding themselves in these circumstances, Jeffs seemed unperturbed.

Many strands of the story had come together in this courtroom. Ross Chatwin, one of the first vocal critics of the FLDS, was present in the gallery, along with Isaac Wyler, who'd been publicly excommunicated from the faith. Neither wanted to be absent if Jeffs, who'd unsuccessfuly tried to rob them of their families and homes, was bound over for trial. To make more room for the public, Engels, Sam Brower, Roger Hoole, Jeffrey Shields, and Bruce Wisan were all seated in the empty jury box across from the defendant. They had a clear shot at eye contact with him, but he'd refuse to accommodate any of them.

If each of these five men was eager to see Warren convicted, not everyone had exactly the same rooting interest. Wisan and Shields had come to watch Elissa's testimony and evaluate her strength as a witness. Before going to the authorities with her information about Jeffs, she'd spoken with Brower and attorney Joanne Suder about taking civil action against the Prophet, his church, and the UEP Trust. In December 2005, she'd filed suit against Jeffs for forcing her into marriage. If she successfully sued him following a criminal trial and received major damages from the trust, and if others filed similar suits and won, Wisan was worried that this could bankrupt the entity he was now in charge of. He wanted to see Jeffs in prison, but also to protect and redistribute the church's assets.

Brower, on the other hand, had been a driving force behind the criminal investigation, the FBI involvement in the hunt for the defendant, *and* the lawsuits filed by the Lost Boys, Brent Jeffs, and Elissa Wall. As the man in the middle of everything during the past three years, he had the broadest perspective of anyone involved in the case.

"Since I started working on all this," he said just before the hearing began, "I've seen a lot of things change. Colorado City has gone from being totally paranoid and freaky and stuck—with nothing being done to help these people—to eight indictments, three civil suits, Warren's arrest, a much improved school system, the possible decertifying of two local police officers and maybe more in the future, a far better tax situation, and the taking away of UEP property from Jeffs. Getting that away from him was one of our major goals."

Sam liked to tell a story about being in college in California, living in a bad neighborhood, and owning a couple of nasty-looking Dobermans who protected his home while he was at school. He said that occasionally, after coming back from classes or a night on the town, he'd notice that some things inside his living quarters had been tampered with, or he'd find torn pieces of clothing scattered about. He never knew exactly what went on there when he was gone, but imagined that somebody had tried to rob him and the Dobermans had gotten the best of the intruder. His possessions were never stolen.

"I think about those of us who got involved with the FLDS during the past few years," he said, "the same way I used to think about those dogs. We can't know what would have happened to the people of Colorado City if we hadn't tried to help them. You don't hear about crimes that got prevented, or bad things that never came about. But I believe we made a difference."

Other victories against the FLDS now seemed possible. Emboldened by Jeffs's imprisonment, several Lost Boys had decided to step forward and bring more attention to their ongoing problems. In January 2007, a group of teenagers who'd been kicked out of the FLDS would travel from St. George up to Salt Lake City's State Capitol complex to share their experience with lawmakers and to ask for funds for housing, food, and clothing for themselves and others in their position.

Washington County attorney Brock Belnap and deputy attorney Ryan Shaum had accumulated more than one thousand documents to support their charges, but the key issue today would not be evidence outlined on paper. Jeffs's legal fate revolved around what three sisters had to say about his actions during the past 30 years—and the emotional power of their memories. Many things made this case unusual, and one was that the state was presenting virtually no direct evidence of criminal behavior against the defendant. The questions in play were far more abstract. Was it a crime to encourage a girl to wed and have sex with someone else at age fourteen—a first cousin, in her case? Was it a crime to tell her to stay in a bad marriage? Had Jeffs committed a felony by persuading a young woman to go along with the decades-old tradition of his religion and culture?

Two of Elissa's older sisters, Teresa and Rebecca, testified first. Each had attended Alta Academy and spoke about Jeffs's insistence on female obedience and about how girls were separated from boys at the school and kept ignorant about all aspects of intimacy. As soon as they were married, their husbands would become their sexual guides and teachers. Rebecca had sewn the lace on Elissa's wedding dress the night before she married Allen in Caliente Hot Springs; the young bride had been with her other sibling in Canada in 2003 when she miscarried for the second time. Both sisters were attractive and articulate, with stylish hair and fashionable clothes, and both had an edge of defiance running just beneath their words. As they paved the way for Elissa's testimony, the FLDS men sat quietly in the rear and stared at the Prophet or uncomfortably at the floor. This clearly wasn't how young women inside their community had been raised to dress or behave. The men shifted on the long wooden bench and exchanged nervous glances. Their enemies were not just apostates or gentiles or those who ran the official LDS Church up in Salt Lake City, but also included the females brought up inside their own religion who'd rebelled beyond anything seen in the FLDS past.

The women on the witness stand had clearly and dramatically changed, not just in their appearance, but in the conviction that they could publicly speak their truth and expose what had been forced on them when they were young. They didn't have to keep sweet any longer. The strength of this realization came through in their body language, their responses when testifying, and the quiet confidence they demonstrated when being cross-examined. A restrained but emphatic revolution was on display in court this morning, and, watching it unfold, the men in the back looked increasingly miserable.

Sara Hammon wasn't sitting in the courtroom itself, but in the room just behind the gallery, which had a glass wall that faced onto the proceedings. She'd driven the forty miles from Mesquite to hear the testimony and show her support for the witnesses and the prosecution. A few weeks prior to Jeffs's capture, Sara had been asked to compare the defendant to earlier church leaders in the border towns when she was growing up there.

"Warren hasn't done anything others before him haven't done," she said, "but he's taken all of it to another level. Before my family left Colorado City and moved to Centennial Park, my father was next in line to be the Prophet and he was a pedophile. No different from Warren. At seventy, my father married a seventeen-year-old. No different from what we're seeing today. It's all about a feeling of being all-powerful, but deep down these are little boys who're scared as hell. They're afraid and they can't deal with that feeling and with their own sense of powerlessness."

Elaine Tyler was in the gallery, unable to stay away from the hearing. She was cautiously optimistic, but not yet ready to celebrate.

"I'll be really happy," she said, "when Warren gets convicted. All this could fall apart when Elissa takes the stand. She's under extreme pressure today, and if she doesn't come through for the prosecution, what are we gonna do? This is our one shot to get Warren and it's gotta work."

44

ELISSA ENTERED THE COURTROOM glowing and swollen with life, due to give birth to her second child soon. With flushed pink cheeks and blonde hair tumbling down to her shoulders, she looked robustly healthy, her appearance causing a stir in the gallery. For months close followers of the case had been trying to guess who she was, but most had been wrong. Months earlier, the state had moved her to an undisclosed location, far away from the FLDS, where no one could tamper with her or her testimony. As the men in the back row stoically watched her vow to tell nothing but the truth, they shifted on the bench and shuffled their feet in anticipation or concern.

When Elissa described her childhood and attending Alta Academy, her composure was intact and her voice remained strong. She explained how in her fourteenth year her mother and father were separated, and she'd been sent to live with Fred Jessop in Hildale. As she began talking about Allen, her bullying first cousin, her face turned red, her shoulders began to tremble, and she tried not to cry. She described her shock at learning that Allen had been selected as her husband and that they were getting married in just a few days. When she told of begging "Uncle Fred" and then Warren not to force her into marrying her cousin, she no longer sounded like a pregnant woman testifying before a judge. Half a dozen years had fallen away, she was fourteen again, and it was the spring of 2001. Her face and words became childlike— she was an overwhelmed and terrified girl. Her voice broke, her upper body swaying and heaving in the witness box, the feelings too raw to be contained. She grabbed for some Kleenex and burst into tears, everything about her making the point that while events come and go, eventually fading into the past, the emotions surrounding them live on beneath the surface until they are encouraged to explode. She hadn't intended to fall apart today, but there was no stopping it now.

Because Elissa had earlier contacted attoneys about a civil case against Jeffs and his church, she was certain to be attacked by Warren's lawyers for going after cash from the Prophet and the FLDS. Prior to her filing a criminal case, Greg and Roger Hoole, the brothers and attorneys from Salt Lake City, had begun exploring a civil suit against Jeffs and the FLDS on Elissa's behalf. She'd also made contact with Baltimore lawyer Joanne Suder, discussing with her the option of suing the Prophet for damages. Greg Hoole would eventually represent Elissa in the civil action against Jeffs and the church. In her proposed settlement with the FLDS, she'd ask for eight building lots in the border towns, four acres in Hildale's Maxwell Canyon, and a $1 million education/assistance fund for displaced teenagers. The lawsuit, Hoole said, was meant to help anyone "trapped in that community to get out."

Financial concerns were part of Elissa's overall legal strategy, but her demeanor this morning went beyond money. As she gave the details of her marriage and sexual initiation with Allen, along with her repeated failed efforts to get help from the defendant, she gave in to more eruptions of sobbing, leaving the gallery encased in silence. It was almost too painful to watch. In time, veteran reporters quit taking notes on her testimony and just listened. The men in the back row had long ago ceased looking at the witness and were leaning forward, elbows on thighs, studying their watches or the walls or their shoes. Jeffs himself never removed his eyes from the young woman on the stand, as if he still believed he could make her quiet or calm her down with the force of his presence. His face carried the same hint of surprise that he'd shown Elissa when she'd first come to him and pleaded with him not to make her marry Allen. He simply couldn't grasp why any young female would feel this way or be so defiant.

Five years later, her hurt and rage had lost none of their sting. They echoed throughout the courtroom, were captured on audiotape, and later played for the nation and the world on CNN. Viewers were used to seeing disturbing pictures of wounded or dead victims of religious or political warfare, but Elissa represented the emotional cost of absolutist thinking, and her cries were just as haunting. Laura Chapman had once said that being sexually molested by her father was "soul murder," and the residue of that pain was lodged in her eyes nearly four decades later. Elissa's outbursts touched the soul as well, but conveyed that change was in the wind everywhere and that those who resisted it the most or refused to adapt were going to feel its wrath.

Before she could finish testifying, Judge Shumate broke for lunch and spectators filed out of the courtroom shaking their heads or giving little shudders. Outside, standing in the clean November sunlight in a dapper gray suit, Gary Engels beamed. He seemed positively joyful about Elissa's testimony and what she was revealing in the courtroom. As he walked jauntily down the sidewalk toward a restaurant, his stride was so effortless that it looked as if he'd never been injured. Grabbing an acquaintaince by the arm, he said, *"Now* you see what this case is all about."

The hearing did not conclude that afternoon; for scheduling reasons it could not resume until December 14, when everybody assembled again to hear the rest of the testimony. In his closing argument, Washington County deputy attorney Ryan Shaum said that because Jeffs was Elissa's former school principal and religious leader, he'd occupied a special position of trust. He'd violated that trust by using psychological and theological pressure to coerce her to obey.

"She was fighting it tooth and nail," Shaum told Judge Shumate, "right up to the marriage ceremony . . . He broke her will down, broke her options down, let her know this was the only way she was going to get to heaven. The only person who could get [Elissa] into this relationship, and that includes a sexual relationship, is that man, Mr. Warren Jeffs."

Walter Bugden countered that if someone doesn't tell a bishop, priest, or rabbi about a problem, "the religious leader can't be held responsible." Elissa had never explicitly told Jeffs that she was being forced to have sexual intercourse against her will. The defendant had merely offered her "generic religious" counsel on marriage. None of that made him an accomplice to rape. Because the judge had no specific proof that Jeffs was aware of Elissa having nonconsensual sex, and because no one was being charged with the rape of the witness, no violation of the law had taken place.

"A person who does not know a crime is occurring," Bugden said, "can't be held liable for it. It doesn't matter if I was encouraging someone to do something if a crime doesn't happen."

He added that in 1998 during a convention in Salt Lake City, the Southern Baptists had adopted the belief that wives were to submit themselves willingly and graciously to their husbands. Wasn't Jeffs merely doing the same thing? And hadn't his quote to Elissa at her wedding about multiplying and replenishing the earth come straight from Genesis in the Bible?

"As some people would say," Bugden concluded, "it's a blessing to have children. A reference in a marriage ceremony to that is not a command to have sexual intercourse tonight or within a month."

To the surprise of no one, Judge Shumate firmly sided with the prosecution.

"To say her [Elissa's] agreement was reluctant," the judge said, "this court finds is very clear."

Even though the girl had never used the term "sexual intercourse" in her discussions with Jeffs, it wasn't a "hard leap" to understand that she was talking about consummating her marriage with Allen. After the wedding, she'd clearly expressed "disdain, reluctance, and opposition" to marital relations with her husband, but the defendant had sent the teenager back home for just this purpose.

With little fanfare, Judge Shumate bound Jeffs over for trial on two counts of accomplice to rape, while setting a court date for late April 2007.

Bugden aggressively took issue with the judge's ruling and later reiterated what he'd been saying since early fall: his client's First Amendment rights were being trampled on by Utah's legal system, and this case was about nothing but the religious persecution of Warren Jeffs.

Both sides began preparing their witnesses. Come spring in Dixie, the lines had been drawn for a classic courtroom battle in St. George. Elissa and others would try to convince a jury that she'd been the victim of a serious crime perpetrated by her faith, her community, and her spiritual leader. Jeffs's attorneys would counter that under the Constitution of the United States—a nation that the accused man had never recognized as having any authority over his religion or congregation—he could not be an accomplice to rape. Because of the governing principle of the separation of church and state, he was innocent of the charges. Like many others who'd scoffed at the American legal system, the Prophet suddenly found himself in an entirely different position. For decades, the FLDS had mocked the country's version of law and order, but Jeffs was now counting on some gifted attorneys, due process, the nation's founding ideals, and the Bill of Rights to keep him out of prison for the rest of his life.

Following the preliminary hearing, two female spectators were heard commenting about this near the courthouse.

"First you bleed the beast," one said, "until you need the beast."

Jury selection was set for Monday, April 23, and for months it seemed that this date would hold up, but nothing would be that predictable. Since taking over as the head of Alta Academy in the 1970s, Jeffs had wielded power by keeping everyone off-balance and uncertain of his next move. He'd now try the same strategy with Judge Shumate and Utah's legal system.

V

FALLEN PROPHET

45

FOR YEARS, Jeffs had predicted to the faithful that he might end up a
martyr in the tradition of Joseph Smith, who'd been murdered in
prison in 1844. While some ex-FLDS members had dismissed this
notion as grandstanding or a plea for more support, with his incarceration
the situation had changed. Jeffs held up fairly well during his first months in
jail, but the longer he'd stayed behind bars, the more he'd begun to deteriorate
mentally and physically.

In Purgatory, the Prophet was threatened with violence and other inmates
let him know he was a target for sexual assault. He was afraid to eat the institution's food, because it could be poisoned or contaminated. Rumors flour-
ished inside the walls that men with AIDS liked to spit into other people's
meals and spread the disease. Instead of taking that chance, Warren began to
fast. His rail-thin 150-pound body dropped to 130. He was afraid to take
showers for fear of rape, and was occasionally kept in a holding cell near the
booking desk, a center of intense activity. The constant noise and the lights,
which were never turned off, made it difficult for him to sleep. His insomnia,
coupled with shredded nerves and lack of nourishment, gradually broke him
down. There was no place to hide in Purgatory, no escape except in prayer.
His goal had always been to control his environment and those within it, but
now it was all he could do to attempt to control himself.

"I don't think Warren is faking his problems in jail," Gary Engels said a
few months after the preliminary hearing. "He was used to having all the attention in the world—with fathers throwing their daughters at him and giving him more money than he knew what to do with. He was used to giving

orders and delivering commands. People worshipped him, but now he's locked in a cell twenty-three hours a day. Everything he does, except when he talks to his lawyers, is monitored. He knows what it feels like to be trapped."

The entrapment went beyond his current incarceration. If he managed to beat the charges in Washington County, he'd likely face another trial for similar offenses in Arizona, plus a federal count for being a fugitive, plus an ongoing corruption probe into the FLDS by the Utah Attorney General's office. Whatever happened to him legally in St. George, his prospects for freedom looked slim.

"I've heard," Ben Bistline said in the winter of 2007, "that Warren has cried out to God for help, and maybe he's gotten some. Maybe he's been told to repent for what he's done to the families of Short Creek, and maybe this is really affecting him. I've heard he's falling apart. There's a history of mental illness on Warren's mother's side, so this isn't really surprising."

As a teenager, Joseph Smith claimed that angels appeared before him and gave him guidance for how to write the Book of Mormon and launch a new faith. In jail, Jeffs believed he was having his own divine visitations, from God. Whatever took place on those long nights of praying on his hard cell floor, they produced a set of revelations and feelings no one could have predicted.

On January 24, 2007, Jeffs shocked members of his congregation by telling them via the jail telephone that the Lord considered him a "wicked man" for immoral acts he'd committed in his youth with a sister and a daughter. He didn't describe these acts or identify the victims, but said that because of what he'd done since age twenty he hadn't held the priesthood inside the FLDS. If he didn't hold the priesthood, he couldn't be the Prophet. He was a false and illegitimate leader.

The following day, his brother, Nephi Jeffs, came to see him and spoke with Warren on the prison phone, their interaction videotaped by jail officials. By now, the inmate looked even thinner than usual and more haggard. He'd been fasting for days and hadn't slept the night before. He talked very slowly to his brother and was under severe emotional strain. After instructing Nephi to take notes, he began to dictate more confessions, blinking and swaying and struggling just to hold himself upright. For long stretches, he said nothing or silently mouthed words into the receiver or paused to stifle his tears.

"I am not the Prophet," he told Nephi. "I never was the Prophet and I have been deceived by the powers of evil. Brother William E. Jessop [another FLDS member in good standing] has been the Prophet since Father's passing. . . . I have been the most wicked man . . . in the eyes of God. In taking charge of my father's family, when the Lord, his God, told him not to because he could not hear him, could not hear His voice, because I did not hold the priesthood.

"And I direct my former family to look to Brother William E. Jessop and I will not be calling [the congregation] today or ever again. . . . As far as I possibly can be, I am sorry from the bottom of my heart. And write this. The Lord, God of Heaven, came to my prison cell two days ago to test and detect me and He saw that I would rather defy Him than obey Him because of the weaknesses of my flesh. I am hesitating while I'm giving this message, as the Lord dictates these words to my mind and heart.

"The Lord whispers to me to have you, Nephi, send this message everywhere you can among the priesthood people and get a copy of this video, letting anyone see it who desires to see it. They will see that I voice these words myself. . . . I yearn for everyone's forgiveness for my aspiring and selfish way of life, in deceiving the elect, breaking the new and everlasting covenant, and being the most wicked man on the face of the Earth."

After stating again that God had come to him, Jeffs said, "He spoke to me, without the powers of evil interfering, so that I could have this opportunity to undo what I have done. And I ask for everyone's forgiveness and say farewell forever to you who are worthy for Zion, for I will not be there."

Then the tears overwhelmed him.

"Yes, you will," Nephi told him. "This is just a test."

"The Lord wants me to . . ." He was unable to finish the sentence.

When he could speak again, he said that he'd "finally shed a tear for the Lord, his God, who has redeemed His son. . . . You can tell He's still dictating to me to tell you, Nephi, before he leaves me to my punishment."

Let everyone see this video, he ordered Nephi, "even apostates and gentiles that they may know that I have been a liar and the truth is not in me. Tell the family I will not be calling anymore, not even today. Thank you."

"We love you," Nephi said. "This is a test. You are the Prophet."

"I say farewell again to all who qualify for Zion. Farewell."

Warren hung up the phone, stood, and motioned to the prison guard that he was ready to return to his cell.

Nephi watched him go and said, "We love you. We love you."

Staring at where his brother had just been sitting, Nephi also began to cry. After putting away his pen and notebook, he got up and leaned against the wall, folding his hands in front of him as if praying.

Three days later, on January 28, Warren tried to hang himself in his cell using his prison clothes. The attempt failed. Surrounded by a SWAT team, he was immediately transported to the Dixie Regional Medical Center, where he was evaluated, driven back to the jail, and placed on suicide watch. Purgatory officials brought in psychiatric consultants to meet with him and calm him down, but he remained overwhelmingly distraught. On January 30, Jeffs began throwing his body against the walls of his cell in order to exact blood atonement on himself for his sins, and end his life. The prison staff now placed him on tranquilizers. A few days after that, he was found banging his head on the wall again, in what a prison psychiatrist called a "cry for help."

As he was disintegrating inside Purgatory, he was becoming a punch line to people on the outside. During the winter, the experimental band Kinkzoid put together a musical parody using an audio clip of his teachings at Alta Academy. The song, broadcast on the Internet, was called "Warren Jeffs Explains" and recorded his hypnotic preaching voice over a bluesy 4/4 beat. The tune featured Jeffs delivering a racist and homophobic rant, asserting that rock music will "rot the soul."

On February 9, about two weeks after the suicide attempts, prosecution and defense lawyers held a conference call with Judge Shumate concerning the inmate's condition, but the transcript of the hearing was kept under seal.

Jeffs's attorneys were carefully monitoring their client and ramping up their defense. First, they contended in a motion that all the materials retrieved from the Cadillac Escalade following the arrest should be thrown out because Trooper Eddie Dutchover had filed a written report stating that the vehicle had displayed no visible license. The temporary license had, in fact, only been partially obscured.

"Upon observing the validity of the tag," the defense motion read, "the justification for stopping the vehicle was satisfied and the occupants should have been free to go."

Jeffs's lawyers then asked the judge to dismiss the accomplice-to-rape charge because it was too vague. Further, they hired Utah pollster Dan Jones to survey two hundred residents in Washington, Iron, and Salt Lake counties (home to Salt Lake City), regarding their views of the defendant. According to the defense, Jones's poll had found "demonstrable prejudice" against Jeffs in Washington County, home to St. George and the site of the trial. Although no crime was specified in the survey, 52 percent of those contacted in Washington County believed the defendant was "definitely guilty," while another 23 percent said he was "probably guilty." In Salt Lake County, only 39 percent felt Jeffs was "definitely guilty." Because of this, the defense asked the judge to move the trial 270 miles north to Salt Lake City.

In the last week of March, Jeffs made his first public appearance before Judge Shumate since mid-December. No reporters and only a few law enforcement personnel had seen him during the past 3 months. When he entered the courtroom and sat down beside Walter Bugden, Tara Issacson, and Las Vegas attorney Richard Wright, people in the gallery were stunned. He appeared feeble, almost unable to stand. He couldn't stay awake during the proceedings, nodding off and drooling on himself. Sixteen of his supporters had once again made the journey from Colorado City to St. George, but he gave them only a brief smile before ignoring them for the rest of hearing. One thing was clear: he wasn't faking his frailty. He was again on the verge of collapse.

Toward the end of the hearing, Judge Shumate made two rulings against the defense, refusing to dismiss the accomplice-to-rape charge and deciding to keep the trial in St. George (he'd later rule on the materials found in the Escalade). As court was about to be adjourned for the day, Jeffs suddenly rose from his chair and asked the judge if he could approach the bench to take care of "one matter." Before lurching toward Shumate, he struggled to rip a sheet of paper from his notepad. The gallery watched in disbelief.

Sam Brower was sitting close to the defense table.

"I was only seven or eight feet away from Warren," he says, "and I can tell you one thing: his lawyers had absolutely no idea he was going to do this. They looked up at him in horror. My own thought was, What the hell is he doing? As Warren tried to tear off the paper, Walter Bugden started rearranging things on his desk. Jeffs's hands were shaking so hard he couldn't rip the page off. The other attorney, Richard Wright, helped him with this and then Bugden grabbed it from both of them before anything else could happen."

The paper had some words scribbled across it.

Judge Shumate, who was also taken aback, refused to accept the page from the defendant, telling him to discuss the matter with his attorneys. The judge quickly departed the bench, Jeffs was hustled away by officers, and the courtroom was cleared. Jeffs then asked a bailiff if he could hold a news conference to read his note to the media. The bailiff relayed the request to Mary Reap, the Washington County Sherrif's Office corrections chief, who turned it down, but his message would get revealed anyway.

In the chaotic moments when Jeffs was addressing the judge, a photographer for the *Deseret Morning News* had snapped a photo of the piece of paper. With editing software and digital enhancement, the *News* was able to make out two sentences that Jeffs had apparently written.

"I haven't been a Prophet," they read. "I'm not the Prophet."

When these words became public, stories began filtering out of Purgatory about Jeffs's January confessions. After FLDS members living at the YFZ Ranch in Texas learned of this, they were so deflated by Jeffs's admission that for two days they turned out all the lights at the compound as a kind of mourning.

These two revelations—one from Warren in prison, the other in court—threatened to knock the case sideways. They raised complex questions that could affect nearly every aspect of the trial, if there was still going to be one. If Jeffs wasn't the Prophet, could his legal defense be built around the theme of religious freedom? If he didn't occupy a special position inside his church, could his lawyers continue to argue that their client's actions were protected under the First Amendment? Was Jeffs creating a pattern of erratic behavior, in jail and in front of the judge, in order to prepare for an insanity defense or a claim that he was incompetent to stand trial? Or was he truly falling apart?

Sam Brower had no doubt that Jeffs was not feigning his condition as part of a legal strategy: "When Warren came to court in March, he looked like he had one foot in the grave."

Judge Shumate scheduled no courtroom proceedings after the March hearing, a common practice when a defendant is seeking to establish mental incompetence so that he can't go to trial. Lloyd Hammon Barlow, part of the vast Barlow clan and a licensed family practitioner and surgeon with a degree from the University of Utah, was Jeffs's personal physician and had met with him at least ten times subsequent to his breakdown, but it wasn't clear what Barlow had treated him for. Following Jeffs's bizarre actions at the hearing,

Warren Jeffs immediately following his arrest just outside Las Vegas in August 2006. The new Cadillac Escalade he was riding in had been pulled over for having an obscured temporary license plate. After months on the run, Jeffs was no longer wearing a disguise. *Photo courtesy of the Nevada State Highway Patrol*

The twin towns nestled against the mesas. *Stephen Singular*

In July 1953, Arizona governor J. Howard Pyle ordered an early morning raid on the polygamous community of Short Creek. Many fathers, including Fred Jessop, whose chair is empty at this table, were taken off to jail. *Getty Images*

Both at the pulpit and as an instructor at Alta Academy, Warren Jeffs insisted that young FLDS girls have nothing to do with boys and treat them "like snakes." *Getty Images*

The family of Rulon Allred, photographed in 1944. In the 1970s, he was murdered by a rival polygamist leader in a dispute over Mormon doctrine. *Getty Images*

A prominent businessman and FLDS leader, Richard Holm was banished from the church and community by Warren Jeffs in 2003. Some of his wives and children were "reassigned" to his brother. *Getty Images*

The FLDS temple in the border towns of Hildale, Utah, and Colorado City, Arizona. In 2004, Warren Jeffs declared the congregation unfit to attend the church and ordered it closed. *Getty Images*

Mojave County criminal investigator Gary Engels attends Warren Jeffs's preliminary hearing in St. George, Utah, in November 2006. *Stephen Singular*

Private investigator Sam Brower was instrumental in the criminal and civil prosecution of Warren Jeffs and in the hunt for him when he was a fugitive. *Stephen Singular*

Salt Lake City certified public accountant Bruce Wisan took over the FLDS trust and property when Warren Jeffs refused to respond to civil suits filed against him and the church. *Stephen Singular*

After taking over as leader of the FLDS in 2002, Warren Jeffs ordered some of his followers to Eldorado, Texas, to establish a new religious compound and build this limestone temple. *Deseret Morning News*

Following the 2005 takeover of FLDS assets by a court-appointed CPA, Isaac Wyler went from house to house in the border towns posting tax notices. Sometimes he needed police protection for his safety. *Getty Images*

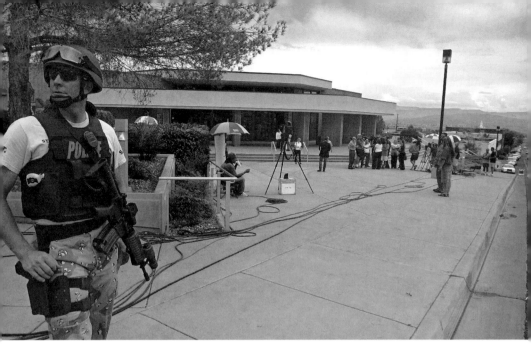

Security was extremely tight at Warren Jeffs's first appearance in a St. George, Utah, courtroom. SWAT teams would remain on hand throughout the duration of his trial. *Getty Images*

At age fourteen, Elissa Wall was forced into marriage with her first cousin, Allen Steed. She became the first person ever to bring criminal charges against Warren Jeffs. *Photo released by her attorney*

Elissa Wall at Warren Jeffs's 2007 trial in St. George, Utah. She was the principal witness against him after the state had charged him with two counts of accomplice to rape. *Deseret Morning News*

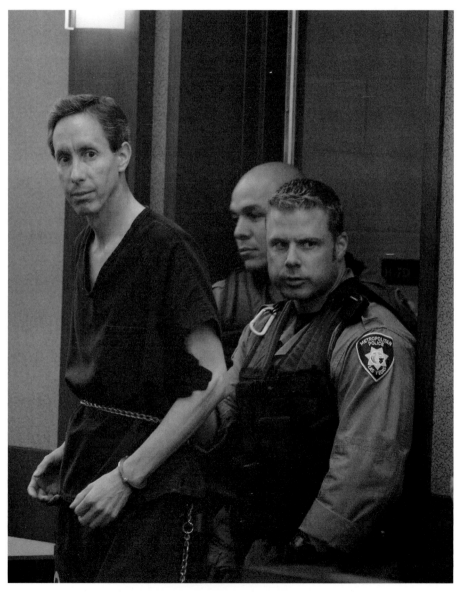

Warren Jeffs occasionally fasted in jail after his arrest in August 2006, losing significant amounts of weight. His physical and mental condition created delays in starting the trial. *Getty Images*

Judge Shumate ordered him to meet with a clinical social worker, Eric Nielsen, a registered agent for Associated Behavior Consultants, a mental health firm in Holladay, Utah. In mid-April, Nielsen delivered a sealed report to the judge on whether the inmate was fit to stand trial, and the media pushed hard to make these findings public.

They weren't alone in their convictions. Both Brower and Engels felt very strongly that everything about Jeffs's courtroom maneuverings should be made available to the outside world.

"Under the Sixth Amendment," Sam said, "legal proceedings are supposed to be public. This thing is being wrapped in secrecy and I don't know why."

"The media," Engels said, "has been great at keeping pressure on the legal system to do the right things in this case and to get the motions unsealed. I never, ever thought I'd say that about the press."

Most of Nielsen's report was eventually released. He'd informed Judge Shumate that Jeffs was not mentally incapacitated but was suffering from depression; he seemed quite aware of both his legal circumstances and his courtroom options as the case had moved forward. According to Nielsen, Jeffs had been very guarded with him, as if concerned about revealing something that might harm him. After receiving this report, the judge ruled that the defendant was competent to stand trial and pronounced him "absolutely healthy." Judge Shumate set early September as the new date for the start of jury selection.

The winter had indeed been filled with unpredictable events, at Purgatory and in the border towns, where respect for Jeffs was crumbling.

46

WITH THEIR LEADER IN JAIL and news of his confession to
Nephi spreading throughout the FLDS, the twin communities
were changing in ways that the authorities could have only
hoped for. In the past three years, they hadn't singled out Colorado City and
Hildale for special prosecution, but merely attempted to enforce the laws
against child abuse and underage marriage that applied to the rest of the
country. It had taken time to catch Jeffs and more time for their legal and financial strategy to start working, but gradually the plan had brought results.
Those results produced more results, and small victories were now cropping
up on every street corner.

Loyal church members had started extending greetings to the "apostates"
whom Jeffs had banished; they even invited them over for a bite to eat. More
children were seen outside playing in their yards and more adults were taking
walks or strolling to the general store. Boys wore shorts and T-shirts while listening to music on headsets, no longer afraid of being hounded by the police
or thrown out of their homes. The sound of barking dogs echoed around
town once again, and local officials would restock the empty zoo with animals. Mark Shurtleff, Terry Goddard, and Gary Engels would all claim that
since Jeffs's incarceration, underage marriages had virtually stopped inside the
FLDS.

Windows blackened since 2002 by heavy drapes, blinds, or cardboard were
being opened to let in the sunlight. Citizens read newspapers and magazines
for the first time in the new millennium, and satellite dishes appeared on a
few homes. In 2005 and 2006, when Isaac Wyler had posted delinquent tax

notices on houses, he'd heard Jeffs's taped sermons on obedience coming from inside nearly every home. By spring 2007, Wyler was picking up the sounds of previously forbidden classical music from several residences, while others played tapes made by Wendell Nielson. Nobody was listening to Jeffs. Nielson ran New Era Manufacturing in Las Vegas, and rumors were spreading that he was replacing Warren as the next church leader. Nielson's picture had begun showing up on the mantels of homes of the faithful, where photos of Jeffs and his father once stood.

That April, Nielsen was spotted in the border towns, dressed in a suit and tie, conducting meetings with leaders in a warehouse and behaving like the new Prophet in everything but name. A pattern established within the FLDS nearly a decade earlier was being reenacted, but with a new twist. In the late 1990s, when Rulon Jeffs had become too ill to run the church, Warren had stepped in for his father, wielding power and making the day-to-day decisions. Now that Jeffs was in jail and his mental health had been called into question, Nielsen was taking over his role. To historian Ben Bistline, this was definitely progress. He felt that Nielsen would be a far more reasonable leader than Jeffs; Nielsen was already encouraging townspeople to let their banned children return home. After years of paranoia and living with a siege mentality, the community was starting to relax. Seven hundred people had come out on Easter 2007 to celebrate together in Colorado City and Hildale, something that hadn't happened since the turn of the century.

"I'm looking for good times ahead," Bistline said.

At the edge of town, a group of polygamous women from Centennial Park had opened a new restaurant called The Merry Wives and were applying for a wine and beer license. Not everyone was happy about these developments, and more hard-core church members, known as "Warrenites," had begun migrating down to Texas, setting up another FLDS outpost near the Panhandle town of Lockney to accompany the one in Eldorado. Those who clung to the hope that Jeffs would get out of prison and return as their leader diligently wrote letters to the inmate from Texas, seeking his advice on spiritual and practical matters.

Border residents were also much friendlier to the men they'd earlier intimidated: Bruce Wisan, Richard Holm, and Isaac Wyler. Hildale and Colorado City officials were at last meeting with the accountant to help him complete a property survey, so Wisan could hand out deeds to new homeowners. Holm and Wyler were no longer tailed by cars each time they left the house. Like Ben Bistline, Holm speculated that since entering the Purgatory jail, Jeffs might have been struck by a genuine attack of conscience for what he'd done to former church members; that was why he tried to tell the judge that he was no longer the Prophet. Under Jeffs's leadership, the FLDS had significantly shrunk. Between those he'd thrown out and those who'd left the church because of him, there were estimates of the faithful decreasing by two thousand members in the twin towns alone. His reign of terror, however, kept reverberating far beyond the border.

In early April 2007, eighteen-year-old Lost Boy Parley Jeffs Dutson was accused of shooting and killing his fifteen-year-old girlfriend, Kara Hopkins, during a party in a Salt Lake City neighborhood. Dutson was the son of Bygnal Dutson, a Colorado City town council member and owner of the Vermillion Deli and Candy Shoppe. Jeffs had excommunicated Parley at sixteen for disobedience. He'd then moved to St. George and met his girlfriend before relocating up north. Other kids attending the Salt Lake party told investigators that Dutson had been smoking marijuana and taking hallucinogenic mushrooms. He and Kara had argued prior to the shooting, after Dutson had insisted that she have sex with him in front of everybody. When she refused and tried to hide behind a guest, according to an affidavit, Dutson shot her in the head and then began taking off her clothing and his own. He was charged with first-degree felony murder and aggravated sexual assault, both counts punishable by life in prison.

For other Lost Boys, though, the news was much better. A small group of them were given an eight-bedroom home in St. George, donated by an anonymous contributor. Johnny Jessop, who'd sued Jeffs in order to be able to locate and speak with his mother, was reconnected with the woman after searching for her for several years. In the first week of April 2007, the seven young men (six Lost Boys and Brent Jeffs) who'd filed the initial 2004 lawsuits against Jeffs and the FLDS—the six alleging they'd been driven away from Colorado City to reduce the competition for plural wives—partially settled their claims. Each plaintiff was awarded a $20,000, three-acre undeveloped lot near a community park in Hildale, with the settlement also calling for a $250,000 fund for education and emergency needs for youngsters banished from the church.

Salt Lake attorney Roger Hoole had represented the seven and released a statement reading, "If these young men could send a message to their families and the FLDS people, it would simply be to stay in your homes, keep your families together, and don't automatically follow the next leaders who will try to exercise control over the people."

The month before, Bruce Wisan had received a default judgment against Jeffs, other UEP trustees, and the FLDS for mismanaging its trust. The state seized a 600-acre dairy and alfalfa spread in the Escalante desert, called Harker Farms, to satisfy this $8.8 million judgment. Wisan now owned a dairy herd, tractors and other farming equipment, 722 heifers, 217 steers, 24 bulls, and 911 milk cows. In the fall of 2007, as Jeffs was going to trial, the CPA would auction it all off for $2 million.

Though Gary Engels, too, was feeling less heat, he wasn't ready to concede that Jeffs was finished as the Prophet. In March, he'd told a group of reporters outside the St. George courthouse that Jeffs still had "influence on the community." But in mid-April Dale Evans Barlow surprised the investigator by pleading no contest to the charges pending against him since 2005, ending the seventh of the eight original cases filed by Mohave County. Until now, FLDS defendants had refused to acknowledge any guilt by taking pleas, and Barlow's actions struck Engels as a significant change of attitude. Church members may have been softening their views toward the legal system, although perhaps not toward Engels himself. On the outskirts of Colorado City, Mohave County had just added a new wing on its multi-use trailer, in the hope that more local women would come in for advice or help—if they didn't have to walk past Engels's office along the way. The strategy worked, with numerous visitors dropping by the new wing or calling its twenty-four-hour hotline, installed to assist victims of polygamy. As a result, more women were breaking away from the FLDS.

"Everything is getting better around here," Engels said in April 2007, "but they still hate me.

"I've gotta admit," he added unexpectedly, "that after I go down to Kingman for a while to work on things besides this case, I start to miss it up here and want to come back."

If the locals continued to shun him, Arizona and Mojave County were showing more of their appreciation and respect. The state had lately bought the investigator a shiny new Chevy TrailBlazer and begun paying more of his living expenses, and that April Arizona Attorney General Terry Goddard presented him with a "White Hat" award for coming to Colorado City on his own, finding the evidence for the eight indictments, and risking his life for a group of strangers.

"He is," Goddard said, praising Engels at the award ceremony, "a one-man law enforcement agency."

Everything about the investigator conveyed his usual modesty, but he couldn't hide how proud he was of the White Hat. Both his mental and physical health had suffered during the past couple of years, yet he'd been determined never to show this to FLDS worshippers, who'd once prayed for his destruction. His bosses knew what Engels had achieved and the price he'd paid. After he'd patiently—and sometimes not so patiently—labored by himself on the border for two and a half years, the Arizona Department of Public Safety and the Mohave County Sheriff's Office were finally assigning more resources and more deputies to Colorado City.

47

IN MAY 2007, Engels went before an Arizona grand jury as the sole witness presenting evidence against Jeffs regarding criminal charges in Mohave County. On May 10, the grand jury quietly indicted Jeffs on two counts of sexual conduct with a minor, both Class 6 felonies, and two counts of incest, Class 4 felonies. Six weeks later, a second Mohave County grand jury indicted Jeffs on two more counts of sexual conduct with a minor and two more counts of incest. These cases involved two new victims, in addition to Elissa Wall, but their names were withheld. Jeffs's legal troubles were spreading in every direction. In Utah, he now faced one felony charge of federal unlawful flight to avoid prosecution; two felony charges of being an accomplice to rape; one lawsuit alleging misconduct as a church trustee; a suit filed by a young woman who alleged harm from a forced marriage; a suit filed by a nephew alleging sexual molestation; and the lawsuit filed by six teenagers who said they were unfairly kicked out of the FLDS community. In Arizona, Jeffs was confronting five felony counts of being an accomplice to sexual conduct with a minor; one felony conspiracy count; and four counts of being an accomplice to incest.

Because of these new charges, Engels needed to travel to Purgatory to serve Jeffs with legal papers. Ever since the investigator had gone to Las Vegas the previous summer and spoken with the Prophet in jail following his arrest, one comment Warren had made had bothered and then angered Engels.

"I forgive you, Gary," Jeffs had told him, "for what you've done to me."

For almost a year, Engels had been living with this remark and simmering over it. If he was ever face-to-face with Jeffs again, he intended to bring it up.

Now the opportunity had come, inside the correctional facility between St. George and Hurricane, and he was eager to confront the prisoner again.

By late spring 2007, Jeffs had recovered from his recent health problems and looked reasonably well and alert. He was paper-thin, but he'd been eating with some regularity and managing to get some sleep. As Engels walked into Purgatory to see him, he was hoping to catch the Prophet on a bad day, when he was feeling lonely or miserable and just wanted someone to talk to. Gary himself was still chewing on those annoying words from last August.

He showed Jeffs the legal papers, which laid out the most current Arizona allegations, and for a few moments they sat together, not saying much. Engels was on edge because of his unfinished business with this man, and he'd never been any good at hiding his feelings or opinions of others.

"Remember when we met before," he asked, "and you said you forgave me for what I'd done?"

The inmate, expressionless as ever, nodded at the investigator.

"What was that all about?"

The Prophet stared at him blankly, the look of someone still not used to having his authority challenged.

Engels was waiting for an answer, and if he got one he didn't like, this time he wouldn't swallow it quietly and walk away.

Jeffs stalled, the silence building between them, and then said he couldn't answer that question without his attorney present.

The investigator felt a rush of disappointment, but he didn't want to push. Leaving the room, he thought that perhaps they'd meet again before too long, in an Arizona courtroom, and then Gary would have a lot to say about the Prophet and his forgiveness.

As Engels and Matt Smith built new cases against Jeffs, Judge Shumate stepped up his role in the impending trial in St. George. He ruled that Jeffs's taped jailhouse confession the previous winter to his brother Nephi was so inflammatory that it could not be played for jurors—a major victory for the defense. But the judge also ordered the defendant to help in the personal struggles of Wendell Musser, who'd been a caretaker for Jeffs when he was on the run. After Musser was picked up for drunk driving, Jeffs had thrown him out of the FLDS and separated him from his wife, Vivian, and their young son, Levi. Jeffs had hidden the mother and child away from Wendell, who'd spent the summer and fall of 2006 looking for his family, traveling to safe houses across Colorado, from Florence to Fort Collins. He moved up to Idaho but continued to search the West without results, filing a missing persons report and then launching a lawsuit against Jeffs, alleging that the defendant had interfered with his parental rights and charging him with "alienation of affection."

After a full year of looking for his family, Musser at last connected with Vivian in Hildale at an arranged meeting, which included Colorado City deputy marshal Helaman Barlow and a pair of Washington County Sheriff's deputies—just in case things turned explosive. Vivian, like Richard Holm's wives in 2003, had been poisoned against her spouse. She refused to see him alone, would not let him hold their son, and claimed that Wendell could have no further relationship with Levi. The devastated husband and father left Colorado City and returned to Idaho, vowing to continue his legal fight. In July 2007, these issues finally came before Judge Shumate, who gave Jeffs one week to aid Musser in reestablishing a permanent relationship with his son. If Jeffs failed to respond to this order, the court would start assessing a $600-plus daily penalty against his commissary account at the Purgatory Correctional Facility, the per-day cost of hiring a private detective to search for the mother and child (Jeffs ignored the order and refused to tell Musser's attorneys anything concerning Vivian and Levi's whereabouts). The judge further ruled that Musser could add the FLDS Church to his complaint and seek judgments against its holdings, including the YFZ Ranch in Texas.

Despite their leader's expanding legal troubles, Jeffs's followers kept showing up at his courtroom appearances. In July, for the first time since his arrest, his mother, Merilyn Steed, attended one. Before taking her seat in the gallery, she mouthed the word "Hi" to her son and this caused a stir, prompting the bailiff to remind observers not to communicate with the defendant.

Judge Shumate was determined to keep the September trial date on track and all the players in line. In mid-July, he issued seven detailed pages of instructions for how reporters and spectators were to behave when court was in session. He laid out provisions about addressing people, what could be said, and what couldn't be read while sitting in the gallery, along with banning cell phones and cameras. Decorum would be critical, security would be extremely tight, and anyone violating any of the judge's rules would find himself on the wrong side of the law.

The challenges facing courtroom observers would be nothing compared to those confronting the twelve jurors selected to weigh the evidence. Juries are carefully instructed not to convict defendants based on gut feelings or preconceived notions about the accused. Jeffs had obviously done despicable things, like dividing families and expelling hundreds of young men from the community, but these weren't the charges against him. Jeffs was on trial for abetting a rape—in a case where the rape itself had not been prosecuted. Would a jury hear and see enough evidence to convict Jeffs when he'd been acting on his own religious beliefs and those of his church? From a legal perspective, the case was hardly black and white.

Nearly a year after Jeffs's arrest, there was still no hint of what else prosecutors might bring against him, besides the impassioned testimony of Elissa Wall, and no clue about what kind of defense his lawyers would mount. While the defendant had been adjusting to life in captivity and struggling with depression, the attorneys had kept silent on his upcoming courtroom battle.

On September 7, 2007, three hundred prospective jurors began answering seventy-five inquiries in writing about their backgrounds, including their religious beliefs, their familiarity with the case, and their opinion of Warren Jeffs. Three days later, they were brought into court in smaller groups to meet the lawyers and be queried individually. For the first time in his career on the bench, Judge Shumate was allowing attorneys to pose highly specific questions to those in the narrowed-down jury pool. Were they squeamish about graphic sexual testimony? How much did they know about the FLDS faith and its followers? Were they practicing members of the mainstream LDS Church, and would that affect their ability to give Jeffs a fair trial? Would they be able to ignore their feelings about polygamy or arranged marriages or the Lost Boys issues, which were not in trial in St. George?

Ten months after Jeffs had first faced his accusers, the media congregated in southern Utah again. If he still looked partially broken from his long winter in jail, his lawyers seemed more than eager to defend his religious freedom and to attack the testimony of Elissa Wall. On September 10, fifty jurors showed up at the courthouse and the questioning began.

VI

OUTLASTING
THE SUN

48

THE NOTED UNION CIVIL WAR general William Tecumseh Sherman once said that if he owned both hell and Texas, he'd live in hell and rent out the Lone Star State. George A. Smith, a cousin of Joseph Smith and a counselor to Brigham Young, applied this line to the area around St. George, a town that would eventually be named after him. Smith must have delivered this opinion about St. George in late summer. As the attorneys and Judge Shumate began assembling a jury, the desert air lay on top of Dixie like a flat iron hand, pressing down harder as the day unfolded, heat building and thickening on the streets and sidewalks, searing the skin.

On the second day of jury selection—September 11, 2007—people throughout the United States were focused on memorials for the terrorist attacks on New York and Washington, D.C., of six years earlier. While Jeffs was looking across the room at his prospective jurors, Osama bin Laden remained on the FBI's Ten Most Wanted List and was releasing more videotapes to the global media, celebrating his freedom and taunting America from a distance. As he mocked the world's last superpower, four hundred visitors gathered in a valley thirty-five miles north of St. George to hold their own memorial for the nation's *other* September 11. They came together on the spot where the 1857 Mountain Meadows Massacre had unfolded 150 years earlier, killing 120 men, women, and children traveling from Arkansas to California. In this valley, the victims' descendants re-created the historical setting with a covered wagon led by two Belgian workhorses, the mourners walking behind the wagon carrying red flags bearing the names of the families of the dead. One hundred and twenty crosses, adorned with black bows, signified those who'd fallen here, along with seventeen red ones for the children who'd survived.

Led by Elder Henry Eyring, a member of the Quorum of Twelve Apostles of the LDS Church, the procession reached the gravesite, and the scorched air was filled with sobbing. Standing before the crowd, Eyring expressed "profound regret" for his faith's role in the carnage of that distant September morning and acknowledged that local Mormon leaders bore the responsibility for recruiting Paiute Indians to take part in the slaughter.

"What was done here long ago by members of our church," he said, "represents a terrible and inexcusable departure from Christian teaching and conduct."

The Paiute would not have participated in the event "without the direction . . . provided by local church members and leaders."

Choking back tears, he added, "We cannot change what happened, but we can remember and honor those who were killed here."

For this occasion, the LDS had reached out to the Native American population. Lora Tom had been invited to represent the Paiute Nation, blamed for so long for the crimes at Mountain Meadows. She got a standing ovation when she said, "For one hundred and fifty years, no one has asked us for our account."

Elaine Tyler was not at the Hope Organization today, but had driven up to the valley to take part in the memorial and to get away from all the requests for pretrial interviews pouring into her office from *Good Morning, America, The View*, National Public Radio, Court TV, the Montel Williams show, and others. Because of Elaine, the women who'd escaped the FLDS, and the charges brought against Jeffs, his church and community were receiving a level of exposure that a few years earlier would have been unimaginable. More intimate exposure was about to come.

As Elaine watched the wagon train wend through the valley, she, too, began to cry. She wondered how long it might be before the LDS in Salt Lake City officially took note of—or apologized to—all the victims produced by the FLDS sect. Would a day come when the mainstream church authorities repented for those who'd been forced into underage marriage, sexually assaulted, or trapped in incestuous relationships inside their own families? Would the LDS ever remove parts of Section 132 from its Doctrines and Covenants? In Verse 61, for example, God says of polygamy, "If any man espouse a virgin, and desire to espouse another, and the first give her consent, and if he espouse the second, and they are virgins, and have vowed to no other man, then is he justified; he cannot commit adultery for they are given unto him."

Were these teachings not the very same guidelines Warren Jeffs had relied upon at Alta Academy and later on when preparing girls for their roles in life as wives and mothers? Would it take another 150 years for the church to address these issues?

For the moment, LDS leaders opted to separate themselves further from the FLDS, issuing yet another proclamation stating that they had nothing whatsoever to do with the fundamentalists down by the border.

While Elaine was at Mountain Meadows, volunteers at the Hope Organization pored over the seventy names on the defense's witness list, trying to figure out who was who. At least one name was easy: Sharon Wall, Elissa's mother, who might be brought in to testify for the Prophet against her own daughter (just as pressure on her parents had shut down Candi Shapley on the witness stand). The list contained thirteen Jessops and twenty-two Barlows, which is where things got confusing. Some of the Barlows and Jessops had the same first names, so you couldn't be sure which one might be called as a witness and which wouldn't. In recent years, some folks in the twin towns had changed their names to avoid contact with the authorities or to avoid being dragged into court, leaving things even more muddled. Gary Engels had attempted to find all the people on the defense list, interview them, and get a sense of what they might say on the stand, but he hadn't had much luck. Unlike under Arizona law, defense witnesses in Utah didn't have to speak to prosecutors or investigators like Engels, and only two of the seventy opted to.

On another front, the situation looked better. As jury selection proceeded in St. George, the Colorado City town council, in a radical departure from the recent past, voted to approve its first subdivision, transferring these homes from the communal trust to private property. "Short Creek Subdivision Plat A" had seventeen lots with twelve houses sitting on them. Bruce Wisan's march toward individual ownership had taken another leap forward, and he'd received 180 petitions from ex-FLDS members for their own land and homes. That September, he sold the first UEP Trust home since 1942, a six-bedroom house for $115,000.

With all this activity unfolding in southern Utah, defense attorney Walter Bugden was asking potential jurors to look into the eyes of Warren Jeffs and presume him innocent of all charges. This added a human touch to a dry and tedious legal process, and one or two people glanced at Jeffs's face before looking away. Part of Budgen's job was to prepare jurors for learning more about— and being more open to—life inside the FLDS. It was the first clue to the defense's strategy, which was not so much to put Jeffs himself on trial, but his church. Unlike in the rest of American society, Bugden explained during jury questioning, "The couple falls in love *after* the marriage." The lawyer had a soft hand with juries and had been refining his courtroom techniques for decades.

The prosecution chose to bring in Craig Barlow, the state's assistant attorney general in the children's justice division. In 1996, Barlow had successfully prosecuted John Chaney on an accomplice to rape charge after Chaney had performed the marriage of his thirteen-year-old daughter to a forty-eight-year-old man. It was the only other accomplice to rape case ever pursued by Utah law enforcement, and Chaney was now serving up to life in prison. Craig Barlow, like the Mormon-raised Sam Brower, came to the Jeffs case not just with an impressive résumé, but also a personal connection. His great-grandfather was a brother of John Y. Barlow, the first mayor of Colorado City, and this seemed to give the prosecutor an extra dose of motivation. The broad-chested Barlow was by far the most aggressive and potent of the three prosecuting attorneys.

Washington County had charged Jeffs with two counts of accomplice to rape, even though there was only one victim. The prosecution alleged that the first crime had occurred between April 23, 2001, when Warren had married Elissa and Allen Steed, and May 12, 2001, the approximate date when the couple had first had sex. The second count was alleged to have taken place during the rest of the marriage, somewhere between May 13, 2001, and September 30, 2003.

During jury selection, one of Craig Barlow's duties was to explain Utah's legal statutes to potential jurors: a fourteen-year-old in that state was capable of consenting to sexual intercourse, but sex was *not* considered consensual if a person under eighteen had intercourse with someone at least three years older. In this case, Allen had been nineteen when he'd married Elissa.

"Regardless of your personal opinion," Barlow said, "are you willing to accept and abide by this rule of law?"

For a variety of reasons, two hundred of the three hundred notified jurors were quickly dismissed from the pool, and there were concerns that the trial might have to be relocated to Salt Lake City. That would be expensive and time-consuming, but the judge was determined to sit a fair-minded jury. After three days of rigorous questioning, seven women and five men on the eight-person jury, (four were alternates) were found to listen to the evidence, and the trial was set to begin. Nancy Volmer, who handled media relations at the courthouse, once again reminded reporters that proper decorum would be mandatory, and Judge Shumate's demands would be backed by nine armed guards constantly circling through the courtroom. The most menacing one was situated behind the attorneys and facing not the judge, but the spectators. Under Shumate's orders there would be no talking, grinning, or smirking when court was in session, and if anyone dared crack a smile, this gigantic fellow would rise from his chair and permanently remove the offender from the courtroom. Police officers stood outside the courthouse, and a SWAT team was stationed across the street. To keep the defendant safe, Jeffs would be flown from Purgatory into St. George by helicopter on occasion, and he'd wear a bulletproof vest during testimony.

With the twelve jurors now chosen, Shumate addressed this relatively young group of men and women and delivered an extraordinary speech celebrating American justice. In decades of professional travels around the country, His Honor had heard a lot of "whining" from other judges about jury decisions, but he felt just the opposite. He'd spent thirty-two years inside the criminal justice system, most of that time on the bench, and in no trial he'd ever presided over had jurors ever made a mistake in terms of their verdict.

"We have committed citizens in this county," he said, "who will come into court and resolve serious issues . . . You heard the attorneys speak with reverence of our Founding Fathers. Does our system have problems? Yeah. Am I part of that sometimes? Yeah . . . [But] I can think of no other system that brings this wealth of experience to bear on the resolution of these issues . . ."

These particular jurors would be confronted with sorting through the legal definition of guilt for accomplice to rape: they had to find from the evidence, beyond a reasonable doubt, that the defendant intentionally, knowingly, and recklessly solicited, requested, commanded, or encouraged another to have sexual intercourse without consent, or aided another in doing so.

With opening arguments set to begin, Shumate admonished the jurors to pay no further attention to the media regarding this case and then offered one final warning: they not only had to presume the defendant innocent of all charges, but "the scales of justice are tilted in his favor, all the way down to the end of the scale."

Jeffs listened to these words expressionless.

49

THE BURDEN OF PROOF in this case did not rest so much on the prosecution as it did on the performance of Elissa Wall. The previous November, her testimony had been overwhelming, reducing some to tears. A young pregnant woman had been revealing her wrenching sexual and emotional history in public for the first time. She'd done so virtually without interruption and the longer she'd talked, the more powerful her story became, overflowing and erupting in a cascade of memories and feelings. Nobody who heard it was unaffected. The prosecution was depending on her to be just as powerful now that the trial was under way.

But on September 13, 2007, as Elissa addressed the jury for the first time, her delivery had lost some of its resonance. The facts were basically the same, but she didn't build as much momentum or unleash the same raw emotion. She was a bit prickly on cross-examination. Reporters and courtroom observers who'd seen her before described this round of testimony with words like "rehearsed" and "defensive." Jeffs's legal team, led by Tara Issacson, regularly interrupted Elissa's words, and she never reached full steam. The anguish of going public in a rape case was clearly wearing her down.

She did provide a few new details about the first time she and Allen had sex. Afterward, she felt "dirty" and "used" by her husband—too upset to go to sleep and too ashamed to talk to her mother or sisters. She got out of bed and went into the bathroom, curled up on the floor, and bawled.

"I felt like a horrible person," she told the jury. "I didn't understand why he had done what he had just done."

From a medicine cabinet, she grabbed a bottle of Tylenol and another of ibuprofen, pouring all the pills down her throat.

"The only thing I wanted to do was die," she said. "I just wanted to die."

Later that night, she threw up the pills.

It was Warren Jeffs, she testified, who'd put her in this situation and he was the only person who could get her out of it. But he refused to do that.

"The Prophet," she said, "was a God to us, a God on earth" who had control over "everything in our lives and we were to follow him as if led by a hair." If you disobeyed him, the strand of hair would break and you'd forfeit your chance at salvation.

Elissa's older sister from Canada, Teresa, briefly testified next, and she was followed by their sister Rebecca, who'd appeared at the preliminary hearing. She was a better witness than she'd been last fall, more focused and with a sharper tongue. In her hairdo and clothing, she resembled several of the young women on the jury, and they listened intently to her while taking notes. That this attractive young woman had married Rulon Jeffs when he was eighty-six was striking, but her testimony was primarily focused on Elissa's wedding. If she'd tried to derail it, Rebecca said, she'd have been deemed "very wicked" by the community and "driven away" from the church. As Rulon's wife at that time, she'd watched the inner workings of the FLDS from inside the Jeffs's Hildale compound, and she echoed Elissa on the subject of who held the ultimate power.

"The one person who could have stopped it," she told the jury, "was Warren Jeffs."

Within the FLDS culture was a slogan that older people often repeated to the youth: "Put your hand into it and your heart will follow." For years Rebecca had tried to obey this dictate, at Alta Academy and later when married to Rulon. But in October 2002 she'd left the church after a series of incidents that had begun with her refusal to perform a sexual act on Rulon when he was past ninety. Her anger only deepened after Warren criticized her for not doing what his father had requested.

"It was extreme evil," she told the jury, "to resist in any way in the bedroom."

Warren had taken her aside and, echoing God in the church doctrines and covenants regarding polygamy, lectured her that under no circumstances "do you ever, ever, ever, tell your husband no. Don't you ever resist him. A wife's duty is to comfort her husband and if she doesn't, she will be destroyed in the flesh."

Rebecca exploded when Jeffs asked her to marry him after Rulon died.

Instead of becoming his wife, she bolted the compound and the faith.

Once again the FLDS made a strong showing at the courthouse. Each morning before the trial went into session, church members lined the walls of the lobby, standing together in their dark suits or old-fashioned, two-toned, Western-cut sport coats, looking like auctioneers or officials at a rodeo. They were usually accompanied by two or three women who stayed close, hands folded in front of their waists, avoiding eye contact with strangers. They wore full-length, pressed, pastel cotton dresses, their hair stacked high in front and braided tightly in back. Pale, with no trace of makeup, they were silent props on display to show support for their imprisoned leader. Blank and squelched, they looked worlds away from the quirky, glamorized suburban depiction of polygamous wives on HBO's *Big Love.*

The FLDS men, on the other hand, carried themselves with a certain smugness. They spoke only among themselves or to Jeffs's lawyers, with whom they were quite friendly. Their red, weather-beaten faces gazed upon the reporters in the small lobby with a mixture of humor and disdain. The men were as polite as they were cold.

Standing alongside the FLDS couples in the lobby were the anti-polygamy women who'd been gathering at the courthouse since jury selection began. Flora Jessop, who'd founded the precursor to the Hope Organization and had rescued several women from the border towns, had made an early showing at the courthouse before disappearing from view. But Elaine Tyler, Sara Hammon, Brenda Jensen, and Laurie Allen were out in force. The latter had escaped from the FLDS as a teenager and gone on to produce a documentary on Colorado City, *Banking on Heaven.* The women had scrambled to get the handful of seats open to the pubic and they all conveyed a sense of mission, but Elaine in particular had on her game face. It was difficult to say who was more determined to see Warren brought down—the three Wall sisters on the stand or the women who were circling the courthouse, listening to the testimony and praying for a conviction.

Early in the trial, attorneys on both sides agreed to play audiotapes of Jeffs instructing girls in a home economics class at Alta Academy in the

1990s (as time went on, the Prophet's disciples had kept up with the latest technological advances; a defense witness would testify that she kept 769 of his teachings on her iPod and listened to one of them every morning). His lessons to the girls were long and repetitive, delivered with almost no feeling or inflection. As his recorded drone filled the courtroom, Warren bowed his head and closed his eyes. The defendant refused to testify or speak with the media, so these unedited teachings were the best available evidence for trying to understand him, and they were the revelation of the trial. His words held no irony or deception. Addressing the girls, he was absolutely solemn and sincere:

"You wake up each day yearning to please your husband . . . In your life are no secrets, but you keep his secrets."

Outsiders tend to focus on sexual relations in their consideration of polygamy: How does all this work in the bedroom? Who sleeps with whom and when? But Jeffs's lessons were utterly sexless. He not only insisted that Alta's boys and girls treat one another "like snakes," but his manner conveyed the opposite of desire and a profound emotional need for control. Girls or women were never to raise their voices, criticize their husbands, or question male authority, never to challenge a man's leadership role. As his soft voice poured forth from the tapes, the fragility of the male psyche screamed out from the recordings:

"If a woman rules over a man, both will lose the spirit of God . . ."

In his ideal world, men would never be hurt by the opposite sex. Inadvertently, he revealed on the tapes just how easily men *could* be hurt by women and how far some would go to try to keep this from happening:

"The very nature of women is that their desire should be for the husband and to completely submit so that he should rule over you."

The tapes had caught Jeffs and his church in an unguarded moment, and their secrets had come tumbling out into the courtroom.

50

WHEN PROSECUTORS SURPRISINGLY rested after presenting only Elissa and her two sisters, Walter Bugden stood and declared that the state had failed to make its case. He asked the judge to dismiss the charges because Jeffs clearly hadn't been an accomplice to rape. This was a common strategy for a defense attorney in the middle of a criminal trial, and Shumate was prepared for it. He ruled against the attorney and revealed some of his own views on what Elissa had experienced on her wedding day. After citing the girl's refusal to take Allen's hand in marriage and say "I do"—not once but twice—the judge declared, "The silence was poignant." Then he told Bugden to call his first witness.

The state had gone out of its way not to put polygamy or the FLDS lifestyle on trial. The prosecution was unconcerned, from a legal standpoint, with Elissa's underage marriage, but only with the crime of accomplice to rape. The defense took the opposite tack. Its first nine witnesses were mostly window dressing—young men and women who came into court to explain, and try to rationalize, the practices of their faith to outsiders. According to their testimony, they'd all willingly entered into arranged marriages and were largely content with their decisions. The women spoke of "turning themselves in" to the Prophet when they were ready to be placed with a husband; then the Prophet, sometimes with input from the women themselves, selected who their partner would be and when the ceremony would occur. After marriage, sexual intercourse was only for procreation, and birth control was not allowed. Nobody, they emphasized to the jury, was forced into anything, and

Warren Jeffs had often been a wise and kind leader when it came to love and intimacy.

For a congregation so committed to privacy, delivering this testimony could only have been excruciating. One wondered what kind of pressure had been applied to get these shy country people to testify about sexual matters on behalf of their Prophet. Regardless of the trial's outcome, the church was being exposed as a result of Jeffs's actions, and that wasn't the only cost. With three high-powered attorneys on the payroll, estimates of Warren's legal fees ran into the hundreds of thousands of dollars.

All the women who testified were at least several years older than Elissa when they'd been wed, all had been eager to have husbands, and all got to choose when they would start marital relations with their spouses; one wife had waited nearly two years before saying yes. Both the men and women agreed that they'd come to matrimony with virtually no knowledge of sex. When one woman was asked how she'd managed to learn a bit about this subject before her placement in marriage, she blushed and said, "We had animals."

Of the nine, Jenny Pipkin was the most convincing. She'd been born in Hildale, had soon moved to Salt Lake City, but then came back to Colorado City before her tenth birthday. When she was seventeen, she wanted to get married, but her father told her to graduate from high school first. Four days after receiving her diploma, she again made this request, and when he began stalling she handed him a mobile phone and told him to call Uncle Rulon and pass along her wishes. She met with Warren instead, who learned that Jenny had already picked out a young man her own age. Once Warren and Rulon had agreed with her choice, the wedding was held the following day. During the next seven and a half years, she had five children, but then came health problems. She badly wanted a break from childbearing and told her husband that he could no longer touch her.

"He nagged me and begged me to be with him again," she testified. "He'd say, 'I need it' and 'It's your duty to comfort me.' I said no. I started to pray and read Scripture and I came across a 1999 Warren Jeffs sermon. I read, 'There is no force in the marriage of Celestial Marriage . . . A man should only have these marital relations with a wife if she invites it.' I realized my husband had no right to be bothering me about this. I realized I was supposed to be in charge, but he kept nagging me."

She wrote Jeffs a letter about her situation and he responded by telling her that she was correct in her beliefs. This deepened her resolve.

"I kept saying no to my husband," she told the court, "and the nagging stopped. But at night in bed he touched me and one night he took my clothes off and was touching me very intimately. I went down and slept on the couch."

When she informed Warren about this latest incident, he followed Scripture and released her from wedlock two days later.

Jenny handled herself bravely on the stand and succeeded in bolstering the defense's claim that the FLDS helped people get out of uncomfortable marriages. The men and women who testified for Jeffs seemed to prefer a more strictly defined approach to male–female relationships. They were convincing, but would the jury consider this applicable to the situation Elissa found herself in at fourteen, when she didn't want to get married or have sex with anyone?

Gary Engels had chosen not to attend the proceedings for reasons he never made clear, except to suggest that he might be unwelcome to the FLDS worshippers sitting in the gallery each day. Passions were indeed running high around the courthouse, even without the investigator. Overheard in the lobby one morning were the following from the anti-polygamy forces:

"Can't we just kill Jeffs and get it over with? Just shoot him?"

"People claim one of Warren's brothers said he'd slit his own wife's throat if the Prophet asked him to."

"Can you imagine going to bed with that bag of bones?"

"I finally got out of my marriage because I was tired of getting beat up."

Despite his absence from the courthouse, Engels's presence was felt in the shadows as he advised potential state witnesses, consulted with Sam Brower, and offered encouragement to the prosecution. He was biding his time and continuing to prepare his own cases against Jeffs in Arizona, planned to get under way once this jury reached a verdict. Despite improving conditions along the border, Gary had lost none of his uneasiness, and he was outraged that the judge had made room in the gallery for ten or more of Warren's supporters every day, while allotting only a couple of seats for those backing Elissa Wall and her sisters.

"What kind of crap is that?" he said.

Utah attorney general Mark Shurtleff appeared for the first part of the prosecution's case. He was still developing his own ideas about how to pursue Jeffs and the FLDS, no matter what happened at this trial. In May 2006, as the Prophet was being placed on the FBI's Ten Most Wanted List, Shurtleff had told the *Deseret Morning News* about an organized crime investigation he was leading into the church regarding alleged financial scams like "double books, cooking the books, offshore accounts, and fraud." After Jeffs was taken into custody that August, the feds and the U.S. Attorney's office in Utah had taken control of most of the items seized from the Cadillac Escalade, including the computers Jeffs had been working on. Shurtleff's investigation had sputtered because he couldn't gain access to the material on those hard drives.

This annoyed many people, none more than Engels.

"The feds are notorious for not sharing information," he said. "We need what's on Jeffs's computers, but they won't give it to us. If we had it, we might be able to file more cases and bring a RICO case against the FLDS and really start to make some changes in Colorado City. If you want to hit a criminal organization hard, you hit 'em in the pocketbook."

5 1

T HE TENTH AND FINAL DEFENSE witness was Allen Steed. With a
ruddy complexion typical of FLDS men, a nervous demeanor, and a
flop of brown hair falling across his forehead, he made a humble appearance as he took the stand, facing the courtroom and public scrutiny for
the first time. Two of the spectators in the gallery this morning were Elissa
and her second husband, Lamont Barlow. In 2006, after Washington County
had filed its case against Jeffs, Allen hired two attorneys, Jim Bradshaw and
Mark Moffat. Since then, the attorneys had met with prosecutors several
times and said that if their client was going to be charged with raping Elissa,
he would voluntarily turn himself in. Washington County officials told them
that no decision had yet been made in this matter, but now prosecutor Brian
Filter and sheriff's investigator Jake Schultz were monitoring both Elissa's
testimony and Steed's.

As Walter Bugden rose from the defense table, he reminded Allen of his
Miranda rights, asking him if he realized that anything he said in court today
might be used against him later on. Steed understood this but wanted to tell
his side of the story and was anxious to deliver his opinion of the Prophet.

"I don't believe," Allen blurted out after being sworn in, "Warren Jeffs has
ever done anything wrong."

Judge Shumate told the jury to disregard this comment and struck it from
the record.

Steed's nerves were causing his body to tremble, and Bugden had to command him repeatedly to raise his volume. Then the judge told him to pretend
that everyone present in the courtroom was deaf. When neither of these

things did much good, Allen stood up in the witness box and addressed the jury from that unusual position, but he remained barely audible in the back of the gallery.

He portrayed himself as a bumbling young husband and a poor communicator with the opposite sex. When Fred Jessop had placed him with Elissa, he was as ignorant of romance as she was: "I didn't know much about how to make a girl like me." On his wedding day, he didn't "particularly love" his wife and their initial weeks together were "rough and rocky." No sexual intimacy had occurred on their honeymoon to Arizona and Carlsbad Caverns, just some kissing and hugging.

"Did she ever ask you to stop?" Bugden said.

"Yes," Allen replied, "and then I did."

After living together for a while, the couple quit going to bed in their sacred undergarments and gradually began having more contact. Steed told jurors the same story Elissa had at the preliminary hearing and the trial, about the two of them going to a park in Hildale one spring evening, laying down on the grass, and looking up at the stars.

"I was enjoying her," he said. "I exposed myself to help move things along and maybe bring her closer."

But this frightened the girl and she went back to Fred's home.

As Allen was describing this scene to the jury, Elissa and Lamont got up and left the courtroom. She was crying and must have sensed what Steed was going to say next.

One night, he returned home exhausted, following a 12-to-15-hour shift at his job as an electrician, so tired he fell into bed in his work clothes. Elissa awakened him, crawled in beside him, and asked Allen if he cared for her. She rubbed up close to him and wanted him to scratch her back. They began hugging and touching, which led to "one thing after the next."

"I felt she was ready to go forward," Steed told the jurors, so they did. Their intimate life had begun and there was "absolutely no force" on that occasion or later on.

This was a radically different account from the one Elissa had given a few days earlier—when she'd said Allen had told her it was "time for you to be a wife" and lay down on top of her while her "whole body was shaking." On the stand, he didn't recall anything like that or that afterward she'd gone into the bathroom, taken two bottles of pills, and then vomited.

"She didn't come right out," he testified, "and say 'stop' or 'no' or 'don't' or at least push away from me or something."

With his unvarnished appearance and his flat, faltering way of speaking, Allen evoked Tom Hanks playing Forrest Gump. He seemed modest and likable and decent—too unsophisticated to even attempt a lie. Steed wasn't just opening up his difficult past to the world but possibly putting himself at legal risk. Elissa had once called him a victim in this case, and many courtroom observers could now see her point. He was trapped in a drama much larger than himself, sympathetic in a way Jeffs had never been. He was also an effective witness, and his testimony raised complex legal issues. Would the jury hesitate to convict Warren because of their concerns that law enforcement might then come after Steed?

It was obvious that Elissa felt strongly that she'd been raped, while her ex-husband felt just as strongly that he'd never sexually assaulted anyone. Their testimonies were credible enough to suggest that perhaps a rape had taken place, but that Allen was unaware of that. If a crime had occurred between the young couple, their environment had sanctioned it.

On the stand, Steed portrayed his young wife as severely disobedient. She was defiant and strong-willed, determined to go to school and work at the local Mark Twain restaurant, despite his view that she could only do well at one or the other. Allen had met alone with Warren Jeffs two or three times in order to seek his counsel about his confounding spouse. The Prophet told him to be "kind and considerate" to Elissa, to "take it slow, try to get close and try to show love." Jeffs told them to pray together, play together, and work together. If Allen did all these things, he might be able to get his wife to "love me so she'd get to the point she'd obey me because she loved me . . . I was patient and tried to show love and support . . ."

When none of this changed her attitude or behavior, he asked her if another man was involved. She said no—that was just an FLDS rumor floating around town. The more Allen reached out to her, the more distant she became. Elissa began spending less and less time at home and stopped taking his calls. Steed prayed for God's help in dealing with his rebellious wife and bringing her back to him, composing heartfelt letters to express his feelings: "Dear Sweetheart, I could write all day the things I think about you . . . I send my love to you always . . ."

One day he found a picture of Elissa and Lamont Barlow enjoying themselves in Las Vegas. Allen was shocked to learn that his suspicions about his wife were true. As he testified about this now, he shook, lowered his head, and began to cry.

"It was her idea to be with that man," he said. "I wanted nothing to do with her. I had a strong desire to get a gun, but knew that wasn't right and left it at that."

He went to Fred Jessop and showed the old man the photo of Elissa and Lamont. That was the end of the marriage.

Craig Barlow stood up for cross-examination, took a few steps toward the witness box, then went on the attack. The defense had already accused Elissa of wanting to help convict Jeffs because that might assist her in collecting damages in her upcoming civil suit against Warren and the FLDS. ("Money," Bugden would tell the jury in his closing argument, "changes everything.") Now Allen came under similar questioning.

Wasn't it true that since his marriage to Elissa had fallen apart, Steed had been single and couldn't have another wife inside the FLDS community unless he was placed in marriage by the Prophet? If he didn't have a wife, he couldn't get into heaven. So didn't Jeffs control not just his marital but also his spiritual future, and didn't that color everything the witness said about the defendant? Wasn't he testifying on Jeffs's behalf today so that the Prophet would help him later on?

"Warren Jeffs," Allen quietly acknowledged, "holds the keys to my eternal salvation."

According to Steed, Elissa had told her husband that she wanted to wait to have sex and children for as long as five years, but within three weeks of their wedding they were having intercourse. Instead of waiting half a decade as his wife had requested, hadn't Allen taken the earliest opportunity to consummate their marriage?

"Yes," the witness said. "Wouldn't you?"

"I'm not you, Mr. Steed," Barlow shot back.

Weren't Allen and Elissa having unprotected sex at that time, in direct violation of the FLDS teaching that intimacy was only for procreation?

Yes, but she couldn't become pregnant because he always pulled out before ejaculation.

Barlow mocked his answer: Did Elissa stop each time in the middle of sex and tell him not "to release the sperm within me during intercourse?" Was that how it worked?

Steed looked confused, unprepared for this kind of grilling. Barlow was just getting started.

Did Allen remember seeing Elissa's blood on the night they lost their virginity?

He shook his head.

Did he ever see bruises on her?

He shook it again.

Did it occur to Allen that his young wife might have been very frightened the first time they made love?

"I didn't really think about it."

What would he do if commanded by an FLDS leader to break the law?

"I believe that he [the Prophet] would never tell me to do anything wrong. I think the Lord would take his life first."

The prosecutor brought up a 1996 Warren Jeffs tape-recorded teaching about John Y. Barlow, the first mayor of Colorado City (and a distant relative of Craig Barlow's). On the tape, Jeffs explained how the authorities had asked the mayor to sign a document saying that he wouldn't perform any more plural marriages. Barlow had signed it, been released from prison, and gone right back to conducting illegal weddings.

What did Allen think about this story?

Groping for an answer and looking more confused, he mumbled something about it being all right to disobey the laws of man if God commanded him to do so.

After watching Steed testify, Sam Brower said, "He didn't just fall on his sword for Warren. He twisted it on the stand."

The defense rested, and the state called a rebuttal witness, Jane Blackmore, a Canadian midwife who'd seen Elissa on three occasions when she'd come north to visit her sister Teresa. Blackmore first spoke to the young woman in December 2002, about eighteen weeks into Elissa's second pregnancy. She'd told the midwife that she hadn't informed her husband about either this pregnancy or her first one, which she had miscarried the previous June.

"She spent most of the time in my office crying," Blackmore testified. "She didn't want to be a mom and be married. She said she'd been forced into getting married and . . . she said, 'My husband won't take no for an answer.' "

Blackmore saw Elissa again near the end of January 2003 and late that February. During their final session, the patient complained of cramps and mentioned that she hadn't felt the baby move for quite a while. She miscarried again.

The midwife had created a couple of pages of medical observations about Elissa, which she presented in court.

"She was feeling guilty," Blackmore said, "for not wanting the pregnancy and thinking this caused the miscarriage. She was adamant about not wanting to go home."

With the end of her testimony, the prosecution rested and the trial came to an abrupt end. On a blistering Wednesday afternoon, with a milky haze settled over the hills and mesas surrounding St. George, the courtroom emptied and Jeffs was transported back to Purgatory for perhaps one of the last times. Given how long it had taken to charge with him with a crime (beginning in Arizona in June 2005); how long it had taken to catch him (more than a year later, in August 2006); and how much time had passed before his trial began (September 2007), the trial itself was startlingly brief. Elaine Tyler and Laurie Allen were concerned about how few witnesses the county had called and believed that other ex-FLDS women should have testified to make the state's case stronger, but that opportunity had passed. Going into the trial, most of the speculation around the courthouse was that the defendant would be convicted. At the end of testimony, the talk was largely about acquittal.

52

I N HIS CLOSING ARGUMENT ON FRIDAY MORNING, September 21, prosecutor Brock Belnap quietly explained that the defendant wasn't just any adult in his community, but the first counselor and the "mouthpiece of God." He had authority over Elissa Wall and because of that and the other testimony they'd heard, the jury's job now was quite simple: follow the law and find Jeffs guilty on both counts.

"If a fourteen-year-old girl doesn't want to do it," Belnap explained, "and someone persuades her to do it, she doesn't even have to say no. No consent, sexual intercourse—rape."

Walter Bugden wasn't as brief, soft-spoken, or predictable as Belnap, choosing to close with a flourish. More than two dozen national and international journalists, he emphasized, had traveled to St. George for the trial, and even Utah attorney general Mark Shurtleff had been in the courtroom.

"This is no small case," the lawyer said. "The state has gone crazy for political reasons."

Utah had "dropped a nuclear bomb on Hildale and Colorado City and charged Mr. Jeffs with rape ... The state can say Warren Steed Jeffs is on trial, but it's his ... church, his religious beliefs, that are on trial here, dressed up as a crime called rape."

What had happened in the bedroom between Allen and Elissa "wasn't different from what happened in other aspects of their lives. She did exactly what she wanted to do"—dropping out of school, working two jobs, having an affair—and the time had arrived to put her character on trial.

"This is not Ms. Submissive," Bugden said. "This is not Ms. Robot, this girl. She was not stripped of her independence. Elissa told no one, absolutely no one, she was being raped," not even her closest sisters. "My client should be judged by the same standard as everyone else in that family. And no one else in that family . . . thought rape was going to take place."

Bugden reminded jurors of the state's failure to charge anyone with rape in this case, of the damages Elissa could receive if successful in her civil suit, and referred to the medical report Jane Blackmore had made when the young woman had visited her during her second pregnancy. Sections of the report were designed to indicate if a patient had abused alcohol or drugs. The defense attorney contended that Blackmore's report determined that Elissa used both of these substances. Coming as it did, at the end of the proceedings, this was a surprising and bold statement.

It was also incorrect. In his rebuttal to Bugden, which was the last thing the jury would hear before starting their deliberations, Belnap pointed out that the defense attorney had misinterpreted Blackmore's findings. Her chart showed that Elissa had in fact not abused drugs or alcohol, but was clean during pregnancy. Bugden had gotten a dramatic ending, if not the one he'd been looking for.

Four jurors were now sent home and the final eight, three of whom were members of the LDS Church, were left to decide the case. The five men and three women all had to reach agreement on either conviction or acquittal regarding both counts, or there would be no verdict. If that happened, Jeffs could be tried again. While reporters waited outside the courthouse looking for any patch of shade, the jury, led by its heavyset, bearded foreman, David Finch, deliberated for the remainder of Friday afternoon before stopping for the weekend. After working most of Monday, they sent the judge a note saying they were deadlocked on the second count and didn't know how to proceed. Judge Shumate's instructions to them were pointed: keep deliberating and order in a pizza for dinner. They followed his directive, but things were getting heated. A nasty argument flared, and one juror threw a pen. When a woman in the room admitted that she hadn't been completely honest about her sexual past on her jury questionnaire, another woman decided to inform the judge about this. He then met with all eight, telling them to end their session and go get some sleep. As they left the courthouse on Monday night, a mistrial had become a distinct possibility.

The next morning, September 25, the judge dismissed the woman who'd misrepresented herself on her questionnaire and brought in a female alternate. Among the journalists covering the trial and on Court TV, which was closely monitoring the verdict, talk of a mistrial was growing. Every few minutes, Nancy Volmer, who was in charge of media relations for Washington County, sent out e-mail bulletins about new developments. Things felt ready to topple.

The jurors had reassembled and asked the newcomer for her input, then sat back and listened. Both her information and her presence were calming, but press reports indicated that nothing would be resolved today. The jury, led by foreman David Finch, forged ahead. They discussed Elissa's credibility versus Allen's and took note of Walter Bugden's misreading of Jane Blackmore's medical chart. Rebecca Musser's testimony had captivated the jury and hinted at darker things about Jeffs's leadership style that hadn't directly come into the trial. He'd long played favorites among the church members, punishing those who weren't completely loyal to him, as with Richard Holm back in 2003. When Warren had had the opportunity to get Jenny Pipkin out of her unhappy marriage, he'd exercised his power and done so. Yet when he could have released Elissa from Allen, he'd refused. Had he denied Elissa's request because Rebecca had defied him and his father so openly? Had he taken revenge on her through her younger sister?

The debate within the jury was complex and intense, but their deliberations avoided the topics that constantly swirled around the FLDS: polygamy, religious doctrine, arranged marriage, and teen marriage. Brock Belnap and Judge Shumate had admonished them to do only one thing—follow the laws of Utah.

After three hours together on Tuesday morning and early afternoon, they'd reached a decision. Forty-five minutes later everyone had gathered in the courtroom, and the defendant was told to stand.

53

J EFFS AND HIS LAWYERS rose from the defense table, the defendant meekly holding his hands in front of his waist, gazing blankly across the courtroom. To observers, he looked sedated, deadened to the process taking place around him. For generations, he and the church had tried to avoid this moment. More than eighty years ago, the FLDS had settled in the remote town of Short Creek precisely so it could distance itself from the reach of the American legal system. For three decades their seclusion had protected them, until Governor Pyle's unsuccessful early-morning raid on the religious community briefly intruded upon its freedom. That resulted in fifty more years of isolation. It was only after a group of rebel FLDS members spoke up, using the powers of government to address underage marriage and sexual assault, that the law finally intervened. This new generation of young men and women launched a series of civil actions against the church, but with disdain for the legal system, Jeffs ignored the suits and the FLDS lost more than $100 million in assets and property in the border towns. Then one teenage girl of a congregation of upwards of ten thousand took the next step and filed criminal charges against the Prophet, forcing him at last to confront his accusers at trial and to face a jury of his peers. Now he could lose much more.

With the courtroom settled into silence, the bailiff read the verdict aloud.

"We the jury," she announced, "find the defendant guilty on count one" and also "guilty on count two."

The words were met with gasps; the courtroom's anti-polygamy spectators could barely contain their joy. The judge had demanded that no matter what the verdict, observers show restraint, so the emotion expressed itself in a rustling of feet and a shifting of bodies, the viewers anxious to escape the courtroom and celebrate among themselves.

Throughout the reading of the verdict, Bugden had swung his head from side to side, glancing first at the jurors, then over at his client, but the Prophet never flinched or made a sound. Even in his detached state, Jeffs could not ignore the implications of the bailiff's words: he could be sent to prison for life. Following Warren's lead, his FLDS followers withheld any visible reaction. Leaving court that afternoon, Bugden muttered to reporters only that he was "disappointed."

Out on the steps of the Fifth District Courthouse and far beyond, jubilation was unleashed.

"This wasn't just lawyering in the courtroom," Elaine Tyler declared. "This was justice."

"I faded to black after the verdict," Sam Brower said when describing his sense of relief. "Given the narrow range of the charges and the small amount of information about Warren the jurors received, they had to make a huge and difficult decision. During their deliberations, I was wringing my hands. The judge in this case was very appeal-conscious, which is good, because I think that will help make this verdict bulletproof on appeal. Warren will get five years to life on each count, but the question is whether these sentences will run consecutively or concurrently. They usually run concurrently but because he was a fugitive for eighteen months and has no remorse about what he's done, his sentences may run back to back. Before this is all over, he's gonna have a lot of time stacked up."

According to Brower, Jeffs would likely come before a parole board in about three years—*if* he served the Utah sentence first and not a potential sentence in Arizona or another one on the federal charge. Brower called the feds' case against him "a slam dunk," which could add another five years of incarceration in Colorado's Supermax prison.

Laura Chapman, watching the verdict on television from another state, took the jury's decision very personally.

"All the death threats I received," she said, "all the moving around I did to escape the FLDS, all the years of not knowing how to navigate in a world I was ill-prepared for—all of it had now paid off. Warren's leadership had been dismantled. If I closed my eyes, I could see a thirteen-year-old girl in a meadow with the sun shining down on her. Girls like to twirl when they're happy and I was twirling like that. I was just free."

As the verdict had been read in court, Elissa cried softly and then smiled. She and Brock Belnap walked out of the courthouse and into the brilliant September light, surrounded by cameras and microphones. The prosecutor told the media that Elissa's courage in coming forward was not just the "highlight" of his career, but his life. She was a "pioneer" who'd withstood the attacks on her reputation with "honor and dignity." When she'd first approached Belnap almost two years earlier and talked about pressing charges against Jeffs, the prosecutor had promised to keep her identity concealed so that the FLDS wouldn't have the chance to influence her or put pressure on her family.

"We had to keep her," as Sam Brower put it, "out of Warren's crosshairs."

It was his promise to Elissa that had kept Belnap from filing any rape charges per se in this case because that would have forced him to release her name. Until the past few days, she'd been known publicly and in court documents only as Jane Doe IV. Throughout the trial, Belnap had taken enormous criticism from the defense and TV commentators, who felt that he couldn't or shouldn't win an accomplice to rape conviction without an underlying rape. But his strategy had worked, and now Elissa had decided to come forward on her own and reveal her name and a wedding photo to the media.

Standing next to Belnap on the courthouse steps and looking thrilled with the verdict, she quoted Emily Dickinson: "Opinion is a fleeting thing, but truth outlasts the sun."

Elissa had prepared a brief speech, which she'd planned to deliver regardless of how the case turned out. As she read it to the reporters, she also addressed her mother, Sharon Wall, and her other relatives who remained inside the FLDS:

> When I was young, my mother taught me that evil flourishes when good men do nothing. This has not been easy. The easy thing would have been to do nothing, but I have followed my heart and spoken the truth. Lamont and I want to convey our love to our families. Mother, I love you and my sisters unconditionally, and will go to the ends of the earth for you. I understand and respect your convictions but I will never give up on you. When you are ready, I am here.
>
> I have very tender feelings for the FLDS people. There is so much good in them. I pray

they will find the strength to step back, re-examine what they have been told to believe and follow their hearts. This trial has not been about religion or a vendetta. It was simply about child abuse and preventing further abuse. I hope that all FLDS girls and women will understand that, no matter what anyone may say, we are created equal.

You do not have to surrender your rights or your spiritual sovereignty. I know how hard it is, but please stand up and fight for your voice and power of choice. I will continue to fight for you. To those who have been there to support and keep Lamont and myself encouraged, words cannot begin to express our gratitude. I hope the FLDS people will feel the same kindness as they make a difficult journey.

For one person, the journey was about to get much harder.

Nearly a week earlier, on the morning of September 19, Allen Steed had testified for the defense. During the lunch break prosecutors informed one of his attorneys, Jim Bradshaw, that they planned to file a rape charge against their client, in part because of his own words on the witness stand. One day after the Jeffs verdict, an arrest warrant was issued for Allen with a $50,000 bond. His lawyers called this amount "grossly excessive," and in court papers they indicated that their client was being punished for his earlier testimony.

"The timing and tone of this arrest warrant," they wrote, "suggests that it is motivated by something other than a desire to protect the safety of the community or the integrity of the process. It is hard to miss the message with respect to the potential consequences for testifying contrary to the interests of the state in the Warren Jeffs matter . . ."

The warrant was unnecessary, they concluded, because Steed had already agreed to appear at the St. George courthouse on October 4 and face the charge against him.

EPILOGUE

A S JOURNALISTS GATHERED OUTSIDE THE COURTHOUSE for Elissa's press conference following the verdict, a SWAT team remained in place across the street and snipers held their positions in the surrounding hills. Jeffs was quietly slipped out of the rear of the building and hustled into a waiting helicopter. The chopper rose up through the cloudless sky and angled toward Purgatory Correctional Facility. From their vantage point, the passengers could see a wide swatch of the Southwest, with Hurricane to the north and beyond that Zion National Park and off in the distance Hildale and Colorado City, nestled against the Vermilion Cliffs, aglow this afternoon in the crisp fall sunlight. Jeffs could take in the horizon in every direction, and in each lay a far-flung FLDS enclave: to the east in Colorado, the west in Nevada, north in South Dakota, and south in Texas.

The Prophet had once controlled this kingdom—the people and their beliefs, their money and most private lives—ruling it as no one ever had before. The faithful had worshipped him by day and secretly transported him at night along the two-lane roads lining this high desert plateau, so that he'd stay outside the reach of the law. They'd treated him like royal blood and delivered him safely from one hiding house to the next, where women were waiting to hear his sermons and meet his every need.

Now he was in handcuffs and chains, gazing down on a fading empire, his shoulders bent and tall frame cramped inside the helicopter's cabin. He knew that Gary Engels was waiting for him in Arizona, armed with more witnesses and accusations of sexual conduct with a minor and incest. After that would be the civil suits, the federal charge, and possibly a RICO investigation. He might try to run the church from prison, as other Prophets had done, but none had ever stayed this long behind bars or made such demands on his congregation. Joseph Smith had died in jail, become a martyr, and been replaced by Brigham Young, and the Mormons had moved westward and gone on without him. Someone else was always waiting to take power from the deposed ruler. Someone would be waiting again.

The dry heat was reaching its late-afternoon climax and the sun was falling as the chopper descended toward Purgatory, kicking up spirals of dust and scattering everything in its path.

On November 20, 2007, the lawyers assembled before Judge Shumate one final time for the sentencing. Walter Bugden asked for leniency for his client, arguing that Jeffs had not committed a severe crime. Prosecutor Ryan Shaum countered by recommending the judge "incapacitate" Jeffs by making his sentences on the two counts run consecutively rather than at the same time. When Elissa had sought help from Jeffs, Shaum reminded the court, his response was to lecture her for disobedience, then send her back home to her husband.

"That in itself screams for consecutive sentences," the attorney said.

According to Shaum, Jeffs had shown no remorse for his crimes and had maintained his innocence to a caseworker putting together a pre-sentence report for the court. The defendant had shown contempt for state laws, yet expected his followers to take hits from Utah.

"It's Mr. Jeffs's turn," Shaum said, "to take the hit without flinching."

Judge Shumate agreed and sentenced the convicted man to two consecutive five-years-to-life terms, plus a fine of $18,500 apiece for each count. He would serve a minimum of ten years. Jeffs was immediately taken to the Utah State Prison in Draper to await further legal developments. His first automatic hearing in front of the Utah Board of Pardons and Parole will be in 2010.

The best thing about the verdict, **Gary Engels** said, was that "Elissa has finally been vindicated. I'm just very happy for her." Warren's conviction had done nothing to dampen the investigator's drive to continue prosecuting the defendant. Engels had other young women whom he was preparing to put on the stand against Jeffs in Arizona.

"As long as the victims will come into court and testify," he said, "we're going forward with our cases."

In October 2007, Engels's employer in Mohave County made a further commitment to the continuing probe for crimes along the border, placing a full-time deputy in Colorado City. The new officer would be stationed in Gary's building, the multi-use trailer at the edge of town, and the move was a reminder to the embattled five-member Colorado City police force that outside law enforcement was now watching them closely. Announcing the arrival of the new deputy, Mohave County sheriff Tom Sheahad declared that with the ongoing decertification of Colorado City police, the locals needed cops they could trust.

Sam Brower would be assisting Arizona's criminal justice system in the upcoming Jeffs cases while helping the Hoole brothers bring their civil actions against Jeffs and the FLDS for expelling young men from the community.

Weeks after the verdict, Sam still sounded exhilarated.

"This has been quite a ride, but we did it. It took an entire team to make this happen and every part of that team had to work properly to put Warren in jail. We had the right victim in Elissa, the right case with her on the stand, and the right prosecutor, in Brock Belnap. Take away one thing and it could have all fallen apart."

Elissa Wall's civil suit was put on hold until the criminal matters had been resolved, but after the trial in St. George, she made a number of public appearances and spoke of her desire for an eventual $1 million settlement against the defendants. This money would go directly into a fund for young people trying to escape the church and start their lives over. She sought to provide them with the freedom of marriage, education, and living that she'd never had.

Elaine Tyler told the media that Jeffs's conviction was "a huge victory, but that does not mean that the abuses occurring in polygamous groups will stop. Until Utah and Arizona government agencies do something to help these victims—and that is highly unlikely—we will still be doing what we can to assist them."

And that meant continuing to solicit help from others. With truckloads of donated goods, the Hope Organization furnished Hildale's new "Affinity House," a huge structure with nineteen bedrooms and twenty-three bathrooms, designed to lodge women, children, and families that had opted to split from the FLDS. Elaine insisted that one of the rooms become a library.

"Knowledge is power," she declared, "and we believe that education is the key to breaking the cycle of abuse." She aimed to get "foster care certification" for Affinity House so it could take in abused, neglected, and abandoned children. Her organization also began furnishing a home in St. George that had been donated to the Lost Boys.

When the local Easter Seals Program assigned a volunteer to work at her office twenty hours a week, Elaine nearly broke into tears of relief. After four years of running Hope full-time, she began to imagine putting in fewer hours. "I look forward to getting my life back," she said.

Laura Chapman kept busy with her social work and appeared at seminars to discuss polygamy, child abuse, and the law. She often began her talks by showing images from *Big Love*, then contrasting them with the far grittier reality that many women face inside the Fundamentalist Mormon Church. Nearly a decade earlier, she'd launched the struggle against polygamy in Utah, confronting the governor about the conditions in his state. Her words in the autumn of 2007 showed that she'd lost none of her fire:

> So much is still lacking in terms of accountability . . . Elissa Wall's parents not only failed to protect her but prepared a child in a wedding dress for her abuser. They are culpable by law and should be charged. If Warren Jeffs has 80 wives, and birth certificates of his 264 children prove this, he should be charged with 79 counts of bigamy . . . He was not charged for violating the Mann Act [taking a minor across state lines for sexual purposes]. Elissa was taken to Nevada to be married. Jeffs should be held accountable for the human trafficking of women and children to Canada . . .
>
> An apology should be issued to the thousands of people, over 160 years, who have lived in extreme conditions of poverty, emotional and spiritual abuse, sexual coercion and assault because of this doctrine that places men as superior over women. Since the LDS Church is one of the wealthiest religious organizations in the world, they should fund nonprofit organizations to provide resources for refugees of polygamy. They should no longer allow a man to be sealed for time and all eternity to more than one woman.

Bolstered by their win in court, Laura and the others who'd resisted the FLDS felt empowered to take on the challenges that remained.

AFTERWORD

D URING THE PAST DECADE, our nation's legal system, voting rights, and protections granted us under the U.S. Constitution have all come under increasing assault. Talk show hosts from coast to coast have decided that due process and jurors' verdicts are far less important than their own opinions. Since the autumn of 2000, countless votes have been lost through ballot problems or electronic malfunctions in both state and national elections, negating the will of the American people. Suspects have been detained in prison for years without the chance to confront their accusers—in violation of the foundation of the law in the United States. Our nation's Founding Fathers wove together the three branches of government so that no single person or group could become too powerful, and the passions of the mob would not prevail in court or at the polls. Balance and restraint were at the core of what they laid out in the Constitution. It was better to use too little force than too much, because the latter could unleash unforeseen and disastrous consequences.

All these things were on my mind in the winter of 2006 when my wife, Joyce, who's helped me with numerous book projects, suggested that I look into the fugitive Mormon fundamentalist Warren Jeffs. He was about to land on the FBI's Ten Most Wanted List, and his picture had begun appearing nightly on television. Jeffs's story was not unfamiliar to me: more than twenty years before, I'd first written about the coming together of fanatical religion and violence. In 1984, Alan Berg, an outspoken Jewish talk show host in Denver, was assassinated by neo-Nazis who also believed they were God's Chosen People. My book about this murder, *Talked to Death*, chronicled what can happen when faith meets terrorism, a topic that in the mid-1980s was still relatively small but has since become a global problem. Despite all this, I initially resisted Joyce's suggestion about Warren Jeffs.

Three years earlier, Jon Krakauer had published his excellent book on the Mormon faith, *Under the Banner of Heaven*. I didn't want to walk over that ground again and didn't know if there were enough other pieces of the Fundamentalist Mormon saga that remained to be covered. After more persuasion from my wife, we decided to drive to southern Utah in the spring of 2006, and I was immediately hooked by the beauty and grandeur of the landscape around Zion National Park. I seemed to be breathing the air of the Old Testament, and it looked like the perfect setting for a spiritual war. The first person I interviewed in Utah was Elaine Tyler, who ran the Hope Organization, which provided assistance to women and teenagers who'd escaped Jeffs's brutal reign. Elaine labored tirelessly on behalf of these people for 50 to 60 hours a week or longer—for free. I was moved by her commitment and her actions, as I'd be moved by others I was about to meet.

She introduced me to numerous women who were trying to contain or undo parts of the damage Jeffs and his church had done to members of their congregation. Some of these women had been sexually assaulted as children or forced into underage marriages, but had found the backbone to flee their religion and start over. In every sense, they made up the heart of the movement to bring Jeffs down. All of these individuals were fighting against homegrown religious terrorism, but with a very different strategy from the one our government was employing abroad in its international War on Terror. No blood had been spilled along the southern Utah–northern Arizona border, and positive change was gradually coming to the region. Small triumphs were appearing, and people were healing from emotional and sexual horrors. After too much neglect for far too long, the two state governments were beginning to use the legal system to root out and prosecute criminals in a hidden corner of America. The Constitution and due process were alive around Zion National Park, where child abuse and forced marriage were starting to be treated as they were everywhere else in the United States.

My wife's instincts had been on target: what was unfolding in Utah and Arizona was the next chapter of the Mormon story, and the further I went into it the more I was struck by one thing. Many of those involved in helping ex-FLDS members seemed to have been looking for a new challenge or a ray of optimism, just as I had. Each time I traveled to Colorado City for more research or interviews, I came away feeling encouraged about the native strength and goodness of my country. The individual accomplishments were important, but another, larger theme had begun to emerge. It had to do with the value of intelligence and restraint in confronting criminal behavior driven by religion—as opposed to launching a broad-based war with undefined goals. Blind force hadn't worked in the twin communities in 1953 and maybe it wasn't the best way to convince others that our side was right. Maybe those working for change on the border had something to teach all of us about confronting global terrorism.

The good feeling I'd first encountered when visiting Elaine Tyler's office was expanding into something more. In several recent high-profile murder cases, government agencies had failed in their responsibilities because they hadn't been able to work well together to solve crimes. Their attitudes and actions generated more confusion than clarity—and less justice for all. In Utah and Arizona, law enforcement and the media were finding a unified purpose and getting results. Cops, investigators, civilians, lawyers, activists, judges, and journalists—each had more to gain by cooperating with the others than by insisting that they had to be right and somebody else wrong. Judge Shumate was astute in praising the American legal system during the case of Utah versus Warren Jeffs.

It's very easy to criticize our government, which is bound to make mistakes when trying to confront and solve entangled problems. But every now and then, those in charge come close to living out the wisdom behind the principles that created the United States. In doing so, they honor the Founding Fathers and our Constitutional heritage—the glue that holds America together as a free nation still pursuing a more perfect union. These people not only give us hope, but the opportunity to think about what power is and the best way to use it.

I believe that heroes have stepped forward in the pages of this book, and we've never needed them more.

ACKNOWLEDGMENTS

I N ADDITION TO MY WIFE, a number of people—Laura Chapman, Elaine Tyler, Flora Jessop, Sara Hammon, John Larsen, Elissa Wall, and Rebecca Musser, among many others—contributed hugely to these pages. Private investigator Sam Brower was very helpful with his psychological insights into Jeffs and his colorful anecdotes, but from the beginning it was Gary Engels who really drew me into the story. I was fascinated by the mission he'd undertaken when going to work in Colorado City and his tenacity in seeing it through. Some people simply will not be defeated. He gave up many hours speaking to me about his professional life while providing background information about the FLDS and his approach to bringing members of the church to justice. Every time I thought Gary was going to fall silent and tell me that he had other, more important things to do, he kept sharing thoughts and feelings about his job. After a while, I figured out that he'd been changed by his experience on the border, and he may have had as much need to talk about this as I did to listen to him.

From the moment I met him, I could feel his passion for his work, his anger at what Jeffs had done to others, and his desire to help victims of the FLDS. I admired him not only for his investigative efforts, but for his caution and refusal to impose himself too heavily on the local population, even when he wanted to. I never sat down with him without learning more about the story—and what it means to play within the rules of the American system of law. This is a much better book because of Gary's participation.

As with most nonfiction projects, newspaper reporters uncovered many of the basic facts that authors later pick up and use. Brooke Adams of the *Salt*

Lake City Tribune laid out various pieces and parts of the raw materials of Jeffs's life, along with other aspects of this story, and that needs to be acknowledged. The *Deseret Morning News* and the *St. George Spectrum* were also important resources for the narrative. So were Ben Bistline's books.

I'd like to thank my agent, Mel Berger of William Morris, for representing this book and finding a home for it at St. Martin's Press. For years I'd heard wonderful things about St. Martin's editor Charlie Spicer, and they all turned out to be true. His enthusiasm and guiding spirit have greatly benefited me and many other writers. Charlie's assistant, Yaniv Soha, did the heavy lifting on this manuscript and was invaluable in keeping me on track with this multifaceted—if not downright messy—tale, with its virtually unlimited cast of characters and story lines. I regularly leaned on Yaniv for advice, and he just as regularly knew what to do to keep the author and the narrative moving forward. He was superb in terms of both the details and the bigger picture, and creating the book with him was a pleasure.